Refugee Reception in Southern Africa

Critical Human Rights Studies

The *Critical Human Rights* Studies series is committed to investigating today's most pressing human rights issues from diverse interdisciplinary and intellectual perspectives. It embraces critically engaged scholarship, methodologies spanning the humanities and social sciences, creative non-fiction writing, co-produced approaches that bridge research and practice in human rights, and work that engages directly with policy. The series interrogates the human rights-related dimensions of phenomena such as colonisation, genocide, ecocide and environmental issues, migration, reconciliation projects, freedom of expression, digital rights, racism, poverty, indigenous peoples' rights, corporate power and extractive industries.

Published in association with the Human Rights Consortium and the Institute of Commonwealth Studies, this series is fully open access and welcomes new proposals in particular from those looking to bring perspectives and approaches from the humanities to address the series' central concerns.

Series Editor

Damien Short, Professor of Human Rights and Environmental Justice, Institute of Commonwealth Studies, University of London, UK.

Recently published

Mapping Crisis: Participation, Datafication and Humanitarianism in the Age of Digital Mapping, edited by Doug Specht (September 2020)
Natural Resource Development and Human Rights in Latin America: State and non-state actors in the promotion of and opposition to extractivism, edited by Malayna Raftopoulos and Radosław Powęska (May 2020)
Reconciling Rwanda: Unity, Nationality and State Control, Jennifer Melvin (May 2020)

Refugee Reception in Southern Africa

National and Local Policies in Zambia and South Africa

Nicholas Maple

Available to purchase in print or download
for free at https://uolpress.co.uk

First published 2024 by
University of London Press
Senate House, Malet St, London WC1E 7HU

© Nicholas Maple 2024

The right of Nicholas Maple to be identified as author of this Work has been asserted in accordance with sections 77 and 78 of the Copyright, Designs and Patents Act 1988.

This book is published under a Creative Commons Attribution-NonCommercial-NoDerivatives 4.0 International (CC BY-NC-ND 4.0) license.

Please note that third-party material reproduced here may not be published under the same license as the rest of this book. If you would like to reuse any third-party material not covered by the book's Creative Commons license, you will need to obtain permission from the copyright holder.

A CIP catalogue record for this book is available from The British Library.

ISBN 978-1-908590-74-9 (hardback)
ISBN 978-1-908590-75-6 (paperback)
ISBN 978-1-908590-77-0 (.epub)
ISBN 978-1-908590-76-3 (.pdf)
ISBN 978-1-912250-62-2 (.html)

DOI https://doi.org/10.14296/wmpx9915

Cover image: "Nelson Mandela Bridge, Johannesburg" by Adele Van Heerden. Adele is based in Cape Town, South Africa.

Cover design for University of London Press by Nicky Borowiec.
Series design by Nicky Borowiec.
Book design by Nigel French.
Text set by Westchester Publishing Services UK in
Meta Serif and Meta, designed by Erik Spiekermann.

Contents

Acknowledgements	vii
List of abbreviations	ix
Introduction	1
1. Framing refugee reception	21
2. Refugee reception policies in Africa	45
3. Investigating state behaviour towards refugees	67
4. Encampment: the maintenance of a camp-based reception in Zambia	89
5. Encampment: post registration in Zambia	117
6. Free settlement: the maintenance of a free-settlement reception in South Africa	149
7. The urban space: post registration in South Africa	179
8. Conclusions and ways forward	205
Bibliography	229
Index	267

Acknowledgements

I would like to extend my deepest thanks to everyone who generously contributed to the work presented in this book. Most importantly, thank you to all in Southern Africa who gave up their precious time for a conversation or to be interviewed. I hope by disseminating my research, I can repay a small part of this debt.

A special thank you to my PhD supervisor and colleague, Professor David Cantor, who has been an exceptional mentor over the past ten years. This includes constant support and guidance, a great deal of patience, as well as opening countless career opportunities and intellectual challenges for me. Without his continued support, this book would not have been possible.

Thank you to Professor Loren Landau and Professor Jo Vearey at the African Centre for Migration and Society (ACMS) for their advice and encouragement over the last seven years. I am particularly indebted to them for their unwavering support during my post-doctoral studies.

At the University of London, Dr Sarah Singer has been a great mentor and friend. I thank Susie Reardon-Smith, for all the advice and for listening to me while walking to get coffee. I am very grateful for the funding received from the School of Advanced Study. In South Africa, I would like to thank everyone at ACMS, with particular mention to Thea, Lenore, Ingrid, Jean-Pierre, Kuda and Becky. In Zambia, thank you to Marja Hinfelaar and her team at the Southern African Institute for Policy (SAIPAR) for their advice and support. Also, to Joseph who drove me to nearly every interview.

Thank you to Professor Sue Onslow, Dr Lucy Hovil, Dr Cory Rodgers and Dr Vickie Knox for sparing time to give constructive feedback on drafts. Thank you also for feedback along the way from Dr Hagar Kotef, Dr Jeff Crisp, Professor Elena Fiddian-Qasmiyeh, Professor James Hathaway and Professor Alex Aleinikoff. Thank you to Professor Jane McAdam, Professor Guy Goodwin-Gill, and everyone else at the Kaldor Centre in Sydney for hosting me and for giving advice. My thanks to everyone else I have not been able to mention, who agreed to a coffee or a meeting. The generosity of time shown by colleagues, friends and strangers continues to amaze me.

Thank you to Megan Cartwright and Caitlin Phillips for reviewing and proof-checking numerous drafts over the years.

A special thank you to Emma Gallon at the University of London Press for her generous support throughout the publication process. Special thanks also to the anonymous reviewers of the manuscript.

I am indebted to friends and family in London, Johannesburg, Cape Town, Lusaka and Sydney who opened their homes to me over the last ten years, as well as being incredibly helpful in so many other ways. This includes Julian, Mahala, Margot, Tina, Eric, Chris, Liz, Riley and Georgia. Special thanks to Sue and Jack Maple-Foster (and family) for going far beyond any required Aunt and Uncle duties.

Finally, and most importantly, thanks to Mum, Dad, Simon and Megan for the incredible support throughout the writing of this, including the many ups and downs.

List of abbreviations

ACMS	African Centre for Migration and Society
ANC	The African National Congress
AU	The African Union
CBI	Cash-based intervention
COR	The Commission for Refugees in Zambia
CRRF	Comprehensive Refugee Response Framework
DA	The Democratic Alliance
DJOC	District Joint Operations Committee
DRC	Democratic Republic of the Congo
INGO	International Non-Governmental Organisation
IOM	International Organisation for Migration
JMAC	Johannesburg Migrants' Advisory Committee
JMAP	Johannesburg Migration Advisory Panel
KIIs	Key Informant Interviews
MCDSS	Ministry of Community Development and Social Services
NEC	National Eligibility Committee
OAU	Organisation of the African Union
PJOC	Provincial Joint Operations Committee
RROs	Refugee Reception Offices
RSD	Refugee Status Determination
SADC	Southern African Development Community
SAIPAR	Southern African Institute for Policy and Research
UN	The United Nations
UNCDF	United Nations Capital Development Fund
UNDP	United Nations Development Programme
UNGA	United Nations General Assembly

UN-Habitat	United Nations Human Settlements Programme
UNHCR	United Nations High Commissioner for Refugees
UNICEF	United Nations Children's Fund
UPND	United Party for National Development
URP	Urban Residency Permit
WFP	World Food Programme
ZDP	Zimbabwean Dispensation Permit
ZEP	Zimbabwean Exemption Permit

Introduction

Countries within Southern Africa regularly host large numbers of refugees and forced migrants, with the United Nations High Commissioner for Refugees (UNHCR) reporting around one million refugees and asylum-seekers in the sub-region in 2023 (UNHCR, 2023a). However, the modes and sites of reception vary greatly between states in Southern Africa, from the confines of refugee camps and settlements to local neighbourhoods in sprawling, contemporary African cities. Most states adopt a form of encampment reception policy, with refugees expected to move to, and reside in, these confined spaces once their stay has been regularised. Yet there is wide variation on the ground in terms of implementation of these approaches. Within many states, movement between refugee camps and rural and urban areas is often permitted, with some refugees even finding official or *de facto* acceptance for settling long term in urban spaces. Conversely, a minority of states adopt a free-settlement approach, whereby newly arrived refugees are permitted – at least in law – to move freely and settle anywhere on the territory, including urban centres.

This variation in state-based reception shapes how, and the extent to which, refugees find protection and formal and informal solutions to displacement in Southern Africa. Furthermore, refugees discover that each of these different reception sites (from the refugee camp to the urban space) has its own unique restrictions and opportunities. Each is shaped by political, bureaucratic and economic factors permeating from the international, national and local levels. These variances are particularly intriguing given that most Southern African Development Community (SADC) member states have signed up to key international and regional conventions related to refugees that all promote a level of uniformity regarding how refugees should be received.

The book develops analysis and understanding of the processes involved in refugee reception policies in Southern Africa. Significantly, we know little about how states make choices regarding refugee reception policies in the context of Africa, including which factors (or stakes) play a role in these policies. Thus, this book examines why states in the sub-region respond to refugee arrivals in such diverse ways – and how these varied reception policies shape a refugee's ability to move around the host state in pursuit of their own personal and economic aims.

These objectives are achieved by analysing two country case studies: Zambia and South Africa. These are the two principal destination countries in Southern Africa for refugees (Crush and Chikanda, 2014), yet maintain dissimilar reception policies. Zambia has retained a dominant camp policy towards receiving refugees since its independence in 1964. In contrast, its close neighbour South Africa continues to diverge from regional trends by adopting a liberal free-settlement policy. Through a state-focused analysis, these opposing approaches to reception are compared in terms of the behaviour of key state and international actors in how refugees access protection and rights within these host states. By asking *why* states behave in specific ways towards refugees, the aspiration is that academia and policy practitioners will be in a better position to understand the realities of reception policy implementation on the ground, and to then offer pragmatic modifications to policy, which will ultimately improve the welcome refugees receive (Betts, 2009b).[1]

This introduction chapter starts by contextualising the topic of the book and providing the justification for the focus on refugee reception, as well as the state-focused approach. Then refugee reception in Southern Africa is introduced within the context of the book's thematic focus. The chapter concludes with an outline of the whole book.

Disparate responses to the reception of refugees

Most states within Africa are party to the core international conventions that underlie the global refugee regime.[2] As such, they have obligations to implement the associated human rights norms, which include rights to employment, provision of travel documents and freedom of movement for refugees. This might be expected to create some conformity among state approaches to the reception of refugees. Certainly, during the 1960s and 1970s there was wide recognition and praise of the 'open door' policy to refugees on the continent (Rutinwa, 2002; van Garderen, 2004). In essence, this involved states maintaining open borders with neighbouring states and affording a generous welcome to refugee and other forced migrant populations. This reception regularly included access to services, markets, and the freedom to move unimpeded around the territory (Crisp, 2000; Rutinwa, 2002).

Yet from the 1980s onwards, approaches to the reception of refugees changed dramatically, with different policies emerging (such as encampment) which restricted many fundamental rights. As a result, implementation of key international norms contained within the global refugee regime, such as freedom of movement, were more readily contested or simply blocked. Today, refugee camps remain the preferred reception choice in the region (UNHCR, 2019b).

Nevertheless, there exists considerable variation in how refugee reception policies operate in practice (Abdelaaty, 2021). As examined in the next chapter, refugee reception in this book is understood as a process. This process encompasses the host state's (and other key actors') behaviour which shape a refugee's ability to engage with local communities and markets when attempting to pursue their own personal and economic aims. Thus, this understanding repositions reception as more than simply an ephemeral moment (such as crossing a border or a formal registration process). Instead, it sees it as a process that reflects the multi-directional and multi-locational dynamics of contemporary refugee arrival including, significantly, the role reception policies play in a refugee's ability to move within the host state and engage with local populations and economies.

By conceptualising reception in this way, it becomes evident that there are significant variations in how host states in Africa *receive* refugees – even though most states maintain dominant encampment-style reception policies. In rare instances, countries have attempted to maintain the more traditional free-settlement approach whereby refugees and asylum-seekers are granted freedom of movement almost immediately upon arrival. In countries which adopt encampment policies, some embrace more development-style settlements, rather than the traditional closed-camp approach, where one of the principal goals is for refugees to become self-reliant within that space. Furthermore, in many countries which adopt encampment approaches, there co-exist state-run policies that permit frequent movement between refugee camps and neighbouring urban and rural areas (Krause and Gato, 2019). In addition, there are the more informal activities that occur at the fringes of implementation of reception policies, whereby host states regularly turn a blind eye to refugees settling in urban spaces in contravention of the dominant encampment policy (Hovil, 2016). Here, refugees can find *de facto* acceptance by the host state via local government structures.[3]

These observed differences in contemporary approaches to the reception of refugees by states provide the motivation for this book. In particular, the book seeks to offer new ways of understanding why states behave in different and specific ways towards the arrival and movement of refugees. The focus is therefore on the role of the state in administering these policies and the effect that different approaches have on refugees' ability to move around the host state in pursuit of their own personal and economic aims. Justification for a state-focused approach to analysing the topic of refugee reception comes from situating this book within the broader body of literature on the differing forms of welcome offered to refugees in Africa.

Specifically, as investigated in Chapters 1 and 2, the academic scholarship on refugee arrival within the continent has traditionally been guided by state responses to this form of cross-border movement, and the modes and spaces of reception these responses dictate. During the 1990s and early 2000s, with states in the majority world[4] and international donors from the minority world preferring strict encampment policies, research within refugee and forced migration studies focused on the refugee camp (Long, 2019). Due to this spatial focus and corresponding lack of attention given to urban refugees by policymakers and practitioners, urban displacement during this period was overlooked by researchers (Schmidt, 2003).[5] However, in the last ten to fifteen years, the focus of relevant academic fields has slowly shifted towards a consideration of the urban space (Maple et al., 2023; Hovil and Maple, 2022). This is at least in part due to academic research now reflecting the realities on the ground, with regional trends of urbanisation meaning more refugees are rejecting the restrictive reception approaches of states and self-settling in cities (Landau, 2018a).

As research on refugee reception has shifted from the refugee camp to include the urban space, the role of the host state has, for the most part, remained underexplored. Instead, emphasis has moved from actors at the international level to those at the local and sub-local level, missing out on the national level (Landau, 2007). During the 1990s, the host state's role was habitually framed as a minor one in the reception of refugees in Africa (Slaughter and Crisp, 2008). Rather, attention remained on UNHCR, with the agency regularly placed in charge of running refugee camps (Schmidt, 2003). When motivations for states' actions were considered in academic literature, there was a tendency to frame host states as 'black boxes' (Betts, 2009b).[6] Thus, states were represented as one complete entity (with blanket inputs and outputs), with all states having similar motivations for how they behaved towards refugees.

The recent shifts in academic scholarship towards engaging with: (i) urban displacement on the continent;[7] and (ii) connections between the camp and urban space have appropriately concentrated on the perspective of the refugee.[8] These contemporary investigations have drawn out novel areas of research looking at alternative forms of welcome, and localised citizenship and resilience (Hovil, 2016; Subulwa, 2019).[9] With these advances have come new understandings of the different actors and their agendas at the ground level (including host communities, refugees and refugee networks). In particular, contemporary research highlights how local networks, refugee-led initiatives and other localised contextual factors (often beyond the reach of the state) can explain how refugees find alternative forms of reception at the local and sub-local level (Berg and Fiddian-Qasmiyeh, 2018).

The new emphasis on the refugee in these situations has, nevertheless, led to the role of host states in the reception of refugees remaining somewhat overlooked. Indeed, in the African context, little is known about how states make choices regarding refugee reception policies and what factors (or stakes) play a role in this (Bakewell and Jónsson, 2011; Milner, 2009; Zanker and Moyo, 2020). This includes the role played by national bodies, national frameworks, local governments and local norms in reception policies (Landau, 2014). By way of illustration, there has been minimal academic work on the juxtaposition between a host state maintaining an overarching refugee camp policy (which demands all refugees remain housed in the camp space), while at the same time implementing policies that permit movement between the camp and urban spaces. A core aim of this book is to complement the existing work on key actors in refugee reception at the ground level, by investigating the role and influence of state bodies and structures at the national and international levels.

This will be achieved by adopting a conceptual framework based on the theory of norm implementation by Betts and Orchard (2014). This framework is utilised to investigate the causal mechanisms embedded within state behaviour (separated into material, ideational and institutional factors) that are influencing the responses of states to the arrival of refugees. By deploying Betts and Orchard's theory, the book sets out an analytical approach to investigate *why* states respond to refugee arrivals in differing ways. Within this framework, the book introduces a multi-scalar approach to investigate the role of the 'state'. This approach acknowledges that host states are not one single uniform entity (nor a 'black-box'), but rather, made up of different structures at different levels, from the local to the provincial and national, all of which can interact, contest and/or influence refugee reception policies. This book therefore contributes to academic learning by adding an important new perspective on this hitherto neglected area of research.

Moreover, ultimately, with a more holistic understanding of what influences the decisions of the plurality of actors involved in refugee reception, the academic community and international policy practitioners will be in a better position to engage with states. This is particularly pertinent if academia and policy advocates seek to encourage alternative ways of welcoming refugees that do not restrict fundamental rights. Indeed, without a nuanced understanding of why states maintain encampment policies, a paradigm shift in how states receive refugees in Africa remains unlikely (Maple et al., 2021; Kagan, 2014; Hovil 2016). As Betts (2009b) observes, anyone who wishes to influence state responses towards refugees must first understand the rationale for their existing behaviour.

To investigate the disparate state responses to the arrival of refugees in Africa, the book sets out to answer two key questions. First, how do we explain the diverse ways in which states receive refugees in their territories? Second, how do the refugee reception policies of host states shape a refugee's ability to pursue their own personal and economic aims?

Refugee reception in Southern Africa

This section starts by outlining the book's central epistemological position and how the case studies derive therefrom. An overarching constructivist epistemological position has been adopted, emphasising the importance and particularity of the domestic sphere. The theoretical approach, the case studies and the methods adopted to investigate the reception of refugees, flow from this position (Crotty, 1998). Specifically, two perspectives linked to a constructivist epistemology have been adopted, namely realist and interpretivist (Gray, 2004; Veroff, 2010b). These are sometimes seen as contrasting epistemes, but in line with the work of Grey (2004) and Veroff (2010b), they have been adopted as compatible perspectives that provide complementary insights. The focus of interpretivists is on 'how members of society understand their own actions', while realism 'involves looking behind appearances to discover laws or mechanisms which explain human behavior' and thus state action (Travers, 2001:10).

By embracing this approach, the aim is two-fold: first, to produce 'thick descriptions' of key actors' experiences with refugee reception policies and investigate the dynamics of bureaucratic and socio-cultural frameworks. Inherent within this interpretivist approach to data collection is the flexibility to consider new issues or concepts during the research process, which may not have been part of the original research focus (Gray, 2004). Second, to develop theory – in other words, to produce 'a set of interrelated categories that describe or explain some phenomenon' (Travers, 2001:10) – around the particularity of state responses towards the arrival of refugees. As examined in Chapter 3, there is no reason why studies that adopt a political science lens cannot balance 'insights of ethnography with the broader comparative insights of political science' (Betts and Orchard, 2014:20).

Indeed, this deliberately inter-disciplinary approach offers a way through which micro-level processes can be followed and understood so as to speak back to macro-level theory.[10]

A direct consequence of this overarching epistemological position is the choice to use comparative case studies of two countries (Zambia and South Africa) from within Southern Africa. Following the work of Merriam (2009) and Stake (2003), the most relevant criterion of case selection should be the opportunity to investigate a phenomenon. Thus, the case studies are investigated from an interpretivist perspective, with the aim of studying contemporary and complex social phenomenon, namely the reception of refugees, in its natural context (Yin, 1994). Consequently, this approach devotes considerable attention to unpacking complex relationships within state and society: in this book, this means examining the relationships between state bodies, refugee policy and refugees' attempts at pursuing personal and economic aims. In line with this position, the clear benefit of a 'few country comparison', rather than a larger sample, is the ability to generate an in-depth and insight-generating study of specific cases (Lor, 2011). By analysing these relationships, a more nuanced understanding of state-based refugee reception within each country emerges. In doing so, the book offers an important contrast with recent large-N quantitative studies and efforts to theorise refugee policy at a global scale.[11]

Southern Africa as a setting for investigating refugee reception

There are several reasons for electing to study refugee reception in Southern Africa. The sheer variety in patterns and dynamics of refugee movement makes it an essential terrain of study: it ranges from mass influxes, constant but small-scale cross-border movements, to multiple forms of 'secondary' movement. In terms of numbers, in 2023 there were around one million refugees and asylum-seekers in Southern Africa (UNHCR, 2023a). Most refugees come from the Great Lakes, the East and Horn of Africa, Central Africa, and SADC countries (UNHCR, 2019c). Refugees normally travel by land, in part because Southern Africa is a porous sub-region of Africa, with large numbers of irregular cross-border movements (Nshimbi and Fiormonti, 2014). Furthermore, a prominent feature of this movement is the large distance many refugees travel, with South Africa hosting sizeable numbers of people coming from Eritrea, Ethiopia and Somalia (Long and Crisp, 2011; World Bank, 2019). These refugee movements are also paralleled by flows of historic and contemporary economic migration into the Southern African region, and in particular, South Africa (Flahaux and De Haas, 2016).

The sub-region is also a useful context within which diverse forms of refugee reception policy can be compared. For instance, many states contest or place formal reservations on specific norms, such as the freedom of movement and employment rights. As a result, countries such as Malawi, Zambia and Botswana house refugees in sites of long-term encampment. In contrast, South Africa, and to a lesser extent Angola, permit refugees to settle immediately in urban spaces as part of their official reception policies. Additionally, the mode of reception can change depending on the composition of a particular refugee population. For example, large, urgent cross-border movements gain the attention of the international humanitarian system and international funding. Consequently, emergency camps and services are often provided. In contrast, sporadic cross-border movements of small groups of refugees are often left to local state structures, local communities and civil society, and thus ignored at the national level and by the wider international community (broadly defined). The urbanisation trend seen in contemporary global refugee movements is also replicated in Southern Africa, with increasing numbers of refugees rejecting camp-based reception policies for urban cities such as Johannesburg (Landau, 2018b; Long and Crisp, 2011).

Lastly, this sub-region of Africa has received relatively limited academic attention in terms of analysis of refugee issues. Indeed, current academic focus in Africa is showing worrying signs of a lack of diversity by disproportionately concentrating on refugee populations solely within a select few countries experiencing medium-intensity conflict and displacement, such as Ethiopia, Kenya and Uganda. Thus, the chosen geographical area is a modest attempt to widen academic knowledge on refugee issues on the continent.

Country case study selection

The book is interested in why states behave differently towards the arrival of refugees. For this reason, within the broader comparative case studies method, a *diverse* case study technique was adopted. As noted by Seawright and Gerring (2008), this technique aims to select two cases which represent the 'maximum variance along relevant dimensions', in this case, state approaches to the reception of refugees. As the individual variable of interest is categorical (that is, the type of reception deployed), an investigator can choose one case from each category (encampment versus free-settlement approach) (Seawright and Gerring, 2008). Thus, a key reason Zambia and South Africa were selected as case studies within the broader

Southern Africa context is because they maintain contrasting approaches to the reception of refugees (encampment versus free-settlement approach).

Zambia is a 'typical case study' in relation to the diverse cases study technique (Gerring, 2008), in that it can be considered a representative case in relation to how states respond to refugees in Southern Africa. The national reception policy, like most states in the sub-region, demands that refugees are housed in a form of encampment. Refugees essentially remain in one of three main refugee settlements after regularising their stay until it is safe to return to their country of origin.

For this book, 'encampment' is understood as a reception policy adopted by states (often in conjunction with international organisations, such as UNHCR), 'which requires refugees to live in a designated area set aside for the exclusive use of refugees, unless they have gained specific permission to live elsewhere' (Bakewell, 2014:129). In turn, refugee camps and (formal) settlements are the modes (and geographical spaces) by which this policy is implemented. In forced migration and refugee studies literature, the terms 'camp' and 'settlement' have traditionally been used interchangeably (Schmidt, 2003). Since the 2000s, academic work has often made clearer distinctions between the two sites, likely at the behest of policymakers and donors keen to emphasise 'new' approaches.[12] For example, planned refugee settlements in Uganda and Kenya (such as the Nakivale and Kalobeyei settlements) are regularly depicted as distinct entities from the more traditional closed-gated refugee camps, such as the Dadaab camp in Kenya.[13]

Nevertheless, in refugee settlements in Africa, freedom of movement is still regularly restricted and for this reason the book adopts the traditional framing and uses the two terms interchangeably. Specifically, the settlements in Zambia are designated areas set aside for the exclusive use of refugees, with refugees expected to reside in them, unless granted express permission to leave. As such, these qualities that severely restrict movement make them take on the character of a camp (Schmidt, 2003). As Malkki (1995) observes, when refugees cannot leave a location whenever they want to, that location has all the hallmarks of a refugee camp, even if it is labelled as a settlement.

Consistent with this approach, the Zambian state has placed reservations on key international norms contained within the Convention relating to the Status of Refugees (1951) ('the 1951 Refugee Convention'), such as freedom of movement. There is also an understanding within the government that refugees are the responsibility of the international community, with UNHCR funding the running costs of the refugee settlements (Bakewell, 2004). Consequently, Zambia is a suitable choice for exploring the underlying causal mechanisms at work that make this approach so popular in Southern Africa and further afield on the continent.

Nonetheless, looking beyond this basic classification, the selection of one Southern African case study is unlikely to be representative of an entire category (Gerring, 2008). As set out in subsequent chapters, it is evident that the reasoning and motivations behind Zambia's responses to refugee movement involves material, ideational and institutional factors, which are particular to the Zambian state and society. For these reasons, and due to the comparative nature of the investigation, the book is focused on the context of particular settings – namely South Africa and Zambia.

Zambia is a landlocked country, bordering eight neighbouring states, meaning it relies heavily on the stability of its neighbours (Subulwa, 2013). The history of Zambia, like so many countries in Africa, is a long history (pre-colonial, colonial and post-colonial) of continuous movement (Subulwa, 2013). Since independence in 1964, major events such as the Angolan and Mozambican liberation struggles, the crisis caused by Rhodesia's unilateral bid for independence, followed by progressive social unrest and economic collapse in Zimbabwe in the late 1990s and 2000s, and ongoing conflicts in the Democratic Republic of the Congo (DRC), have affected geopolitical dynamics and social stability in Zambia (Burnell, 2005). As Subulwa (2013) notes, of Zambia's eight neighbours, five have been directly involved in serious conflicts and associated mass migration in recent times (namely Zimbabwe, Mozambique, Angola, Namibia and the DRC). Due to these geopolitical factors, Zambia has hosted refugees for generations, even if officially the hosting of refugees, as defined by the 1951 Refugee Convention, only started in the 1960s.

This contemporary understanding of receiving 'refugees' coincided with the start of the much-celebrated 'open door policy' on the continent (van Garderen and Ebenstein, 2011). Yet, this 'open door policy' also occurred at the same time as the wars of liberation in countries such as South Africa, Namibia, Mozambique, Angola and Zimbabwe, which saw hundreds of thousands of refugees fleeing to neighbouring states (Rutinwa, 2002). For this reason, the initial reception offered to refugees in Zambia during this period took the form of an encampment policy (Hansen, 1979). This approach to reception has continued to this day.

The country witnessed a peak in refugee numbers in 2001, with around 300,000 refugees living mostly in camps and settlements (with others self-settled in rural and border areas and cities). This peak was due to the intensity of the conflict in the DRC, and political repression and economic tumult in Zimbabwe (Frischkorn, 2013). During this time there were six camps and settlements (Darwin, 2005).[14] As the numbers of refugees reduced (mainly due to the end of civil unrest in Angola, Rwanda and, for a period, the DRC), several of the camps and settlements closed. According to UNHCR figures, Zambia currently hosts around 94,618 persons of concern (UNHCR, 2022), with most refugees residing in the three main settlements, Meheba, Mayukwayukwa and Mantapala.[15]

Since 2018, Zambia has shown signs of potentially relaxing the encampment reception policy. Following the New York Declaration for Refugees and Migrants in 2016 and the formal adoption of the Global Compact on Refugees (which consists of a plan of action and the Comprehensive Refugee Response Framework (CRRF)), the now former president, Edgar Lungu made public commitments to *consider* allowing more freedom of movement and enhancing measures to enable refugees to engage in income-generating activities (Carciotto and Ferraro, 2020).[16] Part of this overall approach was the establishment of the Mantapala settlement in the north-east of the country in early 2018. The intention has been for this settlement to realise a more inclusive approach to housing refugees, with locals given land next to refugees in the settlement (Maple, 2018; Carciotto and Ferraro, 2020).

In terms of recent economic history, Zambia still bears the legacy of the colonial state's extractive political economy, and the 'hollowing out of the state' during the Structural Adjustment period (1980s–1990s) (Onuoha, 2008; Jepson and Henderson, 2016). Indeed, the country ranks amongst those with the highest levels of poverty and inequality globally. In 2015, 58 per cent of Zambia's 16.6 million people were earning less than the international poverty line of $1.90 per day (compared to 41 per cent across Africa) (World Bank, 2019). In respect of governance, Zambia is a unitary state with two levels of government: the National (or Central) and Local. There is also technically a provincial level, although in practice this is seen as an extension of the national government (Mutesa and Nchito, 2003; UN-Habitat, 2012). Power and responsibility for refugee matters are predominantly retained within the national government, although some relevant services are the responsibility of local government, such as public transport (UNHCR, 2012).[17]

From 2016 to 2021, under the presidency of Edgar Lungu, Zambia moved towards an authoritarian (or dominant) style of political settlement (Bebbington, et al., 2017; Phiri, 2016). Opposition political parties were threatened and their members imprisoned (Siachiwena, 2021a). In addition, civil society was increasingly silenced and the independent press shut down (Quak, 2019). As a result of this democratic 'backsliding', the president became less concerned about the risk of losing re-election (Quak, 2019) and was implementing long-term planning based on political self-interest and ideological commitments, such as pan-Africanism. It was, therefore, a surprise to many political commentators, that in 2021 Lungu lost the national election to Hakainde Hichilema of the United Party for National Development (UPND) (Siachiwena, 2021a). Siachiwena (2021a) calls the election a 'silent revolution'. With the democratic space essentially closed, there was no open or public agitation for change. Yet behind closed doors, Zambians had lost confidence in the president. Since the election, there exists some optimism that the new president can reverse the authoritarian shifts and oversee a refiguration of the country's political settlement (Siachiwena, 2021b). Early signs, however, are not encouraging in terms of greater freedom for civil society or the press (USDS, 2023). Similarly, time will tell if Hichilema will follow-up on the state's recent international commitments regarding more inclusion for refugees. The removal of all reference to refugees in the recent 8th Zambian National Development Plan raises concerns in this regard (8NDP, 2022).

In contrast to Zambia, South Africa can be seen as a 'deviant' case study in the context of Southern Africa (Gerring, 2008). A deviant case is selected to demonstrate a 'surprising' value, in this case, the decision by the state to maintain a broad free-settlement approach to refugee reception, when most neighbouring countries in Southern Africa adopt camp-based approaches. A key purpose of a deviant case study is, therefore, 'to probe for new – but as yet unspecified – explanations' to understand why the case defies the general approach or understanding (Gerring, 2008:106).

A free-settlement approach, while varying in implementation, can be understood as a reception policy, where upon arrival or once their stay has been formalised, refugees are permitted to freely move and settle in the host state (Masuku and Nkala, 2018). Thus, in the context of South Africa, refugees can move and reside wherever they choose. By selecting these two countries, the book can uniquely investigate two disparate overarching refugee reception policies, as well as two very different geographical reception sites (the refugee camp and the urban space) within the same sub-region of Africa.

South Africa has a comparatively short history of involvement with the global refugee regime, with institutionalisation at the national level commencing in the early 1990s. Equally, while post-apartheid South Africa is a party to the 1951 Refugee Convention, the state maintains an arms-length approach to UN agencies such as UNHCR (Landau and Segatti, 2009). Regardless of this tense relationship with global refugee regime institutions, the state maintains a generous approach to refugee reception, with no restrictions (at least in law) on freedom of movement for asylum-seekers or refugees. Even at times of crisis – for example with the large intake of forced migrants from Zimbabwe between 2003 and 2010 – the state avoided using encampment policies (Crush and Chikanda, 2014).[18]

In terms of numbers, UNHCR reported 250,250 persons of concern in the country in 2023 (UNHCR, 2023b). The real number, however, is higher due to the number of refugees living in cities like Johannesburg without documentation (Segatti, 2011). Due to patterns of mixed migration in the region, there are also large numbers of forced migrants living without formal documentation (Tati, 2008; Crisp and Kiragu, 2010). Since 2010/2011, reception policies at the national and local level have, however, noticeably shifted, with the Department of Home Affairs implementing several policies and regulations that have begun to shrink the asylum space (Crush et al., 2017). Furthermore, recent policy recommendations at the national level have proposed the creation of reception centres in border areas, which would severely restrict freedom of movement for asylum-seekers and refugees (Moyo, 2020).

In respect of recent economic history, as one of the richest countries on the continent, South Africa is at a different stage of socio-economic development to Zambia (AWR, 2020). Yet, it also represents a unique fusion of mature socio-economic and bureaucratic development, and a developing state with limited capacity and acute needs (Mulaudzi, 2015). Advancements in poverty reduction have slowed recently, with the $1.90 per day poverty rate increasing from 16.8 per cent to 18.8 per cent between 2011 and 2015. A key challenge remains unemployment, standing at 27.6 per cent in the first quarter of 2019 (World Bank, 2019).

Modern-day South Africa is a constitutional democracy with a three-tier system of government (national, provincial and local).[19] Each level has legislative and executive authority in specific spheres, with local government including eight metropolitan municipalities, such as Johannesburg and Cape Town (SAgov, 2020). The primary needs of refugees including shelter, access to education, health and economic opportunities are the responsibility of the national government (and to a lesser extent, the provincial government) (Landau et al., 2011). Nevertheless, some key services such as public clinics do fall under the purview of the local government (Musuva, 2015).

Despite the post-1994 political dominance of the African National Congress (ANC) at the national level, post-apartheid South Africa can be characterised as a competitive state with power dispersed across political parties (Levy et al., 2015). However, twenty years after the end of the apartheid regime, cracks in the political settlement are showing, with risks of internal conflict ever-present. Nevertheless, with recent local municipality elections being won by political parties opposing the ANC, for now the settlement remains competitive with elites focusing on short-term goals (Levy et al., 2015).[20] Finally, with the ruling competitive political settlement willing to listen to xenophobic attitudes within the voting public, refugees have recently found that the reception offered is increasingly restrictive (Fauvelle-Aymar and Segatti, 2011; Misago et al., 2010).

As set out above, it is evident that there are significant differences in approach to the reception of refugees between the two countries. The intention, therefore, is to develop an understanding of the reasons behind these alternative responses through a state-focused analysis. Notwithstanding, it also becomes apparent that as well as differences, there are also numerous themes and concepts that connect the two neighbouring states, both of which share the task of welcoming considerable numbers of refugees onto their territory. These connections will be utilised to draw out a conceptualisation of refugee reception in Southern Africa at the end of the book.

Potential limitations of comparative case studies

Concerns raised about in-depth case studies commonly relate to selection bias, which occurs when a project intentionally chooses the countries that are to be compared (Collier, 1995). In essence, selection bias can under- or over-emphasise the relationship between variables and is likely to be particularly misleading when findings are generalised to a wider setting (Collier and Mahoney, 1996). As will be examined further in Chapter 3, small sample case studies produce insights with a limited capacity to generalise beyond the specific cases. To minimise this risk, any attempts in the book to generalise the findings beyond the chosen countries and sub-region are deliberately modest. Indeed, the assertion is that the two cases, in and of themselves, are of sufficient academic interest rather than just being bearers of a set of variables.[21] Despite being close neighbours, they adopt divergent national refugee reception policies, they exhibit contrasting relationships with the global refugee regime (including the implementation of global refugee norms and engagement with UNHCR) and there have been recent noticeable (and divergent) signs of shifts in approaches to reception policies in each country.

Finally, inherent in these discussions are concerns about verification bias. This is the belief that case studies contain a bias toward verification, meaning a tendency to frame a project in a specific way so that it confirms a researcher's preconceived notions. To guard against this possibility, a researcher needs to remain open to alternative explanations. Indeed, if conducted correctly, an advantage of the case study approach can be that it 'closes in' on real life situations and tests 'views directly in relation to phenomena as they unfold in practice' (Flyvbjerg, 2006:19). In this way, it is common for case material to test and subsequently show

how preconceived assumptions and concepts were wrong, and in doing so force researchers to re-evaluate their understanding of an issue (Bennett, 2004; Flyvbjerg, 2006). As examined in future chapters, pre-existing assumptions I held about why states respond to refugee arrivals in specific ways were tested by the book's case material. For example, preconceived notions regarding the role and importance of the global refugee regime in reception policies in Southern Africa were continually tested and had to be re-evaluated in light of the empirical evidence.

The structure of the book

Chapter 1 examines the notion of reception in relation to the arrival of refugees within the country of asylum. The chapter's emphasis is on urban and camp spaces as reception sites. The chapter outlines a working understanding of refugee 'reception' that frames it as a *process* whereby state, international and local actors shape a refugee's ability to engage with local communities and markets when attempting to pursue their own personal and economic aims. In this way, reception is more than just a one-off event, or the end to a singular journey or the act of finding immediate shelter. It can be all these things, but it also includes the process of refugees engaging with local networks and structures to settle within a particular area.

On this basis, the first chapter introduces the book's conceptual framework. By adopting Betts and Orchard's (2014) theory of norm implementation as a conceptual framework, the book sets out an analytical approach to investigating why states respond to refugee arrivals in divergent ways. At the heart of this framework is a heuristic tripartite model that outlines key 'causal mechanisms' (namely ideational, material and institutional factors) embedded within state behaviour that can constrain, alter or aid in the implementation of core global refugee regime norms. This *trilogy of factors* is adopted to analyse key variables that are influencing the responses of states to the arrival of refugees. The theory of norm implementation suggests that finding neat and constant causal links between a factor (or factors) and a state-run refugee reception policy is, nevertheless, improbable. Rather, the creation and continual implementation of reception policies are likely to reflect ongoing processes of negotiation and renegotiation between institutional actors. During these 'negotiations', different factors interact, reinforce and/or contest with each other to create a given response. This explains why reception policies are often prone to incremental or sudden shifts over time.

Chapter 2 examines three academic debates that are key to framing an understanding of why states receive refugees in different ways. The debates have been selected because they attempt to identify and explain wider factors that influence the reception of refugees in Africa. The first debate investigates why, since the 1980s, the majority of states in the region have shifted from free-settlement to encampment reception policies. The 'democracy-asylum' nexus is introduced as a credible reason for these behaviours. In essence, the nexus idea posits a negative correlation between democratic structures and the accessibility of asylum measures. As states on the continent introduced more democratic processes in the 1980s, the space for asylum started to shrink, with refugees increasingly being moved to refugee camps. The chapter highlights how the 'democracy-asylum' nexus concept can be applied to explain contemporary refugee reception policies. This forms the platform for subsequent chapters to investigate links between the disruptive role refugee movement can have on urban spaces and democratic structures (including electoral accountability) in the host state.

The second debate considers how the 'global' inserts itself into the national and local levels. Specifically, the section examines the continuing influence of the global refugee regime (via its international governance frameworks and main actor, UNHCR) in the context of refugee reception in Africa. In contrast to the regime's apparently dominant presence in refugee camps, the section questions the regime's continued relevance in the everyday practice of reception in urban spaces. The third debate addresses the ongoing influence of 'securitisation' theory in research on state responses to refugee movement (including both cross-border and within territory movement). The section raises concerns about how contemporary academic studies can at times appear one-dimensional, namely by portraying states as seeing *all* cross-border movement of low-skilled migrants/refugees as negative when viewed through a security lens. The chapter introduces a complementary 'stability' lens to that of security as necessary to bring more nuance to discussions on the relationship between refugee movements, state structures and reception policies. Subsequent chapters will develop understanding related to these three debates through their examination of reception policies in Southern Africa.

Chapter 3 explores how the methodology for the book was developed from the conceptual investigation of refugee reception and the examination of the literature on state responses to refugee arrivals in Africa. Specifically, the chapter builds on the previous two chapters, by explaining the research methodology step-by-step through the distinct phases of the project, from choosing the research design through to collecting and analysing the data. The chapter also offers a critical reflection on the methodological and ethical choices made during the life of the book project.

By taking this systematic approach to methodology, the chapter aims to be a model for future work by scholars developing and designing similar projects.

Chapters 4 to 7 examine the empirical data collected concerning the urban and camp spaces as reception sites in the two case studies. Analysis in these chapters is predominantly conducted from the perspective of the 'state', with a focus on the dominant national-level refugee reception policy. Nevertheless, incorporating a multi-scalar approach to the state perspective enables engagement with processes relating to refugee reception at different levels of analysis (the international, the national, the local and sub-local). This allows for possible variations in reception policy at different levels of the state to also be examined.

Chapter 4 questions why Zambia has adopted and maintained an encampment policy for receiving refugees over the last sixty years. The chapter highlights the importance of national refugee legal frameworks in relation to the implementation of policies at initial registration.[22] Indeed, a former legal framework, which focuses entirely on the creation and maintenance of refugee settlements, continues to inform and influence the understanding of refugees at the national level. As a result, refugees are essentially understood by large portions of the national government as 'regime refugees', who reside within the confines of the settlements.

Even so, the chapter shows how, in Zambia, the refugee camp is profoundly connected to the urban space, with the Commission for Refugees (COR) allowing a certain number of refugees to leave the camp space either to engage with nearby communities or to travel to large urban areas. The empirical evidence shows that the aim of the dominant camp reception policy is not about stopping all movement of refugees; rather, it can be understood as a filter to regulate and manage the numbers of refugees in urban spaces. In this way, the chapter highlights how, paradoxically, the adoption of camp-based reception creates sufficient stability for *some* movement. Finally, because of this perceived stability (via the managing of refugee movement), the camp reception policy continues to help prevent the emergence of top-down and bottom-up securitisation of refugees in Zambia.

Chapter 5 investigates post-registration reception in Zambia. The chapter engages primarily with the behaviour of key actors from the international and national level inside and outside the settlements. International protection in Zambia – as implemented by UNHCR – is essentially restricted to the refugee camp. Indeed, the UN agency is reluctant to work with, or assist, refugees outside of the settlements. This stance essentially confines the global refugee regime to the camp space. Therefore, for many refugees, they have little choice but to give up certain key rights and freedoms to gain access to essential humanitarian services. In contrast, urban refugees in Zambia are understood by both the state and UNHCR to have full human agency. As such, they are seen as fundamentally distinct from the 'regime refugees' in the settlements. By conducting journeys to the urban space in their attempts to pursue personal and economic goals, refugees are in effect moving outside of the construct of a refugee in Zambia. In this way, the chapter shows how urban refugees are slowly being shifted away from the refugee label (and the associated protections of the global refugee regime that this brings), towards a more general (and often illegal) migrant label.

Chapter 6 moves to consider the second case study, South Africa, and examines the initial registration of refugees. With South Africa currently adopting a free-settlement reception approach, the geographical focus of the chapter is on the urban space. The initial welcome granted to refugees – in law at least – is particularly generous, with no spatial restrictions, meaning refugees are free to move unimpeded around the territory. Here, the chapter again highlights the role and influence of the national refugee legal framework in the implementation of reception policies. Indeed, the 1998 Refugee Act, in combination with ideologies based on pan-Africanism and notions of fairness stemming from the need to find distance from the old apartheid regime, are helping to contest recent pushes by elements of the national government to move to a more camp-based approach to reception. In contrast, key elements of the global refugee regime, namely UNHCR, are ostensibly held at arm's length by the ruling political settlement at this initial stage of reception.

The maintenance of a free-settlement approach to reception is not, however immune to institutional and material contestation. Since the 2010s, concerns surrounding instability brought on by increased cross-border movement have started to gain momentum. As the chapter observes, unrestricted movement of non-citizens is always likely to cause a reaction. The result of these concerns has been the adoption of a security lens at the national level to frame the movement of refugees (and other cross-border African migrants) into urban areas. As explained using the 'democracy-asylum' nexus, increased numbers of asylum-seekers and refugees has created negative democratic loops, whereby perceived additional competition for resources has created resentment amongst host populations, thus the state becomes politically motivated to move away from ideals based on solidarity and pan-Africanism, to ones framing migrants as a 'problem'.

Chapter 7 analyses the self-settlement policy in South Africa after initial registration. Significantly, due to the length of journeys typically taken to arrive in cities like Johannesburg, coupled with the granting of freedom of movement and some employment rights, urban refugees are constructed as an entirely self-sufficient category of migrants by the national government and UNHCR. We therefore again see urban refugees in Southern Africa diverging from the framing of 'regime refugees' seen in camp spaces in the sub-region. This framing is then seen as justification by the national government and UNHCR for their choice to abandon several key obligations relating to protection and integration as set out by the global refugee regime. Instead, a delicate, if highly contested, relationship emerges between host and guest in the urban space, whereby the bulk of obligations falls on the visitor. Refugees are granted temporary access to cities as visitors, with an implicit understanding that they remain essentially invisible and unproblematic.

The focus on refugee movement at the level of the city nevertheless conflicts with the current broader national approach investigated in the previous chapter. Here a security lens is gradually being applied to all forms of cross-border movement. Thus, if there is too much perceived movement into urban spaces, this will likely cause contestation or even a rupture in the delicate host/guest relationship at the level of the city. A precarious and conditional form of reception therefore emerges in urban spaces.

The Conclusions chapter is split into four parts, each examining key conceptual and analytical findings from across both case studies. Firstly, the chapter questions current understandings of 'reception' by outlining a contemporary conceptualisation of refugee reception in Southern Africa. Secondly, the chapter interrogates the analytical benefits and limitations of the theory of norm implementation in this book. Thirdly, the chapter establishes the main contributions to academic knowledge made by the book in relation to the three debates about refugee responses in Southern Africa that are outlined in Chapter 2. Those findings are then utilised in the final section to examine the key implications of the book for national and international actors and advocates working on issues related to the reception of refugees in Southern Africa.

Notes

1. See also Arar and FitzGerald (2023).
2. These include the Convention relating to the Status of Refugees (1951) and the OAU [Organisation of the African Union] Convention Governing Specific Aspects of Refugee Problems in Africa.
3. Large numbers of refugees in Africa avoid or reject state reception policies by settling informally (d'Orsi, 2019).

4. This book replaces 'global north' with minority world and 'global south' with majority world. This is to emphasise how the privileged global north holds the minority of the global population, while the global south holds the majority (Alam, 2008; Punch, 2016).

5. There were notable exceptions: Kibreab (1996); Sommers (1999).

6. See Jaquenod (2014).

7. See Omata and Kaplan (2013).

8. See Fiddian-Qasmiyeh (2015, 2016); Basok (2009); Varsanyi (2006); Landau (2014); Sanyal (2017).

9. See also Landau (2018a); Fiddian-Qasmiyeh (2015, 2016).

10. This is not to imply that political science vs. anthropology differences align with macro- vs. micro-level theories.

11. For example, see Abdelaaty (2021).

12. See Betts et al. (2018); Omata and Kaplan (2013); Betts et al. (2019).

13. This distinction is often based on the willingness of states to permit activities beyond humanitarian assistance (Omata and Kaplan, 2013).

14. Mayukwayukwa, Meheba, Kala, Mwange, Nangweshi and Ukwimi.

15. The number is higher when you include self-settled refugees in urban and border areas.

16. See UNGA (2016); UNGA (2018).

17. Both Zambia and South Africa governance structures are (in different ways) the result of European structures and concepts being 'grafted onto them' during colonial times. Yet, while these structures may look like Western norms, they develop politically, economically and culturally into unique hybrid entities (Somerville, 2017; Chabal and Daloz, 1999).

18. See Betts and Kaytaz (2009).

19. Debate remains over whether South Africa is a unitary or federal state (Schwella, 2016).

20. Power has started to shift at the city level in South Africa, with the Democratic Alliance (DA) winning control of Cape Town in 2006 and Johannesburg in 2016.

21. See Lor (2011); Ragin (1987).

22. For each country, analysis is broadly separated out into two stages – namely, 'registration stage' and 'post-registration stage', with a chapter for each stage. As examined later, there is analytical value in separating out reception into these phases. Nevertheless, at times these stages merge or become hard to distinguish. Additionally, refugees may remain indefinitely in the 'registration stage'.

Chapter 1

Framing refugee reception

The idea of 'reception' is at the very heart of refugeehood: it speaks directly to the forms of welcome and protection offered to persons seeking refuge in host states. Yet the notion of reception itself remains ill-defined both conceptually and in practice. This is true in international law, in the policy norms and practice of host states and international organisations, and within academia more broadly.[1] When reception is examined in literature, it is often seen as an ephemeral moment (such as registration) of a much larger interaction between refugee and host state. Yet this portrayal does not reflect the multi-directional and multi-locational dynamics of contemporary refugee arrival, particularly the role reception policies play in a refugee's ability to move within the host state and engage with local populations and markets in pursuit of their personal and economic aims.

The aim of this chapter is to provide the theoretical underpinnings of the book. Specifically, the chapter's task is to develop – by taking a state-focused approach – a preliminary understanding of reception and to set out a conceptual framework that can respond to the question of why states receive refugees in different ways.[2] This is achieved by utilising literature from refugee and forced migration studies and associated fields that have investigated the arrival and initial welcome of refugees.

The chapter is split into two parts, investigating distinctive but overlapping conceptual aspects of reception. The first half of the chapter examines a range of interdisciplinary literature to develop an initial conceptual understanding of refugee reception. This body of work understands reception as a *process*. This process encompasses the host state's and other key actors' behaviours, which interact with a refugee's ability to engage with local communities and markets when attempting to pursue their own personal and economic aims. The first half of the chapter then moves to consider how states understand this form of cross-border arrival. It is important to do this, given the global trends showing that states are increasingly adopting reception policies that are in direct conflict with the international commitments they made when they became party to the global refugee regime. The first half of the chapter ends with an investigation of how key reception sites (the camp and urban space) can be understood in terms of state responses to refugee arrival, as well as how these sites shape a refugee's ability to settle. Taken together, these three strands of analysis set out an approach to understanding refugee reception, which will then be developed throughout the book, with the goal of establishing a grounded conceptualisation of refugee reception in the context of Southern Africa.

The second half of the chapter introduces the book's conceptual framework through which the notion of reception will be analysed. The adoption and adaption of Betts and Orchard's theory of norm implementation as the book's conceptual framework is a result of the literature reviewed for this project.[3] Accordingly, the literature canvassed in the first half of this chapter is drawn upon to identify key concepts (and the connections between them) that are relevant to understanding refugee reception and differing state reception policies. This, along with the initial fieldwork phase, informed the selection of a fitting conceptual framework within which to embed the study.[4]

Understanding reception

The concept of reception remains largely elusive within the fields of refugee and forced migration studies. When it is discussed, it is regularly framed as an ephemeral moment or one element, such as a registration procedure, of a larger set of interactions between the refugee and the host state. This is perhaps understandable in mass influx contexts. In these situations, with the setting up of emergency camps, the idea of reception can appear self-evident. Registration, accommodation and aid are all supplied at the point of entry onto the territory. This 'reception phase' then ends when refugees move from emergency transit camps to more permanent camps or are permitted into urban areas.[5]

This scenario, nevertheless, does not fully reflect the role reception policies play in the contemporary dynamics of refugee arrival and attempts by refugees to meet basic needs and find economic opportunities within the host state – particularly in the majority world. In contrast to the – at times highly managed – arrivals at emergency transit camps, states regularly encounter more sporadic and/or circular patterns of refugee movement

(Landau, 2018a). In these situations, the notion of reception is much harder to articulate. For example, refugees in many regions of Africa frequently move back and forth across a border between a 'home' state and host state (Bakewell, 2014). They may settle for periods of time within a local host population in border areas during times of unrest, and then return 'home' when conditions across the border calm down.[6] Equally, refugees regularly find their way independently to urban spaces in host states. In these urban sprawls, the idea of refugee reception is equally hard to determine, especially as there is often no formal policy or practice in place beyond initial registration (Polzer, 2009; Hovil and Maple, 2022).[7]

Consequently, a lack of clarity surrounding the concept of reception itself persists. Indeed, fundamental questions such as 'what *is* reception in the context of cross-border movement of refugees?' and 'what does reception involve?' remain unanswered. Equally, from the perspective of key actors, do understandings of reception fluctuate at different levels of analysis (that is, between the global and national or the national and the local)? For instance, how does a host state's framing of reception compare to a more global understanding of reception by UNHCR actors, based on the implementation of international norms contained within the global refugee regime? Finally, when narrowing attention to specific reception sites, further questions arise, such as 'how should refugee reception in urban spaces be understood or conceptualised?' With the line between camp and local areas often becoming blurred, is a simple understanding of reception (such as a refugee's stay being formalised before being moved to a refugee camp) any longer sufficient? These varied questions remain highly significant as state-based reception policies unquestionably play a key role in how refugees settle in host states. Yet, without first addressing the initial conceptual queries about what reception *is*, it is difficult to move on to more developed enquiries concerning the *role* of reception in determining how refugees settle and engage with local communities and economies.

The 'context of reception' approach

To generate an understanding of refugee reception, the book takes its lead from the 'context of reception' approach, as introduced by Portes and Böröcz (1989). Acquired from migration studies, this approach is primarily interested in the host state and its methods of integrating migrants into the local labour force (Guarnizo et al., 1999; Portes and Landolt 1996; van Amersfoort and van Niekerk, 2006).[8] At the heart of this perspective is the belief that to understand reception you need to investigate 'how state policies shape newcomers' experiences when attempting to integrate and their opportunities for mobility' (Asad, 2015:282). This can range from how government policies affect a migrant's access to labour markets, to how policy interacts with changing perceptions of the public (Grosfoguel, 2004).

This understanding of cross-border reception acknowledges that the ruling political settlement's role is not exclusive. In addition to the national government, the actions of a multiplicity of actors, at different levels within society, can all play an important part. Indeed, state policy designed to constrain or control migrant movement is often modified or contested by the 'countervailing actions of other participants in the process' (Portes and Böröcz, 1989:626). Reception is therefore framed as a *process* informed by a multitude of factors (including cultural and social ones) at different levels of the state. With this assertion, the 'context of reception' approach diverges in two key regards from more traditional understandings of refugee reception and refugee movement: firstly, in how it frames the host state in terms of arrival and secondly, by viewing reception as a process rather than an 'event'.

A multi-scalar lens

Taking these points in turn, research that investigates host states in terms of refugee-hosting and protection often remains broad in focus, with a tendency to draw holistic conclusions that create an image of a 'black box' state (Betts, 2009b). Through this lens, states are seen as acting in self-interest, with their identity and actions fixed and interests pre-defined (Betts, 2009b). There are undoubtedly benefits to generalising actions when examining and attempting to map and/or predict state behaviour. Nevertheless, this approach regularly misses the complexity of situations within individual states (Ravenhill, 1990).

In contrast, by utilising the 'context of reception' approach, this book can incorporate a multi-scalar lens to understanding state responses to refugees.[9] At its core, this lens allows research to probe into how reception policies are conceived, shaped and implemented at different levels of the state. For these purposes, policy and practice are examined at these different levels: the international level – for example, the global refugee regime, the 1951 Refugee Convention and global UNHCR policy; the national level – for example, national refugee law and national refugee policies; the local level – for example, local level or municipality policy and practice; and finally the sub-local level – for example, the role and impact of other refugees and local communities.[10] In this way, a multi-scalar analysis underlines the importance of recognising the 'plurality of actors involved' in the reception of refugees (Fiddian-Qasmiyeh, 2019:40).

Despite this, the focus of the 'context of reception' approach remains predominantly at the national level. Indeed, alternative forms of reception at the sub-local and local levels are still 'nested in larger geopolitical hierarchies' (Jaworsky et al., 2012:4). This justification for a state-focused understanding of reception is not, however, a dismissal of the role of the 'global' or 'local'. Rather, it is a starting point for further research into a more dynamic concept of reception. Indeed, as examined below, the local level can be a site of real divergence from the national in terms of how reception policies are implemented. Concurrently, it also illustrates how each level is deeply connected to the welcome refugees receive in a host state. For example, where refugee movement into urban spaces becomes associated with a sense of instability, the resulting community tensions (particularly when expressed through violence towards forced migrants) can feed into politics played out at the national level.

Thus, localised attitudes regularly 'scale up' and contribute to policy change at the national level. At the other end of the scale, the global refugee regime (via international legal frameworks, key regime norms and international actors) can also 'cascade down' and play an influential role in reception policies at the national and local level. The adoption of this alternative, multi-scalar method of examining host states in relation to the implementation of refugee policies, is developed further when the chapter introduces the book's conceptual framework below.

Reception as a process

Turning to the second point, the 'context of reception' approach conceptualises reception as a process rather than a one-off event. As highlighted above, when reception has previously been discussed in the fields of refugee and forced migration studies, it has traditionally been portrayed as a mere moment in time, such as the crossing of a border or gaining status via registration procedures. In contrast, there are no definite parameters in terms of duration to reception within this broader migration approach. Instead, reception is seen as a process whereby the state (and other actors) interacts with a migrant's ability to move and engage with local communities and settle. Indeed, as argued below, reception (and by extension reception policies) at the national and local level reflects ongoing processes of negotiation and renegotiation between different key actors.

Contemporary research on refugee movement and mobility does highlight a point of departure from Portes and Böröcz's (1989) original work. While the 'context of reception' approach sees reception as an ongoing process, it nevertheless understands migrant movement as *unilinear* (one-directional) until the point of arrival, when movement effectively ends

(Grosfoguel, 2004). In contrast, recent academic work within the context of the majority world shows that refugee movement is often circular or pendular, sporadic and unpredictable (Omata and Kaplan, 2013; Chapotera, 2018). This is particularly evident in the environs of modern-day cities in Africa (Landau, 2018b; Omata and Kaplan, 2013). For example, many refugees continuously move between different urban spaces (in-country and between host states) in search of better social and economic opportunities (Landau, 2018a). This indicates that purely destination-focused understandings of reception need to be modified (Collyer and King, 2016; Flahaux and De Haas, 2016).

Appraisal of the 'context of reception' approach

By integrating the 'context of reception' approach with contemporary research that questions more traditional notions of refugee movement, the previous section has set out an initial working understanding of *reception*. Accordingly, it will act as the foundation and guide for developing a conceptualisation of refugee reception in specific settings in future chapters. The adoption of a state-focused lens to reception nevertheless also brings challenges, particularly concerning the role of other actors. Firstly, the 'context of reception' approach has been critiqued for being too state-centric, with the role of the international and local often dismissed or overlooked (Grosfoguel, 2003). Portes and Böröcz (1989) do acknowledge the influence of international governance systems which, as noted above, are incorporated into the book's analysis and indeed form a core element of the adopted conceptual framework. Also, this area of scholarship has developed and expanded in recent years (Jaworsky et al., 2012). Specifically, this understanding of reception has been applied at lower levels, such as cities (Cadge and Ecklund, 2007; Bloemraad, 2006; Guarnizo et al., 1999). At this level, the role of contextual factors (such as local networks and social capital in reception) has also been examined (Waldinger, 2001).

Secondly, the 'context of reception' model stresses the importance of understanding 'how state policies shape newcomers' experiences when attempting to *integrate* and their opportunities for mobility' (Asad, 2015:282, emphasis added). Based on the research carried out for this book, the book substitutes 'pursue their own personal and economic aims' for 'integration'. This is because, as examined thoroughly in future chapters, it is evident that not all refugees and forced migrants choose to 'integrate' into local communities. Many refugees in Southern Africa understand urban spaces in host states more as resources than new 'homes'. As a result, 'integration' has become a contested term in some of the recent scholarship on urban displacement in Africa (Landau, 2018a). Equally, for the purpose of this book, at a minimum, 'personal and economic aims' is understood as the social and economic ability of a refugee to meet their urgent needs, which may include accessing protection and assistance from local, national and international structures.[11]

Notwithstanding this shift in terminology and understanding, the emphasis nevertheless remains on state responses. Specifically, this conceptualisation of reception is concerned with the implications of state-based reception policies on refugees' attempts to pursue their own personal and economic aims. Attention, therefore, remains at the state level rather than taking a more localised approach and looking at how refugees experience reception. Thus, in the next two sections, understanding is developed around a key element of this initial discussion of refugee reception: namely *the processes by which host state policy shapes* refugees' experiences and responses when attempting to settle in the host state.

How states understand refugee reception

The chapter now examines how host states (as the key actors in this book) understand this form of cross-border arrival. Specifically, this section asks whether there is something inherent within the construction of the refugee figure that makes states' attitudes to their reception unique. This will be addressed by investigating an emerging body of literature within the fields of forced migration and human geography that examines how host states conceptualise the *offer* of reception to refugees. In doing so, this section continues to develop and integrate different strands of understanding surrounding state-based refugee reception.

Taking inspiration from the work of Derrida (2000), Pitt-Rivers (2012) and Nancy (2000), a growing body of research has started to conceptualise *state-offered* reception (also discussed in terms of hosting or hospitality) in terms of the limitations inherent within the offer (Collyer, 2014). This 'qualified' welcome normally manifests itself in two ways: firstly, reception is usually temporary in nature and excludes any claim to a right to residence per se; secondly, acceptance into the host's territory confers conditional rights *and* obligations to the migrant via international and domestic law and policy. Thus, beyond an initial welcome, reception can normally be understood as conditional and restrictive (Stronks, 2012).[12] As observed by Fiddian-Qasmiyeh and Berg (2018:3), this conditional component of state reception often has a spatial dimension, for example, a refugee camp.[13]

The conditional and temporary aspects of the welcome offered to refugees can be traced back to the creation of the global refugee regime. The modern system of states is based on the notion of 'sovereign' states, whereby membership of a state is required before rights and protections can be forthcoming (Arendt, 1951). When refugees cross a border, they effectively arrive without such 'membership' and hence are perceived as victims or 'objects of pity', who need to be welcomed by a political community in order to have an identity as a right-bearer (Aleinikoff, 1995). This goes to a paradox at the heart of the refugee definition. By becoming formally recognised as a refugee, an individual accrues the rights and norms contained within the global refugee regime. Indeed, member states party to the global regime have an obligation to incorporate these international norms into their reception policies. However, in practice refugees often also must give up certain rights – and ultimately dehumanise themselves – to gain other fundamental ones. This is because refugees, as 'people on the move', are less threatening to states than other migrants, as they can legitimately be contained. They have lost the protection and membership of their home state and so to seek protection from another, they become guests with little choice but to submit to the conditional reception offered (Aleinikoff, 1995).

This understanding of the refugee, and the temporary and restricted spatial nature of the welcome regularly afforded to them, can be observed in host states in both the minority world and the majority world. In Africa, states have been praised for their 'generous' welcome towards refugees. Nevertheless, as examined in the next chapter, this essentially amounts to maintaining an 'open door' policy towards forced migrants since the end of colonial regimes (Rutinwa, 1999; Fielden, 2008; van Garderen and Ebenstein, 2011). However, once a refugee moves past this initial 'welcome' (that is, being allowed entry at the border), reception policies are usually conditional and restrictive. For example, the welcome afforded to refugees in countries such as Malawi and Zambia is provisional and based on the expectation that they remain in refugee camps (Lindley, 2011; Darwin, 2005).

Within many refugee-hosting states in the majority world, this conditional approach to reception equally applies to UNHCR and the global refugee regime more broadly. As Banerjee and Samaddar (2018) note, humanitarianism in post-colonial countries is often a double-edged sword. It saves lives but also regularly reduces the persons involved to objects of charity. Indeed, refugees are often only able to access core norms and services attached to the regime if they remain within the confines of a refugee camp (Schmidt, 2014).

In host countries in the minority world, reception policies can appear to be very different, with refugees regularly granted a range of key global refugee regime norms, including freedom of movement (Zieck, 2018).[14] As such, at least in policy and law, state-offered reception in these states can seem magnanimous. Nevertheless, even when a refugee has access to large urban centres, host states (at various levels) often find ways of reminding the refugee that they remain a guest and as such that the city is not 'theirs' (Sanyal, 2014; Hovil and Maple, 2022). Similar to the refugee camp, where space is demarcated or 'walled', within the perceived chaos of modern cities sovereign power is still likely to be asserted (Darling, 2009; Pasquetti and Picker, 2017; Sanyal, 2014). Moreover, in both the minority and majority world, gaining a form of permanent legal status is often very difficult (Daley, 2013; Manby, 2016), the result being that refugees stay as permanent guests, regardless of the time they spend in the territory.

Pugh (2011:6) goes further in commenting on this guest and host dynamic, by referring to an 'invisibility bargain' whereby international migrants are expected to conform to a set of unwritten expectations. Within this unspoken agreement, the state tolerates the presence of some migrants (even some without legal documentation) if they bring economic value while simultaneously remaining politically and socially invisible. In essence, migrants are not expected to make 'political demands on the government, and ... they essentially are relegated to serving, but not participating as equals, within the host society' (Pugh, 2011:6).

This book builds on this existing body of work by investigating how obligations relating to arrival and reception are divided between the host (the state) and the guest (the refugee) in Southern Africa. By way of illustration, a host state may incorporate international norms and rights from the global refugee regime into their national frameworks, yet reception policies (*de jure* or *de facto*) on the ground, via processes of negotiation, may in effect 'dissuade' refugees from demanding these rights while they attempt to settle in the host state.

The observation that reception is implicitly conditional is nevertheless open to critique. Firstly, Fiddian-Qasmiyeh (2016) suggests that it is not always inevitable that a 'welcome' will bring some form of tension or conditionality. Secondly, within these discussions, the national government is generally framed as the sole gatekeeper, with unique powers to permit and/ or restrict varying forms of 'membership' within the state. Yet, practices occur at the lower levels of the state that may resist these 'fatalistic invocations' of hosting refugees and migrants (Fiddian-Qasmiyeh and Berg, 2018:3), for example, the invaluable role local communities and settled refugees play in the reception of new arrivals (Fiddian-Qasmiyeh, 2015).

Such criticisms largely stem from an objection to seeing the state as a 'black box' and framing reception (or hosting or hospitality) solely from the perspective of the national government. Indeed, seen in this way, the critiques serve as a valuable prompt to reflect on the multitude of networks and structures (at different levels) that refugees utilise when attempting to settle in a host country. However, these critiques appear to stop short of directly engaging with the assertion that reception policies adopted at the national level are likely to contain inherent limits to reception (for example, spatial restrictions). This issue will be addressed in future chapters by interrogating these concepts via a state-focused analysis, as well as through acknowledging the role of lower levels in creating alternative forms of reception and welcome. Moreover, by adopting the conceptual framework that will be set out in the second half of this chapter, the book develops this area of work further by examining the key factors *behind* how the relationships and power dynamics between state actors and other key stakeholders evolve.

Understanding reception sites

This section examines relevant contemporary research to draw out key understandings regarding the refugee camp and the urban space as reception sites.[15] Specifically, academic work from the fields of forced migration studies and human geography are used to show how refugee camps and urban areas as geographical spaces inform and contest the host state's offer of reception; the relationship that forms between these spaces via reception policies and refugee movement; and how these spaces interact with refugees' attempts to pursue their own personal and economic aims. In this way, the section will incorporate concepts from the previous two sections, including the conditionality of reception, while concurrently developing new strands of understanding around refugee reception.

There is, however, a significant discrepancy between the quantity of academic work conducted on these two geographical areas. Research on the camp space is extensive, with refugee camps more broadly remaining the focus of academia in relation to refugee arrivals throughout the 1990s and early 2000s (Da Costa, 2006; Crisp, 2017).[16] In contrast, little work has looked at the urban space as a site of *state-based reception* for refugees, particularly in the context of Africa. Instead, literature in this area has focused on topics such as self-settlement, local networks, and localised forms of hospitality (Hovil, 2007, 2016; Subulwa, 2019). Nevertheless, by engaging with literature that has investigated the movement of refugees into urban spaces from a ground-level perspective, some key insights relevant to this book can be gleaned.

The refugee camp as a site of reception

For the purposes of understanding the refugee camp as a site of reception, a key starting point in the literature is the considerable body of research that has adopted the work of modern political philosophers such as Foucault (1979), Arendt (1958) and Agamben (1998, 2005). Certainly, Agamben's work (1998) has generated a substantial amount of research (Owens, 2009; Ramadan, 2013; Turner, 2016; Martin 2015). A full exploration of this literature is not within the scope of this book. Nevertheless, it is illuminating to introduce specific elements of Agamben's work that have been popularised in forced migration literature as they are relevant to analysing the refugee camp as a site of reception, and ultimately to the question of why states respond to refugees in particular ways.

One of Agamben's key contributions has been in framing how governments situate the camp space as a geographical and political space removed from the interior and political life of the host state. According to Agamben, refugees are a 'disquieting element' to the normal order of states, nations and citizens (Agamben, 2000:21). As a way of removing the 'problem', refugees are relocated to designated and separate spaces. Relying on the work of Hannah Arendt, who saw camps as the denial of political space (Nyers, 2006:17), Agamben (1998) argues that inside refugee camps, refugees are solely biological beings – as mere animals – without political rights. As Bauman (2002) puts it, they are 'in' national spaces, but they are not 'of' these spaces.[17] This construction of refugee camps sees refugees reduced to 'bare life', in permanent 'states of exception' outside the law (Owens, 2009).

There is a wealth of academic literature on refugee camps that has adopted these concepts to analyse the separation of refugees from the interior and the political life of the host state (Owens, 2009; Ramadan, 2013; Malkki, 1992; Diken and Laustsen, 2005). Key observations within the wider field that draw from these concepts include how UNHCR regularly becomes a 'surrogate state' in terms of running refugee camps (Slaughter and Crisp, 2008). In doing so, these humanitarian spaces relieve the host state of its obligations towards refugees within its territory (Hyndman, 2000). In essence, by placing refugees in camps, the responsibility to care for their well-being is transferred to international actors. In these humanitarian spaces, refugees are warehoused and 'managed', with little political space (Sanyal, 2017; Hyndman, 2000; Minca, 2015).

This type of representation of the camp space has nevertheless been challenged and reappraised in recent years (Martin, 2015; Ramadan, 2013). Critical geographers have particularly questioned these portrayals of the refugee and the geographical space (Sanyal, 2014). Firstly, the depiction of 'bare life' in refugee camps diminishes the role of the human agency in creating political and economic opportunities, despite the inherent limitations within these sites of reception (Owens, 2009). Far from being devoid of political activity, unique forms of politics regularly emerge in these spaces (Sanyal, 2014; Ramadan, 2013; Darling, 2009; Newhouse, 2015). Secondly, academics have observed how 'spaces of exception' tend to spread out into their neighbouring environments (Martin, 2015; Sanyal, 2014). As Sanyal (2017) notes, camps in Kenya, Lebanon and Jordan may have started as tents during emergency responses, but over time permanent structures are built and informal economies begin to grow.[18] The evolution of the refugee camp in many countries in the majority world has led academics to question how we understand and conceptualise these complex reception sites (Agier, 2008; Montclos and Kagwanja, 2000; Sanyal, 2014).

These critiques are well-grounded, indeed a great deal of empirical evidence now directly contradicts fatalistic conceptualisations of the camp space (Hyndman, 2000; Turner, 2016). Furthermore, purely in relation to academic benefit, Crisp (2015) raises concerns around the 'over-intellectualisation' of the refugee camp. He notes how a considerable amount of contemporary work based on post-modernist social theory, such as Agamben's work, is at times almost impenetrable. There nevertheless remains analytical value in engaging with key concepts from Agamben (1998, 2005) as a *starting point* for discussions exploring this site of reception. This is particularly pertinent when investigating reception from the perspective of the host state, rather than responses to official camp policy by refugees or local populations. For example, a host state's overarching reception policy may aim to frame the refugee camp as a place of exception through which most refugees are removed from the interior – even if the reality on the ground is different.

The urban space as a site of reception

In contrast to refugee camps, the urban space as a site of refugee reception has until recently remained under-researched. Practical issues play a role in this bias towards studying encampment practices, for instance, national laws can be analysed and access to sedentary populations can be secured in camps or government-run settlements. Conversely, refugees who self-settle in urban spaces are often harder to locate and less willing to come forward (Schmidt, 2003; Sommers, 2001). Furthermore, state responses to refugees in urban spaces, particularly in the majority world, are often realised more through local-level practices than recorded in national policy or set out in national law (Schmidt, 2014).

In the last decade, with refugee movements increasingly following global patterns of urbanisation, research on urban displacement more broadly has nevertheless begun to grow substantially (Landau, 2018a). Indeed, key insights into urban reception can be extracted from recent work focusing on vast global cities, such as Beirut, Istanbul and Johannesburg, which have all witnessed substantial increases in forced migrant movements (Martin, 2015; UNHCR, 2018b). However, this emerging area of research has predominantly focused on the local and sub-local level, rather than at the state level (Landau, 2018a).

Firstly, contemporary research has investigated the role of mobility and agency in refugees finding their own form of *de facto* local integration (Long, 2014, 2009; Adepoju et al., 2007; Sturridge, 2011; De Haas, 2009) and/or 'urban citizenship' via local networks and localised hospitality (Basok, 2009; Varsanyi, 2006; Hovil, 2016; Landau, 2014; Sanyal, 2017; Porter et al., 2019). The modern-day city cannot always be seen as a place of real social cohesion, yet migrants are still able to negotiate 'alternative forms of inclusion' (Bakewell, 2018:235). These local negotiations between refugees and local power holders place refugees and their hosts at the centre of this understanding of 'reception' (Polzer, 2009). Thus, refugees are framed as political actors using political leverage like other local groups or communities (Polzer, 2009). By extension, this understanding from the ground up of reception in the urban space (particularly in the majority world) relegates national bodies and international actors like UNHCR to minor roles (Landau, 2007). Landau and Amit (2014:547) go further, suggesting that for these self-settled refugees, the international refugee regime and national refugee policy may be 'something akin to a distant weather pattern with only indirect (and rarely determinative) effects on local actions'.

Secondly, forced migration studies and connected migration fields have also started to scrutinise the role of local authorities in reception (Darling, 2017; Walker, 2014; Squire, 2011). In particular, there has been an emphasis on the role municipalities can play in refugee arrivals when policies at the national level continue to shrink the asylum space (Darling, 2017). Large urban spaces have the potential for a different kind of 'cosmopolitan, egalitarian model of rights and ethical responsibility towards others' (Darling, 2009:649), for example, as 'sanctuary cities' (Basok, 2009; Varsanyi, 2006), 'cities of refuge' (Darling, 2009) or 'welcoming communities' for refugees and migrants (Bucklaschuk, 2015). Indeed, by engaging with city-level institutions and bureaucracies, it is possible to observe how concepts of localised citizenship are often replicated in local-level governance and urban planning (Guarnizo, 2011).

By adopting a multi-scalar approach to analysing reception, the 'local' becomes more than just a sovereign site of '(in)hospitable decisions' (Darling, 2009:649). It may be that, but it can also be a space of 'local citizenship' and local solutions to protracted displacement (Hovil, 2007). Indeed, it is conceivable to reimagine the urban space as a political space of rupture, where core global refugee regime norms that were blocked at the national level can re-emerge.

There is a risk, nevertheless, that this recent academic attention to the city as a site of reception is reconceptualising the urban space into one of unconditional hospitality and kindness. As observed by Samaddar (2018), on the ground in cities such as Johannesburg, refugees and migrants often gain social and political space only through persistence and hardship, rather than this being benevolently offered to them by the city or even locals. Equally, similarly to refugee camps, forms of confinement regularly appear in urban spaces. These can result directly from national and local reception policies or indirectly from more general policy that creates barriers to access. Indeed, threats of bribes, eviction, detention and the temporality of legal documents can all limit the movement of individuals in urban areas (Pasquetti and Picker, 2017; Chekero, 2023).

Links between the two reception sites

Finally, a persistent theme within the literature concerning these different reception sites has been the emphasis on the *locational distinctions* between the refugee camp and the urban space (Sanyal, 2014).[19] Thus, during the 1990s and early 2000s, research often ended up in 'geographical silos', resulting in little interrogation beyond a binary analysis of refugee camps and urban spaces as diametrically opposed to each other. However, recent shifts in academic focus and the adoption of different conceptual lenses have added new depth and nuance to our knowledge about these geographical sites. Contemporary research shows how the camp space is in fact regularly connected to the urban space (Omata and Kaplan, 2013; Chapotera, 2018). In situ, in Africa, the camp and urban spaces are linked daily via movement and technology (Betts et al., 2017; Omata and Kaplan, 2013). As Bakewell (2014) suggests, there is a need to recognise the fluidity between refugee camps and urban and rural areas, as people continue to find ways to move between these different reception sites.

Subsequent chapters reassess these two spaces from the viewpoint of reception, and in doing so build on contemporary research that challenges the notion that these sites are diametrically opposed to each other. In contrast to previous work, however, the book will approach the topic from the perspective of the host state. An assumption inherent within some existing research is that the movement that regularly connects these two spaces is either conducted covertly (that is, without permission and conflicts with the national reception policy) or with the state turning a blind eye to the movement of the refugee(s). The subsequent analysis highlights the possibility that some of this circular movement is accepted or even encouraged by state bodies and actors as part of the 'bargain' host states make with refugees when receiving them. In line with Polzer (2009), there is also the possibility that the form reception takes continues to evolve (including the acceptance of additional refugee movement) due to ongoing negotiations between key actors and entities in these spaces.

In summary, the first half of this chapter has utilised different but connected bodies of work to elucidate the concept of refugee reception. In doing so, it suggests that understanding the core concept of refugee reception requires an appreciation of it as a process, rather than a singular moment or set of requirements to regularise status. Thus, it resists the notion that reception ends with the regularly praised 'open door' policy of many states in the majority world.[20] As a complex process, reception involves negotiations between the state and other key actors that ultimately shape a refugee's ability to engage with local communities and markets in pursuit of their own personal and economic aims. Consequently, the state-focused perspective taken acknowledges the plurality of actors involved at the different levels of the state, while retaining a focus on state-run reception policies and practice. In this way, the architecture of reception (such as policy designed to permit or constrain movement) is regularly contested or modified by the behaviour of different participants in the process.

Using Betts and Orchard's theory of norm implementation, the remainder of this chapter will now turn to developing the book's conceptual framework. This is employed to advance an understanding of the processes by which global refugee regime norms are implemented, altered or contested at the national level. Member states that are party to the global refugee regime have an obligation to implement international norms in their reception policies. This suggests that in theory at least, a degree of uniformity might be expected to be observed in how states receive refugees. However, reception is not fixed but regularly negotiated and renegotiated between various actors in different reception spaces. As such, diverse factors at different levels of the state may influence policy and in doing so contest implementation of international norms, creating unique outcomes in terms of how refugees are received and treated.

The implementation of refugee reception policies

Betts and Orchard's (2014) theory of norm implementation is concerned with how international norms are implemented and how they play out in practice at the national level. The theory is based on a constructivist understanding of regimes, international norms and institutions. Importance is therefore placed on domestic normative and ideational structures, with identity, shared beliefs and values all exerting influence on political and social action (Hurd, 2008; Reus-Smit, 2005). As such, norms can develop, evolve and ultimately shape political discourses (Reus-Smit, 2005). This can occur at the international level through a process of socialisation whereby states can be persuaded to amend their views and behaviour over time (Betts, 2009a). It can also occur at the national and local levels, whereby a state's identity is shaped through interactions with its own society and the various identities that make up that society (Jackson, Sørensen and Møller, 2019).[21]

The theory of norm implementation also argues that to understand the level at which norms impact on outcomes, there is a need to know how they are implemented as prescribed actions at the national level (Job and Shesterinina, 2014). Taking the 1951 Refugee Convention as an example, member states have an obligation to allow refugees particular freedoms. These include the freedom of movement; to own and dispose of property; and the right to seek employment (Crisp, 2004).[22] Equally, Article 34 envisages forms of integration and the potential for citizenship. Yet, implementation of regime norms is left to states, resulting in practice being hugely varied between regions and individual states (Canefe, 2010).

As a way of examining and explaining these variances, Betts and Orchard (2014) suggest that the process of norm implementation at the domestic level opens up political contestation, with norms then becoming subject to reinterpretation and redefinition, and even being ignored by state actors. This can result in differing understandings of key regime norms developing and ultimately lead to different approaches to the reception of refugees in practice. Indeed, when two states ratify the 1951 Refugee Convention and incorporate the norms it contains into domestic law, it is not axiomatic that these norms will come to be implemented in the same way in practice.

Betts and Orchard (2014) also distinguish 'implementation' from the concept of 'compliance'. Constructivists see compliance as the *act* of rule-following itself, not the mechanisms through which compliance is achieved. In other words, a state either complies with a norm or does not. Implementation on the other hand is a process which furthers the adoption of a new norm. The norm implementation framework is therefore concerned with *why* a state obeys or ignores a norm rather than *if* a state adopts the norm into national law.[23]

Ultimately, the theory of norm implementation by Betts and Orchard (2014) was adopted as the book's conceptual framework for the following reasons: the theory is fundamentally interested in *why* states behave in specific ways, as opposed to *how* states should behave; factors that can influence state behaviour and policy are not framed as mutually exclusive but rather have the potential to engage and contest with each other, resulting in unique localised outcomes.

Adopting the theory of norm implementation to investigate refugee reception policies

To frame and scrutinise variations in responses to refugees (that is, *why* states respond to refugees in the way they do) and the role these approaches have on refugees' ability to pursue their own personal and economic aims, the book utilises the theory of norm implementation. In essence, an implementation lens is adopted that is broadly based on member states' obligations to implement the core norms contained within the global refugee regime. This is achieved by integrating the heuristic tripartite model that lies at the heart of Betts and Orchard's (2014) work. This model sets out three key 'causal mechanisms' that can 'constrain or constitute implementation efforts driven by particular actors' (Betts and Orchard, 2014:12): as per Figure 1.1. These three mechanisms are composed of ideational, material and institutional factors.

These three factors are not mutually exclusive, yet they 'provide a way of identifying critical implementation mechanisms that can then be examined as operationalizable variables' by in-depth qualitative research (Betts and Orchard, 2014:13). Each of the 'factors' in turn may play a role in *altering* or *constraining* regime norms 'by enabling or limiting its impact and salience within domestic policy and practice' (p. 13). Thus, this trilogy of factors will be employed to help identify key variables that are influencing responses of states to the arrival of refugees in Southern Africa.

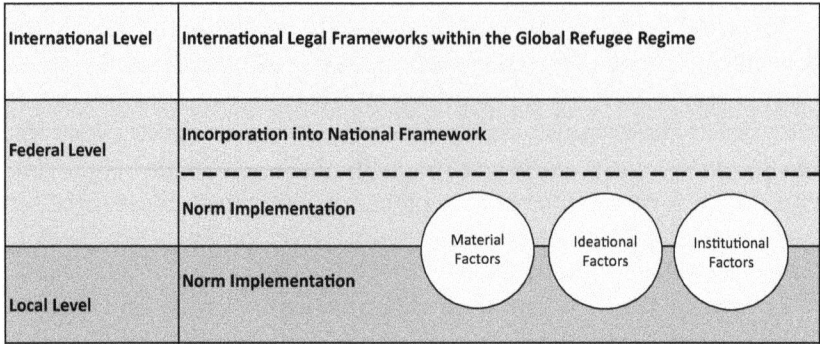

Figure 1.1: A conceptual framework examining implementation of refugee reception policies

Firstly, ideational factors can modify or change the implementation of norms through the cultural context of domestic politics. In this way, an international norm can mean very different things at a national level when combined with the pre-existing cultural and historical setting of the individual state. Thus, cultural ideas and identity, shared beliefs, national institutions and legal frameworks may all constrain or shape international norms during the implementation process. As Cortell and Davis (2005) note, constructivism sees international norms having more impact when they have domestic salience, meaning when they mirror or support local values, beliefs and practice.

Acharya (2004) suggests that contestation can also occur between international norms and pre-existing regional normative social orders. As Cortell and Davis (2005) observe, when international norms conflict with local beliefs and understanding, actors may find that relying on international norms to support a policy may be ineffective. Equally, the national legal system may also influence the implementation process by 'serving as a constraining ideational structure in legitimising (or not) different international norms and allowing them to take effect' (Betts and Orchard, 2014:15). For example, variables such as whether the national system is based on common law or statute, the perceived strength of the rule of law and the number of lawyers in the country, may all interact with the international norm resulting in differing practices at the national level.

Secondly, material factors such as the capacity of the state also affect the implementation of the global refugee regime at the national and local levels. The effectiveness of techniques such as pressure or persuasion, deployed by other states, donors, institutions and non-state actors, will also be strongly influenced by capacity issues. For example, the ability to ensure all refugees receive full protection as set out in the 1951 Refugee

Convention will depend greatly on the ability of the host state to respond through financial, humanitarian and developmental assistance. Political pressure applied by minority world states on states in the majority world to implement elements of the refugee regime, will mean little if it comes without financial support and if host states simply do not have the capacity to respond (Hovil and Maple, 2022; Arar and Fitzgerald, 2023). Other material factors such as genuine security concerns may also influence the implementation of key norms.

Finally, institutional structures that interact with the implementation of norms at the national level will differ greatly between states and potentially also between specific districts of an individual country, which in turn will affect how a norm is interpreted at the national and local level. For example, how government departments split responsibility for a particular policy between the national and local level can influence the implementation of a norm.

Bureaucratic contestation may also play a role in deciding which aspects of a norm will be implemented and which will be ignored. For example, inter-agency conflicts and competition for resources across national and local-level ministries can result in variations in how an international norm is translated into practice. National institutions and bureaucracy have received less attention in relation to how states respond to refugee movement than have issues relating to material structures such as capacity and security. Nevertheless, specific bureaucratic identities and contestation at different levels of government can affect the way the refugee regime is implemented within a state.[24] Furthermore, as Deere (2009) notes, bureaucratic contestation brings international institutions into the implementation process, whereby international actors interact with national actors to shape and contest international norms.

A multi-scalar understanding of host states' responses to refugees

By adopting Betts and Orchard's theory of norm implementation as the conceptual framework, emphasis is again placed on a multi-scalar understanding of the host state. Betts and Orchard (2014:274) acknowledge the role that individuals can play in enabling implementation (using terms such as 'enablers of implementation' and 'norm implementators'). This book goes further by placing particular importance on the applicability of the trilogy of factors at the international, national and the local level. This method allows greater flexibility in analysis to incorporate reasons why specific policies are implemented, contested, changed or recast at 'various levels of power and in different sites' (Williamson, 2015:17). For example, refugees can receive different treatment at the local level in their interactions with local authorities or partners, compared to more restrictive national approaches. As observed above, this suggests that the global refugee regime (and its core norms) may skip levels when blocked at the national level and reappear at lower levels. Equally, the 'regime is its practice' – meaning changes to the regime at the local level have the potential to feed back into the national level (and even into regional or global levels) (Schmidt, 2003).

Betts and Orchard (2014) also keep analysis at different levels separate (especially between the international and national levels). In contrast, this book is interested in how international, national and local dynamics may interact and tussle with one another to create structural mechanisms that shape the implementation of regime norms and policies. A multi-scalar lens enables such an examination to take place, focusing in particular on how processes are influenced within different levels of governance, how they interact between levels, and the effect this has on refugee reception.[25] The outcome of these different dynamics can be seen in shifting approaches to refugee arrivals, and the way that their acceptance in spaces (such as urban areas) may run contrary to the formal national legal framework. Thus, 'implementation' is informed by the 'enmeshment of international and domestic or local logics and practices' (Schmidt, 2014:267). Indeed, the book argues that reception policies of host states are not fixed constructs, but rather continual processes that are constantly shaped by the different factors at different levels of analysis.

A critical reflection on the book's conceptual framework

There are some potential limitations in utilising this approach to investigate the issue of refugee reception. Firstly, the framework focuses on how and why reception policies operate as they do in practice, rather than on addressing the question of how reception *should* operate. In doing this, an argument can be made that it provides few criteria with which to evaluate the information it offers (Shapcott, 2010). Yet as examined above, the difference between how state practices express core norms and how they are set out in the 1951 Refugee Convention, makes answering the question of how a regime norm *should* operate extremely complex. Indeed, state practice alters how regime norms are understood. Equally, by examining what a state is doing (and why) concerning policies and specific reception sites, the book references explicitly how and why states are either *obeying* or *ignoring* key regime norms such as freedom of movement or employment rights. Finally, by improving the understanding around state responses to the arrival of refugees, the hope is that academia is then better equipped to be able to suggest new pragmatic methods and techniques for improving the implementation of core regime norms.

Secondly, it is fair to say that great importance is placed on the 'global' within Betts and Orchard's model. This emphasis risks assigning more weight to the role of the global refugee regime in reception policies in Africa than is warranted. Similarly, the prominence given to the 'global' risks ignoring the role of the 'local' in shaping reception policy on the ground. Indeed, as previously noted, recent work in the urban space in Southern Africa suggests that some refugees have little to no interactions with national legal frameworks or global governance regimes. A multi-scalar approach mitigates these risks by enabling the framework to investigate the applicability of global governance frameworks and national reception policies at the level of the city. Furthermore, rather than dismissing or ignoring the existing body of scholarly work looking at local and sub-local levels, future chapters will build on and complement this body of research to gain a more holistic picture of reception in Africa.

Finally, the heuristic tripartite model – as a core element of the framework – sets out the key causal mechanisms that can affect the implementation of refugee reception policies. On one level, this 'trilogy of factors' can be seen as a purely descriptive set of factors or categories, which are intrinsically difficult to critique: they are highly logical and relevant sets of typology. To move analysis beyond mere categorisation and to develop understanding around causation, a reflexive methodological approach was adopted to ensure impartial evaluation (which acknowledges preconceptions and assumptions) and to test the validity of the overarching conceptual framework. Put differently, to utilise the framework in a fruitful way, the methodological approach selected for the book needed to be sufficiently reflexive to be open to opposing arguments and alternative factors emerging through the fieldwork, rather than being tied to a strict typology of prescribed factors. This reflexive research approach is expanded upon in Chapter 3.

With regards to causation specifically, the reality on the ground means that it is unlikely that the research will reveal neat causal links between a factor or a combination of a factors and a state-run refugee reception policy. Rather, in using this framework there is an expectation of reception policies at the national and local level being formed and/or contested via the result of ongoing and highly contingent processes of negotiation between institutional actors (Betts and Orchard, 2014). During these 'negotiations', specific factors – such as material ones (that is, capacity) – may conflict with others – such as ideational ones (legal and normative obligations to implement human rights ideals). In this way, the reception of refugees is understood as 'a political process of contestation in which a range of structures and actors share and channel what norms do in practice' (Betts and Orchard, 2014:281). As Ragin (1987) notes in relation to the intricacies of social phenomena, *refugee reception* is not merely a function of the many factors that account for the ultimate result. The specific response to refugees stems from the effects of circumstances, whereby 'a particular combination of factors have to merge before a given effect can occur' (Lor, 2011:14).

In closing, this chapter has situated the disparate responses to refugee arrivals seen in Southern Africa, within a theoretical context. By using a state-focused lens and incorporating literature from connected academic fields, the chapter advances a preliminary understanding of 'reception': an understanding that is relatively unique for refugee studies, due to the field generally overlooking or minimising the topic in the past. In turn, a conceptual framework has been introduced that is suitable to respond to the question of why states receive refugees in different ways. The next chapter builds on this analysis, by evaluating broader academic debates within the fields of refugee and forced migration studies that allude to why states in Africa, even close neighbours, have such dissimilar reception policies.

Notes

1. It is interpreted in European case law: EU law affirms that reception begins once an asylum application is made (ESRC, 2017).
2. The chapter is concerned with the reception offered to refugees by a host state. Other forms of reception at the local and sub-local level will nonetheless be discussed.
3. See van der Waldt (2020).
4. See Ravitch and Riggan (2016).
5. See Schmidt (2014); Deardorff (2009).
6. During this time there is little to no interaction with formal state infrastructures (at least at the national level) nor with the global refugee regime.
7. Even these systems of registration can be ad hoc.
8. See Portes and Rumbaut (2006); Jaworsky et al. (2012).
9. Based on the work of Castles (2015).
10. See Williamson (2015). In the context of the two case studies there are other levels of analysis: the regional level (for example, the influence of the African Union (AU)); the sub-regional level (for example, the influence of SADC); and the mezzanine level of the provincial government. While touched on in the book, these levels

are not key priorities due to the minor role they play in refugee reception in Zambia and South Africa.

11. Thus, while taking core elements from the term 'self-reliance', the book attempts to avoid the implication that a refugee's intention is always to be independent from the moment of arrival (UNHCR, 2005).

12. See also Derrida (2005).

13. See also Derrida (2000); Derrida and Dufourmantelle (2000).

14. This 'generous' reception is only offered to the lucky few who are granted refugee status. Donor states in the minority world have devised numerous policies to evade responsibility sharing and 'contain' forced migrants in the majority world (Hovil and Maple, 2022).

15. These geographical spaces are selected due to their popularity and dominance as official and unofficial spaces of reception for refugees and forced migrants in the chosen case studies. Nevertheless, border and rural areas will also be examined where relevant to drawing out a more complete picture of reception in Southern Africa.

16. As a sample see Harrell-Bond (1998); Black (1998); Crisp and Jacobsen (1998); Crisp (2000); Jamal (2003); Smith (2004).

17. See also Bloch and Donà (2018).

18. See also Jansen (2016); Newhouse (2015).

19. There are notable exceptions to these approaches (Hyndman, 2000; Crisp, 2008).

20. Meaning that reception appears to be framed as the act of allowing a refugee onto a host state's territory.

21. The approach of Betts and Orchards (2014) complements the work of Finnemore and Sikkink (1998) who were interested in how norms are formed at the international level.

22. In relation to the international refugee regime, it is generally understood that the most important norms, principles and rules can be found in the 1951 Refugee Convention and the Statute of UNHCR (Betts, 2009a).

23. See also Alderson (2001); Arar and FitzGerald (2023).

24. See Schmidt (2014); Landau and Amit (2014).

25. See Delaney and Leitner (1997).

Chapter 2
Refugee reception policies in Africa

This chapter presents and reflects upon current academic explanations of why states in Africa adopt specific refugee reception policies. It is structured around three academic debates which illustrate existing ways in which, via bigger picture trends, research has endeavoured to explain responses to refugee arrivals in Africa. The chapter starts by investigating the 'democracy-asylum' nexus, which observes a negative correlation between democracy and states' approaches to asylum. The nexus has previously been employed to help explain the remarkable shift in reception policies witnessed on the continent over the last sixty years. The section sets out a case for reinvigorating this area of research by proposing new avenues for investigation in relation to the reception of refugees in Southern Africa.

Next, the chapter shifts to examine the role of the 'global' at the national and local levels, in the context of Africa. The section investigates the influence of international legal frameworks and UNHCR on reception policies, with a considerable body of research having been developed over the past two decades on the role of the global refugee regime and specifically UNHCR in the day-to-day practice of reception. Nonetheless, more contemporary work has begun to question the regime's continuing relevance for many refugees on the ground in Africa.

Finally, the chapter reviews research that has adopted a security lens to explain state responses to refugees. This analysis shows how the increasingly popular framing of migrant movement as a security threat inevitably influences the implementation of refugee reception policies. Yet, the chapter also questions whether there now exists an overreliance on a security lens to explain all state responses to refugees. As a response, a stability lens is introduced to help draw out a more nuanced discussion on how states understand the arrival and movement of refugees on their territory.

In terms of the selection of the debates, the scope of the literature reviewed for this chapter has been refined by the adoption of Betts and Orchard's theory of norm implementation as the book's conceptual framework.[1] As such, the chapter interrogates specific themes identified through the process of selecting and adapting the framework. Thus, the three debates were chosen as they each speak to why state reception policies in the region regularly diverge from international regime norms. Indeed, by examining relevant literature it is possible to elicit key causal mechanisms (that is, material, ideational and institutional factors) that appear to regularly contest, alter or stop the implementation of regime norms, thus creating unique reception policies on the ground for refugees in this region. By critically engaging with each of these contemporary academic discussions, the intention of the chapter is to elucidate key themes and factors that influence states' responses to the arrival of refugees.

The 'democratic-aslyum' nexus: shifting policies to refugees in Africa

The political and spatial dynamics of refugee reception in Africa have changed dramatically over the last sixty years (van Garderen and Ebenstein, 2011; Crisp, 2010). Between the 1960s and 1980s, states traditionally maintained an open-door policy towards refugees. Rutinwa (1999) sees the period following the adoption of the OAU Convention Governing Specific Aspects of Refugee Problems in Africa ('1969 OAU Refugee Convention') as the 'golden age' of asylum in Africa. The period embraced a free-settlement approach which, while varying in implementation, is a reception policy whereby refugees are permitted to freely move within the host state and select their place of residence (Masuku and Nkala, 2018).

The enduring nature of the free-settlement approach during these decades can be understood through the ideational concepts of pan-Africanism and anti-colonialism, economic prosperity and the characteristics of refugee movements seen during that period. Many refugees during this time were 'the product of independence struggles and wars of national liberation, most notably in countries such as Angola, Guinea-Bissau, Mozambique, Rhodesia, South Africa and South-West Africa' (Crisp, 2000:3). This was also helped by resilient and politically stable leaders such as Kenneth Kaunda in Zambia, who set positive examples in their refugee policies (Crisp, 2000). In addition, during the years immediately after independence, the size of refugee populations remained modest, and individual economies were relatively prosperous. Indeed, there were around a million refugees in Africa in the early 1970s (Crisp, 2000). The combination of these factors meant host states were happy to give generous hospitality to refugees. In turn, local communities generally saw these refugees as victims of colonial rule and thus received them warmly (Lindley, 2011).

In contrast, the 1990s witnessed sweeping shifts in reception policies, with states beginning to favour methods of containment and the refugee camp emerging as the dominant approach to welcoming refugees within the continent. Key reasons for this shift in policy are well established. Firstly, the sheer size of the refugee populations, and their unequal distribution between host countries, created problems. To illustrate this, the refugee population had rapidly grown to almost six million people by the early 1990s (van Garderen and Ebenstein, 2011). Secondly, a lack of economic growth in the region added to the strain of absorbing new populations into host communities (Crisp, 2000).[2] A third reason, which has perhaps received less academic attention than it warrants, is the 'democracy turn' observed on the continent during the 1980s and 1990s. This has also played a significant role in shifting attitudes towards the form of welcome given to refugees.

Indeed, what can be understood as the 'democracy-asylum' nexus may still be playing a significant role in how states respond to refugee arrival and movement. In essence, this nexus refers to the observed association between increases in democratic structures and practices within a state and the deteriorating attitudes and responses to asylum (Milner, 2009). This apparently negative association between the practices of democracy and asylum appears to run counter to the assumption that democracy is indispensable for the effective exercise of fundamental freedoms and human rights.

The loss of popularity of free-settlement reception policies in the 1990s occurred during the same period as the introduction of democratic structures and shifts away from authoritarian political settlements towards more competitive ruling political settlements.[3] When ruling political parties move towards democratic ideologies and become competitive, elites within the government become more concerned with short-term goals, such as re-election (Khan, 2011; Abdulai and Hickey, 2016). Thus, political elites tend to prioritise engaging and reacting to public opinion. This time of democratic change on the continent coincided with shifting attitudes seen among local populations who were exercising new voting power. During the period of decolonisation in Africa (1950s–1960s), refugees were perceived as kin and as 'brothers' linked in the fight against an external power. However, by the 1990s, the reasons for flight were changing and becoming about ongoing civil wars or aspirations of economic betterment. This in turn led to an ideational shift occurring whereby refugees began being seen solely as outsiders and/or as a threat to limited resources (Crisp, 2000). It is perhaps not, therefore, surprising that xenophobia towards refugees and forced migrants emerged in the 1990s, 'at a time when most of Africa [was] democratising and governments [were] compelled to take into account public opinion in formulating various policies' (Rutinwa, 1999:2).

In response to this shift in attitudes and with the added pressures of re-election, governments started closing borders and severely restricting the rights of refugees (Crisp, 2000). In essence, as governing political settlements on the continent moved from authoritarian rule towards democratic and competitive political approaches, the space for asylum started to shrink. As a result, refugees were increasingly confined to geographical spaces away from large urban areas and the voting public.

The 'democracy-asylum' nexus accordingly helps explain why states within Africa shifted from more open reception policies to more closed camp-based approaches in which the constraint of movement became the new norm on the continent. In addition, the shift from long-term integration to new forms of temporary reception was intended to facilitate the eventual return of refugees to their home states. Yet with internal conflicts persisting for decades, repatriation never materialised as a workable option for most refugees (Deardorff, 2009). Thus, this switch of reception approach left millions of refugees in limbo in protracted situations (Schmidt, 2003; Deardorff, 2009; Zetter, 2015).

Based on this observed nexus, Milner in 2009 noted that 'the relationship between democratization and asylum policies in Africa is not always good for human rights' (p. 178). Yet despite this noteworthy – if troubling – finding, the 'democracy-asylum' nexus has received little attention in the literature since Milner's work in the late 2000s. To investigate the continued relevance of the nexus today, the book examines connections between democratic structures and how host states in Southern Africa respond to refugee arrival and movement. Subsequent chapters will develop this work in three key areas: firstly, by examining the significance of the nexus in the context of the two selected reception sites in Southern Africa, specifically its continued relevance in the maintenance of camp policies and its influence over national reception policy and practice relating to urban spaces; in particular it will consider the increasing urbanisation of refugee populations and the potentially disruptive role increased refugee movement can have in contemporary African cities.

Secondly, the association between democracy and asylum will be investigated at the local level. Given the global trend of decentralisation witnessed on the African continent since the early 2000s, increased powers at the city level are likely to affect the form of reception refugees receive in urban spaces. As explored by academics such as Hickey et al. (2015), decentralisation can create the possibility of achieving improved implementation of development projects and international norms at sub-national levels, even when there is a lack of political will at the national level.[4] At the same time, increased democratic power at the local level also raises the possibility that any reception offered could deteriorate if the local population becomes hostile to forced migrants and refugees (Kihato and Landau, 2016).

Finally, the book interrogates the possibility of the *reverse situation* to the historical one observed by Milner also holding true (2009), that is, can a slide to a more authoritarian style of political settlement open up the possibility of improved reception conditions for refugees? According to some political theorists, when a political settlement moves towards an authoritarian style of governance, the state is free to implement long-term programmes based on self-interest and ideological commitments, without being overly concerned about opposition parties or losing re-election (Khan, 2010). If a state is experiencing 'democratic backsliding' and has a president who subscribes to the ideology of pan-Africanism – as was witnessed in Zambia between 2016 and 2021 – could this potentially assist in initiating long-term improvements in the implementation of regime norms within national refugee reception policies? Future chapters will investigate this contrary hypothesis inferred by the 'democracy-asylum' nexus.

The role of the global refugee regime in shaping refugee reception policies

The global refugee regime is in essence made up of three components: the regime's main international legal framework – the 1951 Refugee Convention; the regime's key global actor – UNHCR; and the common principles and norms that govern how states should treat refugees, such as guaranteeing the right to seek asylum (Loescher et al., 2008; Maple et al., 2023). Traditionally, a great deal of academic attention has focused on the first two elements when research has investigated refugee displacement in Africa. In fact, the level of importance placed on the global regime has meant that the host state is commonly framed as a secondary actor in the initial welcome given to refugees on the continent. In addition, academic attention has also mainly concentrated on examining refugee camps, and UNHCR's role in overseeing them. In the last ten years, with research on refugee arrivals shifting more towards urban displacement, a growing body of work has begun to debate the regime's continuing relevance in the urban spaces of Africa. The following subsections interrogate these connected areas of research pertaining to camp and urban reception spaces, to assess the extent to which the global refugee regime continues to shape refugee reception policies in the region.

Role of the global in the reception of refugees: the refugee camp

A key debate that has dominated academic scholarship engaged with refugee protection on the African continent over the last twenty years has been the role of UNHCR in responding to refugee displacement. As noted above, attention has concentrated on the refugee camp, and on the role of UNHCR, as guardian of the 1951 Refugee Convention,[5] in setting up and maintaining the camp system (Slaughter and Crisp, 2008).[6] Certainly, since the 1980s, UNHCR (and by extension the global refugee regime) has been profoundly involved in the architecture of refugee reception in Africa.[7]

UNHCR is regularly compelled by host states in the majority world to offer protection and assistance to refugees within the confines of refugee camps (Crisp and Jacobsen, 1998). Two material factors emerge in explaining why host states have so readily handed responsibility for refugee reception (and effectively for a portion of their territory) to UNHCR: capacity and security concerns. In terms of capacity, developing countries host over 84 per cent of the world's refugees (UNHCR, 2017b). As van Garderen and Ebenstein (2011) note, this highly skewed distribution of refugees has had pronounced effects on host countries. As a result, many states in the majority world find themselves ill-equipped to carry out their duties towards refugees (Field, 2010).

In Africa, the absence of equitable burden-sharing (Rutinwa, 1999) results in states viewing encampment as a smarter and more visible strategy for gaining international support than allowing for integration (Kagan, 2011; Jamal, 2003).[8] For the donor states in the minority world, funding refugee camps allows them to 'pay' their way out of burden-sharing (Hovil and Maple, 2022). Meaning, while offering the basics of humanitarianism, this approach is also based on the reasoning of control, to prevent large numbers of refugees from moving to the minority world (FitzGerald, 2019; Arar and FitzGerald, 2023).[9]

In terms of security, as examined fully below, various security worries frequently arise when large numbers of refugees cross a border (Milner, 2009). Concerns ranging from the fear of armed elements infiltrating the refugee population, to the additional stresses being placed on infrastructure and services mean that the refugee figure quickly becomes framed as a disquieting element to the normal order of states and citizens (Agamben, 1998).[10] For these reasons, refugees are placed in camps, stripped of social and political rights and left to be governed and regulated outside the state's normal legal framework (Owens, 2009; Nyers, 2006). Thus, security and capacity concerns at the national level become contained and reduced when refugees are excluded and placed in refugee camps (where they become the responsibility of global refugee regime actors).[11]

These imposed locational dynamics to reception leave UNHCR in a precarious situation. By acquiescing to the pressures favouring encampment, fundamental regime norms are relinquished by the agency. For instance, freedom of movement is surrendered to focus purely on the right to life and the principle of *non-refoulement* (Verdirame and Harrell-Bond, 2005). This 'care and maintenance' approach to the reception of refugees has been critiqued by scholars (Verdirame and Harrell-Bond, 2005; Crisp and Jacobsen, 1998). Chief amongst the criticisms has been the accusation that violations of refugees' right to freedom of movement are often too readily accepted by UNHCR as part of a state's right to manage their own territory (Jamal, 2000).

UNHCR's involvement in reception policies on the ground is also complicated by a lack of political or legal power. Indeed, it has to rely on moral authority, persuasion and inducement in its dealings with sovereign states (Lewis, 2012).[12] This lack of power is coupled with working within a political landscape where 'power and interests dominate and define outcomes' (Loescher et al., 2008:2).[13] Put another way, it is difficult to persuade host states to implement global refuge regime norms when key material factors, such as capacity and national security concerns, continue to take precedence over the fundamental freedoms of newly arrived guests. In addition, as already noted, pressure comes from donors, who regularly fund UNHCR projects in the majority world, to grant certain rights to refugees but at the same time severely limit forms of movement (Barutciski, 2013).

In summary, the research on UNHCR and refugee camps in the last twenty years has been extensive. Much of it has been largely critical, despite the fact that many authors recognise the unenviable position that the UN agency is regularly placed in. In terms of the overarching themes of the book, this body of literature highlights several issues relevant to investigating state-based reception policies. These include the common perception that refugees are the responsibility of the international community. Some key contradictions are also revealed. On the one hand, there is a broad understanding that refugee camps are insisted upon by many host states (for the reasons set out above) leaving UNHCR in a difficult position in relation to offering protection and global regime norms in these countries. On the other hand, due to the UN agency regularly accepting spatial restrictions on reception (and taking responsibility for managing, funding and running refugee camps), the host state has constantly been framed as a secondary or minor player in the reception of refugees on the continent.[14] The result is that: (1) the role of the global refugee regime (and UNHCR) is regularly elevated, despite appearing at times to be entirely confined to the refugee camp; and (2) little research has investigated the role of national actors or national frameworks, beyond the initial request that camps be set up.

These interrelated points are especially pertinent when you consider how contemporary research highlights the various ways that the refugee camp and the urban space are connected on the continent (Fábos and Kibreab, 2007). With movement regularly seen (and often *permitted* by key state bodies) between these different sites of reception, it calls into question whether the host state's role (in terms of policy and actors) in camp-based reception is as hands-off as some of the literature implies. Equally, if refugees are regularly moving between these reception spaces, yet the global regime (and its international actors) remains confined to the refugee camp, where does this leave the regime in terms of ongoing relevance in Africa? These lines of enquiry will be developed throughout the book.

Role of the global in the reception of refugees: the urban space

In Africa, the role and influence of the global refugee regime outside of the refugee camp remains less clear than it does within it. Certainly, relatively little work has been conducted looking at the influence of the regime in the urban space on the continent (Maple et al., 2023). Work that does exist consists of preliminary investigations into recent UNHCR global policies on urban protection and general critiques concerning the lack of UNHCR's involvement in these spaces (Ward, 2014; Crisp, 2017; Landau, 2018a; Pavanello et al., 2010).

Turning first to consider the influence of international frameworks, the global refugee regime is represented in national legislation, national discourse and national institutions (Schmidt, 2014). Indeed, most African states have signed both the 1951 Refugee Convention and the 1969 OAU Refugee Convention (Maple, 2016). Nevertheless, incorporation of the global regime into domestic legal frameworks has been patchier, with the domestic legislation of some states lacking reference to either convention (Canefe, 2010).[15] Furthermore, as observed in the last chapter, the implementation of core norms from the 1951 Refugee Convention into policy on the ground appears to be regularly contested. As Schmidt (2014) notes, traditionally the implementation of the refugee regime on the African continent within national institutions has been seen as high in normative content but low in practical application.

Beyond the refugee camp, available research suggests that the influence of the global refugee regime (in terms of implementing international norms) remains weak. Additionally, implementation of national refugee legal frameworks, or even written policy documents relating to refugee reception, is seen as poor on the ground in Africa (Schmidt, 2014). Indeed, state responses to refugees in urban spaces often appear to come about through ad hoc local level policy and practice (Landau, 2018a; Schmidt, 2014). This understanding, of reception policies being conducted via impromptu methods rather than being influenced by the global refugee regime or national frameworks, makes the shortage of empirical data at the national and local government level surprising.

Conversely, the role of global actors in the urban space has received more academic attention than international and regional governance frameworks. Until recently, however, this body of research has remained quite broad and has been largely critical (Landau and Amit, 2014), in a way that is reminiscent of the work done on UNHCR's more customary role in the camp space. Unquestionably, the UN agency has been slow to react to key trends in the urbanisation of refugee populations (Kagan, 2013). Large transnational cities in Africa, like Kampala, Nairobi and Johannesburg, have always received refugees and forced migrants. Indeed, they have in many respects been reshaped by the arrival of international migrants (Landau, 2014). Yet, UNHCR has either ignored urban refugees (concentrating on refugee camps instead) or viewed their claims for refugee status with mistrust (Sanyal, 2019; Landau, 2014). In the case of Southern Africa, for example, large numbers of refugees who move through the sub-region originate from counties in eastern Africa and the Horn of Africa. These patterns of movement denote passage through numerous other 'safe' countries, and as a result UNHCR regularly labels this form of movement as 'secondary', 'irregular' or 'onward' (UNHCR, 2004; UNHCR, 2015c). This kind of perspective on urban refugees in Southern Africa on the part of the global refugee regime's key international actor inevitably has implications for reception policies in these spaces.

This perceived historical indifference to the urban space is exemplified by UNHCR first publishing a workable global urban policy only in 2009.[16] In the 2009 Urban Policy the agency did finally acknowledge that most refugees worldwide live in cities (Sanyal, 2019). The document also emphasised the need to assist refugees where you find them, rather than *telling them where to go* (Kagan, 2013). Yet in the same document, refugees still theoretically need a 'good reason' to justify living in an urban setting (Verdirame and Pobjoy, 2013).[17]

Since the publication of the 2009 Urban Policy (UNHCR, 2009) and the subsequent 2014 'Policy on alternatives to camps' (UNHCR, 2014a), there has been a growing body of literature that consistently highlights the protection issues and challenges faced by urban refugees on the continent (Pavanello et al., 2010; Kihato and Landau, 2016). Nevertheless, UNHCR continues to struggle to adapt programming and interventions specifically for the urban space (Crisp, 2017). Equally, as observed by Crisp (2017:94), policy shifts on paper do not automatically translate into support and training for UNHCR staff on the ground. Agency officials are often 'expected to engage much more thoroughly with urban refugees but have not been given the capacity to do so'.

In defence of UNHCR, the urban space is a highly politicised space, making the role and position of the agency in assisting with reception complex and often extremely delicate. Essentially, this geographical space is still 'new' to UNHCR and because of this, forming partnerships with urban partners (such as mayors, municipal councils, civil society and development actors who work with the urban poor) has proved harder than anticipated (Crisp, 2017). Equally, the agency's role in cities in Africa is further complicated if the host state maintains a dominant camp-based reception policy.

Finally, recent attempts by UN bodies to implement initiatives on the African continent under the normative frameworks of the New York Declaration for Refugees and Migrants, Global Compact on Refugees and the CRRF, do show some promise in terms of UNHCR attempting to improve reception in urban spaces. Yet even with the momentum of these new global frameworks, initiatives supported by UNHCR in many CRRF implementing countries (including Djibouti, Uganda and Kenya) are still chiefly focused in refugee camps (Carciotto and Ferraro, 2020).

The analysis of the role of the 'global' in refugee reception in Africa thus identifies several important themes and ideas pertinent to the question of why states respond to refugees in specific ways. For example, key material and ideational factors emerge that appear to influence states' preference for maintaining encampment policies, including the ability to shift responsibility and costs for hosting refugee populations, at least in part, onto the international community. The section has also raised several topics which to date have been under-explored within the literature owing to the global refugee regime having traditionally dominated a considerable amount of the research surrounding refugee arrival on the continent. This attention appears justified in terms of the setting-up and management of refugee camps for the last twenty years, nevertheless, this dominance has meant that national legal and policy frameworks and institutions are regularly ignored or dismissed as irrelevant. With evidence consistently showing how the implementation of the 1951 Refugee Convention on the continent is patchy at best, and how movement regularly connects the refugee camp to the urban space, this lack of attention to national law, policy and local norms is somewhat surprising.

Also, research continues to adopt a critical stance to UNHCR's role in Africa, perceiving an over-engagement in the camp space, at the expense of other reception sites, such as the urban space. This juxtaposition between inactivity in cities and towns versus activity in refugee camps suggests the potential for the geographical confinement of the global refugee regime in Africa. In turn, the lack of the 'global' in urban spaces raises questions about the continuing relevance of the global refugee regime in the everyday practice of refugee reception and UNHCR's attitude and decision-making concerning refugee movement and agency. By not proactively engaging with urban refugees, UNHCR run the risk of merely reinforcing the concept of the refugee figure as a helpless sedentary victim.

The security and stability nexus

Security is a recurring issue within research that attempts to understand why states continue to respond to new arrivals in specific ways, often in direct contravention of their commitments to the global refugee regime. Research ranges from examining the material factors (such as direct and indirect security concerns) associated with the arrival of refugee populations in the host country, to looking at the increasingly globalised practice of states securitising all forms of cross-border movement. In contrast, there has been less work on the concept of stability (and its inverse, instability). The importance placed on the perception of stability by host states appears worthy of further exploration. Importantly, this can shed light on how states understand the effect refugees (and crucially their *movement*) have on host communities and national and local political structures. While intrinsically connected to security concerns, a stability lens is also able to move discussions beyond the popular yet binary notion that all refugee movement is understood by states via a security prism.

Security and securitisation

Security issues have long been discussed in reference to state responses to refugee movement in Africa. The concept itself, though, is often left ill-defined or employed broadly in order to cover a multitude of issues (such as the infiltration of refugee warriors into a refugee population or the risks of increased crime in urban spaces). To gain more precision, particularly in relation to the role security plays in reception policies, the book utilises Milner's (2009) distinction between: (1) direct security concerns; (2) indirect security concerns; and (3) securitisation. Milner sees direct security concerns as those that relate to *who* is coming into the host country. In contrast, indirect security concerns refer to increased levels of insecurity or crime within the areas that refugees settle. These initial two categorisations (direct and indirect threats) are valuable, as they can help to identify genuine security issues facing host states. This contrasts with political securitisation agendas that target refugee movements in order to justify restrictive reception policies and/or to 'scapegoat' refugees.

Direct security concerns

Numerous security issues potentially arise when refugees cross a border. This is particularly so in situations of mass influx, when armed elements may be able to infiltrate refugee camps or local communities (Milner, 2000, 2009). In the African context, the frequency of civil unrest, war and liberation movements since the 1960s have meant that states are particularly cognisant of these issues (Crisp, 2006). Thus, the separation of refugees from the local population by setting up refugee camps, at least during an emergency period, can be regarded as a state defending its territory against perceived external threats (Newman, 2003).

Equally, however, the refugee camp itself can become the location of direct security concerns. Zolberg et al. (1989) notably documented the issue of 'refugee warriors' infiltrating refugee camps close to the border to recruit soldiers during the 1980s and 1990s. Thus, refugee camps can become 'a breeding ground for refugee warriors: disaffected individuals, who . . . equip themselves for battle to retrieve an idealized, mythical lost community' (Stedman and Tanner, 2004:3). This manipulation of the refugee camp and the refugee regime inevitably has had ramifications for national and international security (Stedman and Tanner, 2004).

The issue of armed elements infiltrating refugee populations has nevertheless not stopped states within Africa and the international community from continuing to utilise encampment as a dominant reception policy. Indeed, the existence of refugee warriors actually reinforces the idea of keeping refugee populations separated from the local population (Adleman, 1998; Milner, 2000). Nonetheless, these direct security concerns have persuaded states and international humanitarian organisations to now construct camps further away from state borders (Crisp, 2006).

As is evident from these discussions, between the 1980s and 1990s security concerns were central to refugee reception policies on the continent. Since the 1990s, incidences of civil wars in Africa had been declining steeply (Straus, 2012). However, due to renewed violence in South Sudan, the DRC, Mozambique, Central African Republic and Somalia, this trend has recently been reversed (UNHCR, 2020).[18] Nonetheless, current conflicts on the continent are generally limited to specific geographic areas (Bakken and Rustad, 2018), meaning that large parts of the continent (including most of Southern Africa) are currently experiencing relative peace. This is not to say states do not retain concerns around who is entering their territory – indeed, many states in Africa remain politically fragile (Bakken and Rustad, 2018). However, the risk of 'refugee warriors' or foreign military infiltrating refugee camps or local populations has been significantly reduced for many countries on the continent over time.

Indirect security concerns

In line with broader trends in the refugee and forced migration fields, indirect security concerns that arise in local populations close to refugee camps, have received a good deal of academic attention. In contrast, similar security concerns relating to the urban space in Africa have typically seen less consideration. This has recently started to change, however, with a growing body of literature now investigating tensions between refugee and host populations in large urban spaces on the continent (Barbelet and Wake, 2017). Work from both streams of research remains largely focused at the ground and local levels, with less work investigating the effect indirect security concerns have on state reception policies – particularly in relation to the refugee camp. The available literature is examined to gain an initial understanding of the concerns of host states in relation to refugee populations present in both reception sites. As will be seen, incorporating state-focused analysis offers a more rounded understanding of how indirect security concerns may influence reception policies.

In terms of the refugee camp, refugees can have an impact on the environment in the host state. This is especially an issue when a refugee population outnumbers the available resources (Whitaker, 2002), for example, when refugees depend on the environment near the refugee camp for firewood, cultivation and fishing (Crisp, 2003; Whitaker, 2002; Martin, 2015).[19] Studies in Tanzania, though, highlight mixed opinions within the local populations living near refugee settlements about the positive effect refugees have on the economy (Kreibaum, 2016; Maystadt and Verwimp, 2014). Similarly, in terms of increased crime and violence around camp spaces, research is mixed (Whitaker, 1999).[20]

Ultimately, it remains uncertain from the literature whether indirect security concerns surrounding established refugee camps influence state reception policy in a profound way. In Kenya, insecurity surrounding the Dadaab Camp has undoubtedly contributed to the repeated threats by the state to close the camp (Chkam, 2016; Cannon and Fujibayashi, 2018). Yet, the securitisation of refugees in Kenya also plays a large role in the response by the state (Abebe et al., 2019). Equally, for these purposes, it is noteworthy that these repeated threats were not focused on shifting to a different reception policy, but rather on the return of refugees to their countries of origin. Finally, if historical incidences of 'refugee warriors' infiltrating refugee camps have not induced drastic changes in reception policy more broadly on the continent, it remains open to debate whether these forms of localised insecurity ever will.

In contrast, relevant contemporary literature has made concrete links between concerns over insecurity in urban spaces and national reception policies. Specifically, the danger of increased insecurity in cities is a key reason cited for the adoption and continued maintenance of refugee camps in Africa (Milner, 2000, 2009). Thus, indirect security concerns appear to hold far greater influence over state-run reception policies within the context of the urban space compared to similar concerns about the refugee camp.

In terms of the empirical evidence to support these fears, it is evident that insecurity can arise when large numbers of refugees arrive en masse into urban areas. Tensions often revolve around competition for employment, health and education, and can be particularly salient over the short-term (Milner, 2000). For example, a surge in demand for basic support needs can create challenges for local social services (Muggah, 2009). Similar effects over time have been observed in relation to the economy and labour market (Maystadt and Verwimp, 2014). Over the longer term, there appears to be a board consensus that any negative short-term effects impacting the labour market are eventually reversed (Muggah, 2009; Grindheim 2013). Yet, this view is not universal and is inevitably context-dependent (Ruiz and Vargas-Silva, 2015). Indeed, the range of findings in relation to the long-term effect of refugees on the urban space suggests that more work is needed in different contexts (Maystadt and Verwimp, 2014).

There has also been a lack of engagement with the role of the host state in these long-term processes (with the emphasis again being on the refugee population and the host community).[21] For example, over the mid-to-long term, the settling of refugees within a local population regularly shows clear benefits for the whole community (Jacobsen, 2017). Yet important questions often remain unasked at the national level, for instance concerning refugees' free access to social services and their ability to contribute to national tax systems. In addition, with competitive political settlements keenly interested in short-term goals such as winning elections, convincing these states of the long-term benefits of integrating refugee populations remains challenging. This is particularly the case if they are likely to experience initial (albeit hopefully temporary) problems relating to increased security concerns.

Securitisation

The two material security concerns that have been set out above also play into a wider ideational factor, namely the broader securitisation of refugees and cross-border movement. Analysis adopting this lens, with notable exceptions, commonly remains at the international level and looks at trends across states, regions or globally.[22] Developed from work conducted by the Copenhagen School in the early 1990s, the securitisation of forms of migration refers to the conception of 'migration' as a security threat to a state or society (Buzan et al., 1998). As Donnelly (2017) notes, the current and dominant response of states to all forms of international migrants is reliant on the language of security and securitisation. In terms of refugees, the past fifteen years have seen a global shift in asylum policy, from a focus on 'humanitarian-driven refugee protection ensconced in international law, to one prioritising the protection of national security interests' (Saunders, 2014:72). Indeed, states and the media have increasingly viewed the movement of refugees as a threat to national security (Hammerstad, 2010; FitzGerald, 2019).[23]

This framing justifies responses that are both rapid and exceptional, such as reception policies that have veered away from norms contained within the global refugee regime (O'Driscoll, 2017). Indeed, the securitisation process (via discourse) produces the threat and *response* – resulting in an implied consensus within the political space over the issue (Oelgemöller, 2017). As UNHCR notes, the viability of the refugee protection regime now 'hinges on its real and perceived impact on international security' (UNHCR, 2006b:63). In this way, states gain public approval for ignoring or constraining key refugee regime norms, such as by keeping refugees in refugee camps (Hammerstad, 2010; Lindley, 2011).

The securitisation of cross-border movement and refugees not only comes from the national and international level but also 'from below'. Hammerstad (2012) observes how grassroots level actors also have the potential to become 'securitisers'. Ground-level sentiments (such as the rising levels of xenophobia seen in Southern Africa) can filter up to the national level, ultimately causing changes in discourse and policy (UNHCR, 2006b). Global tendencies towards neo-liberal economics and democratisation support this 'from below' construction of refugees as a security risk. As observed via the 'democracy-asylum' nexus, the shift in the 1980s and 1990s from authoritarian-style political settlements to more competitive ones on the continent has led states to become more amenable and reactive to anti-refugee and anti-immigrant feelings in the local population (Crisp, 2000; Seidman-Zager, 2010).

The incorporation of a security lens into discussions on how states respond to refugee movement has generated a wealth of understanding in terms of explaining the slow decline seen globally in the overall treatment of refugees. Nevertheless, this body of literature is not immune from critique. Firstly, within the context of Africa, academic work on securitisation often remains focused on how mobility on the continent informs understanding around security borders in the minority world (Mayblin and Turner, 2020; Obi, 2010; Zanker, 2019). Secondly, McGahan (2009) suggests there is a need to examine the dynamics of individual host countries when analysing the securitisation of refugees. Common positions taken in the literature see analysis remain at the international level, observing broad trends or applying these broad trends to the national context, without fully engaging in the social, economic and political dynamics of a particular state. Or as O'Driscoll (2017) notes, there is a need to understand how these in-country specificities impact on *how* and *what* issues are securitised. Giving attention to the state-level is particularly pertinent in relation to the question of why states have adopted specific refugee reception policies that contest or undermine the implementation of core regime norms such as freedom of movement.

Thirdly, research that focuses on the securitisation of refugee movement can be one-dimensional (Vigneswaran and Quirk, 2015). By insisting that host states are increasingly seeing refugee movement solely as a security threat, the resulting analysis remains relatively inflexible. For example, it is unclear how a security lens can fully explain why states with security concerns regarding the movement of refugees regularly allow *some* movement between refugee camps and urban spaces.

The concept of stability

Interconnected with the ideational factor of securitisation, is the notion of stability (Weiner, 1992). This concept (and its converse, instability) has not received a great deal of attention within the forced migration literature. When it is discussed, it is typically mentioned within a broader discussion on potential insecurity concerns linked to migrant movement into urban spaces. Yet, recent research has started to investigate the concept of stability as a way to critique the perceived overreliance on a security lens in the literature. By developing the work on stability as a complementary concept to the prevalent security lens, the book aims to draw out a more grounded state-focused understanding of refugee movement. This in turn will help to develop further clarity about how states respond (in the form of policy) to refugee movement at the point of reception.

The 'problem' of refugees and their movement

The 'problem' of refugees can be understood conceptually as instability (Maple et al., 2021).[24] That is to say, the belief or perception that instability of some kind will result from the cross-border movement of forced migrants (particularly those arriving en masse). This is particularly apparent with regards to the destabilising impact that refugee and migrant movements into large urban spaces are understood to have. Too many new arrivals into the urban space are deemed to cause instability for state structures and infrastructure, as well as creating additional competition for scarce resources with the local population (Jacobsen, 2002).[25] This is particularly acute when host states are facing ongoing economic problems and/or political uncertainty before the new arrivals (UNHCR, 2006b). In recent years, states have responded to concerns about influxes of migrants by slowly replacing concepts such as universal human rights with a 'new ideological rival', that is, one of stability (Kagan, 2014). States 'view more freedom for non-citizens (including movement) as creating chaos', and because of this, maintaining the status quo is often seen as the best answer (Maple et al., 2021:11).

In response to this ideological shift in state behaviour, the literature explored above has shown how the cross-border and internal movement of refugees is increasingly being seen as a uniquely political concern via the process of securitisation (Bakewell, 2018; Betts, 2009b). As Vigneswaran and Quirk (2015:2) highlight, this approach *solely* frames refugee movement in terms of 'government efforts first to prevent and then – when official efforts prove ineffective – to cope with unwanted movements across sovereign territorial borders'. This narrative is frequently adopted by states through the reception policies that emerge in response to refugee movement. Nevertheless, the emphasis in the research on the idea that stopping *all* movement (particularly in relation to forced migrants and refugees) is a state's ultimate aim has meant that analysis often remains narrow. This stance tends to overlook several other key components of the relationship between refugee movement, reception policies and the host state. As Vigneswaran and Quirk (2015:2) acknowledge, movement plays a foundational role in 'what states look like as spatial and political entities, how they accumulate power and resources, what types of policies and strategies they pursue, and how they relate to their peers and other political, social, and economic actors'.

In terms of reception within Africa, refugee and other forced migrant movement inevitably plays a role in the construction and the day-to-day running of host states. For example, at the level of the urban African city, these geographical spaces are not home to sedentary homogeneous populations which simply submit or conform to the will of the state. Refugees regularly move to avoid interacting with state structures entirely and find alternative forms of 'local citizenship' in urban spaces (Landau, 2018a). Equally, the movement of refugees can also engage with state structures (at the local and national levels) irrespective of whether that movement is officially permitted or is more illicit.

A central tenet of this book is that stopping all movement is rarely the overarching aim of a reception policy. Rather, it is about constraining or managing movement with the aim of maintaining the status quo and a resemblance of stability, particularly within the urban space. As a result, controlling movement is often balanced with efforts to exploit movement and the opportunities that it can ultimately create (Vigneswaran and Quirk, 2015). This juxtaposition of dissimilar goals is particularly apparent when analysis shifts from seeing the state as a unique unitary actor, to analysing it in a multi-scalar way (for example, across the international, national, local and even sub-local levels).

Stability and the paradox of human movement

This sub-section builds on these ideas surrounding states' understanding of movement and stability by introducing the recent work of Kotef (2015). Kotef's work offers insights into the apparently conflicting and contesting approaches to refugee reception displayed by host states. For example, a common occurrence in Africa is that a state will maintain a dominant refugee camp reception policy, but at the same time permit (by express or tacit agreement) considerable numbers of refugees to move and settle in urban spaces (Bakewell, 2014; Maple, 2016). Put differently, this area of research helps to examine and explain the balancing act that is seen between controlling the movement of new arrivals, while also exploiting the potential and opportunities that it can create. In addition, Kotef's work ties directly into the debates highlighted above in relation to the material and ideational factors (such as security) that are influencing state approaches to the arrival of refugees.

Movement within a sovereign state has never been entirely seen as unrestrained or 'free', but rather secured by 'many anchors that provided it with some stability' (Kotef, 2015:4). Even in the most liberal states, there has always been a reaction to movement that seeks to stop it from being unrestrained. Such reactions are ultimately understood as being about creating or maintaining stability and even freedom. All key thinkers on the 'state' have regarded methods such as erecting walls or enclosures as a precondition for freedom, rather than necessarily being in direct opposition to the free movement of persons (Kotef, 2015). Conceptualisations of movement are therefore not conceivable in the modern world without the possibility of its management. According to Kotef (2015): 'Regimes of movement are thus never simply a way to control, to regulate, or to incite movement; regimes of movement are integral to the formation of different modes of being.'

This complementary process can be explained in two steps. Firstly, citizenship is dependent on constraining and regulating movement to support the 'sedentarist ideology' of the nation state, even if in reality people are always mobile (Sassen, 1999). Secondly, once this image of stability has been achieved, citizens are granted more freedom to express their growing mobility. As such, movement and stability work hand in hand. Refugees and other forced migrants rupture this ongoing symbiotic relationship between citizens, movement and the state. Refugees are not citizens nor what Kotef refers to as 'rooted' people. For this reason, their movement is seen as a threat. This synopsis highlights the paradox of human movement today:

> Movement here is seen both as a manifestation of freedom and as an interruption, as a threat to order. One of the functions of the state is, therefore, to craft a concept of order, stability and security that is reconcilable with its concept of freedom and its concept of movement. (Mbembe, 2018:1)

The movement of citizens of a state is deemed as an essential part of being 'modern' and as such is protected. In contrast, the movement of outsiders, such as refugees, regularly falls into the second category – namely that of an interruption or a threat. Indeed, refugees who refuse to remain sedentary are often perceived as a threat to the peace and stability of the host state.

For Kotef, the idea of stability (and with it controlled or managed movement) is based on a core relationship with the geographical space. People who have land and who are 'rooted' can be permitted to move freely, and this right needs to be protected. The state is at ease with this form of self-regulated movement because here movement is framed as being in moderation and regulated. In contrast, for others ('non-rooted people') who have no fixed relationship with the land (such as refugees), movement may be restricted. This restriction is not conceived as an infringement upon a freedom, but rather as controlling a security problem. As Mbembe (2018:1) notes, to the state, these people are often 'enemies, both of freedom, because they do not exercise it with restraint, and of security and order'. As discussed previously, stability in this sense has become a new ideology: one that rivals human rights and democracy (Kagan, 2014). Excessive refugee movement can be seen as a threat to this stability and as such, while some movement is regarded as a permissible freedom, other forms are deemed as a threat (Mbembe, 2018). These points also add further nuance to previous discussions on the role of the 'democracy-asylum' nexus, whereby violations of the rights of non-voting individuals can be reframed as in the interests of protecting the rights and freedoms of the 'rooted' voting public.

In line with this understanding, reception spaces become political spaces for refugees via the movements they allow and prevent (Kotef, 2015). Movement is thus inextricably linked to the form of reception afforded to the new arrival (Gill et al., 2011). For example, the literature has long observed how encampment policies provoke a reaction, whereby refugees reject this enforced immobility to self-settle illicitly (Darling, 2017; Basok, 2009; Varsanyi, 2006). Equally, the mobility strategies adopted by refugees trigger reactions by states, regardless of whether the strategies are broadly in line with a state's reception policy or adopted as a way to resist repressive reception policies. In South Africa, refugees and asylum-seekers have adopted mobility strategies in large numbers, in line with the official reception policy. Yet as long as this form of movement remains unchecked or unmanaged, a political reaction that restrains and brings some order to this movement is likely. Thus, a delicate balance emerges between the movement of refugees and host states, with some movement accepted and even encouraged as long as it adds 'value' and does not reach a level perceived to be unstable. In this way, the movement of refugees (particularly into the urban space) informs the conditional nature of refugee reception, which was examined in the previous chapter.

Current academic literature shows how security and stability, at both a material and an ideational level, continue to play a significant role in reception policies in Africa. Indeed, due to the complex relationship between these concepts and refugee movement, reception policies regularly diverge from international commitments. This is seen starkly in the case of freedom of movement, with many states in Africa still understanding encampment as the most rational way of combating forms of insecurity and instability linked to the arrival of refugee populations. Nevertheless, key gaps in the literature exist, particularly in relation to this kind of state behaviour. Using a state-focused lens, the book will develop a deeper understanding about the influence that concepts related to security and stability have on state-based responses to the arrival of refugees.

The chapter has set out three key academic debates in which research has attempted to explain approaches to reception in Africa through reference to broader trends. In doing so, the chapter has made significant observations pertinent to the book's core aim of investigating the disparate state responses to the arrival of refugees in Africa. It has also highlighted some key gaps in the research that are worthy of further examination. Finally, through the debates presented in this chapter several key material, ideational and institutional factors have been introduced that seem to influence state-based reception policies and influence the degree of implementation of regime norms. Equally, due to the volatility of specific factors (such as security and stability concerns), the analysis recognises the possibility that reception policies are likely to be subject to change and revision via contestation between different factors. These observations and hypothesis are interrogated and developed through the two case studies of Zambia and South Africa that follow the next chapter, which considers the methodology used to examine reception in the two countries.

Notes

1. See van der Waldt (2020).
2. See also Okoth-Obbo (2001); UNHCR (1997).
3. A political settlement is defined as 'informal and formal processes, agreements, and practices that help consolidate politics, rather than violence, as a means for dealing with disagreements about interests, ideas and the distribution of and use of power' (Laws, 2012:1). Ultimately, 'analysing political settlements supports a more detailed understanding of how the interests, ideas and relations of power among leaders, elites and coalitions can assist or obstruct the process of positive change' (Laws and Leftwich, 2014:1).
4. See Levy et al. (2015).
5. See Loescher et al. (2008).
6. UNHCR remains involved in the running of many RSD (Refugee Status Determination) processes in Africa (Kagan, 2011, 2013).
7. Although key actors attached to the global refugee regime have been assisting states in offering protection to refugees since the 1950s (Glasman, 2017; Rahal and White, 2022).
8. The visibility of refugees also delays the onset of donor fatigue (Jamal, 2003; Crisp, 2003).

9. See also Agier (2011); Hyndman and Giles (2011). States in Africa nonetheless appear cognisant of the uncomfortable truth that these spaces are funded as part of broader containment policies (Hovil and Maple, 2022; FitzGerald, 2019). See the work on refugee commodification (Tsourapas, 2019; Freier et al., 2021).

10. See also van Garderen and Ebenstein (2011).

11. See Malkki (1992:34). The significance of applying the global regime in the host state can be seen as transferring refugees from the political realm to the supposedly non-political or humanitarian realm (Karadawi, 1999).

12. See also Saunders (2014).

13. See also Chimni (2009); Betts (2009a).

14. Often the running of refugee camps has been left entirely to UNHCR (Slaughter and Crisp, 2008).

15. See Cantor and Chikwanha (2019).

16. In 1997, UNHCR published a 'Policy on Refugees in Urban Areas' but this was widely criticised (Kagan, 2013).

17. Therefore, in some situations, camps are deemed as a necessity (UNHCR, 2009).

18. In the last ten years, the number of refugees in Africa has tripled to over 6 million (UNHCR, 2020).

19. See Whitaker (2002); Milner (2000).

20. See also Amuedo-Dorantes et al. (2018).

21. There are notable exceptions, see Kibreab (2007).

22. See Hammerstad (2010, 2012).

23. The securitisation of refugees was first looked at in the 1990s (Loescher, 1992; Weiner, 1992).

24. See Kotef (2015); Maple et al. (2021).

25. See also Hove et al. (2013).

Chapter 3

Investigating state behaviour towards refugees

This chapter explores the methodology and research methods used to investigate variations in state responses to the arrival of refugees in Southern Africa. Specifically, the chapter examines the book's adopted methodology in a piecemeal way through the distinct phases of the project, from choosing the research design to collecting and analysing the data. In doing so, the intention is for the chapter to be a working model for future work by scholars developing and designing similar projects. This should be of particular interest for scholars studying refugee reception policy but also for those in related fields who are interested in research methods, triangulation and comparative case studies.

The chapter starts with an explanation of the overarching methodological approach of the book. It then broadly follows the steps set out by Hentschel (1998) in relation to producing a robust research design, by outlining the overall research design, then moving on to examine the approaches taken in respect of data collection, data analysis and data interpretation. At each stage, time is spent critically reflecting on the decisions made, and how certain approaches were selected over others. In the second half of the chapter, the timing of the research, positionality and potential limitations to the study are explored. Key ethical considerations inherent to a project aimed at understanding state policies related to refugees are also examined. Engaging with an emerging body of literature on this topic, the chapter considers relevant ethical concerns and how they were mitigated in the project. At the same time, the chapter does not purport to have solutions to all ethical challenges that emerge in forced migration research (Müller-Funk, 2021). There are no easy answers when addressing these issues. Rather, it remains a constant balancing act, with the principle of 'do no harm' needing to be the starting point for all decisions.

The book is predominantly based on three prolonged stays in Southern Africa that took place between 2016 and 2018 and draws from a range of sources (both oral and written). Initial library research, conducted at the University of the Witwatersrand in Johannesburg in late 2016 generated a focused literature review of key topics and a collection of published law and policy relating to refugee reception on the African continent and specifically concerning South Africa and Zambia. In addition, informal interviews were conducted with local academics, and meetings and events between state officials and civil society were attended. During this first visit, the design of the project was finalised.

In 2017 and 2018, two further extended visits were undertaken in South Africa and Zambia. The methods used for data collection were: (1) key informant interviews (KIIs); (2) informal interviews and attendance at state body and civil society meetings and events; and (3) review of national legal and policy documents. This amounted to over seventy hours of formal and informal interviews, attendance at more than twenty public meetings and events with government officials and/or civil society and the review of a considerable quantity of policy documentation. Between 2018 and 2022, three years of post-doctoral study were completed at the African Centre for Migration and Society (ACMS), University of the Witwatersrand. During this time, initial analysis was revised and updated to reflect political shifts in Southern Africa and recent developments in academic literature.

Overarching methodological stance

In line with the overarching epistemological position set out in the Introduction, the qualitative methodological approach that underpins this book is a broad constructivist one. In contrast to a positivist stance, which aims for objective and universal knowledge, this approach acknowledges the constructed nature of the social reality that is embedded in decision-making and power relations concerning state reception policies. Within this broad constructivist stance, there is the scope for both 'thick descriptions' of key actors' experiences at the national and local level (Neimeyer and Levitt, 2001), as well as advancing knowledge via the process of theory-building (Gray, 2013). As proposed by Betts and Orchard (2014), this can be achieved through balancing the in-depth insights of ethnography with wider insights from political science.

The use of KIIs as the primary method of data collection closely fits this overall approach. The aim of KIIs is to uncover participants' perceptions (Crouch and McKenzie, 2006) and specific motivations and behaviours relating to a particular topic (Kumar, 1989). Thus, the goal is to generate insights into the stakeholders' involvement with the reception of refugees. Furthermore, under constructivism, contradictions between KIIs indicates differences of perspective and remain valid and insightful rather than indicative of inaccuracies. These insights were supplemented by quasi-ethnographic methods, namely residing on and off in the target region for over four years, undertaking informal interviews with local 'experts' and attending a large number of events, meetings and conferences relating to the reception and movement of migrants in the sub-region (referred to hereafter as 'informal interviews and symposia'). The use of the term 'quasi-ethnographic' is due to the frequency of visits to the sub-region (Murtagh, 2007). Ethnographic studies have customarily involved the researcher being immersed in one setting for a long period of time (Bryman, 2004), whereas this book conducted a study in a small number of settings. Nevertheless, since the 1990s, 'multi-sited ethnography' has been widely accepted (Marcus, 1995). Consistent with Murtagh's (2007) understanding of quasi-ethnography, while the use of multi-sites does have implications in terms of less time spent in each setting, it nevertheless facilitates the opportunity to explore refugee reception from two perspectives and to generate a rich array of data and processual connections.

Research design

An overarching explanatory research design was chosen because the book asks 'why' and 'how' questions about refugee reception (Gray, 2013). As explored in the previous chapter, knowledge already exists on specific aspects of the reception of refugees in Africa. Thus, a more exploratory research design was rejected (Robson, 2002).[1] Instead, the book builds on previous work within the fields of refugee and forced migration studies to understand specifically why states respond to refugees in different ways.

To investigate the disparate state responses to the arrival of refugees in Africa, the book sets out to answer two key questions. First, how do we explain the diverse ways in which states receive refugees in their territories? Second, how do the refugee reception policies of host states shape a refugee's ability to pursue their own personal and economic aims? The need to ask these 'how' questions has a bearing on all aspects of the research design, including the methods chosen for data collection (Crotty, 1998). Nevertheless, as examined next, the development of these research questions themselves was an iterative process, with findings during the framing exercise and initial stages of fieldwork being fed back into this process and informing the finalised questions above (Creswell, 2009). Lastly, when determining the research design, care was taken to make sure it also fitted with the chosen comparative case study model, as presented in the Introduction; the book's conceptual framework, as set out in Chapter 1; and the overarching methodological approach, as discussed above.

The framing exercise, September 2016

The first visit to Southern Africa lasted for four months. It took place in 2016 and was based at ACMS. The purpose of this initial visit was to undertake a framing exercise. This amounted to the completion of several preliminary activities to determine the make-up of the research design. Firstly, six informal interviews were conducted with academics working in the field of migration studies in South Africa.[2] Secondly, an affiliation with ACMS permitted access to the daily activities of the centre, which included a multitude of workshops and lectures relating to human mobility and migration in Southern Africa. Finally, the affiliation also allowed access to civil society meetings with government bodies, as well as to presentations and conferences hosted and run by the Department of Home Affairs in South Africa. The overarching aims of the framing exercise were to develop and refine original research questions; to develop a comprehensive literature review in order to locate an adequate conceptual framework through which to respond to the research questions; and to select the most appropriate methods to answer the research questions.[3]

The initial focus of the project (derived from a Masters' dissertation completed in 2013) was on state attitudes towards the right to freedom of movement for refugees at the point of arrival using a socio-legal lens.[4] The first iterations of the research questions were tentative, yet also useful as a tool for setting out the primary aims of the research (Agee, 2009). Through the framing exercise, the research questions evolved, becoming more focused on the rationale *behind* state-run reception policies and the potential implications for refugees. In this way, the concept of the 'state' became more layered in terms of the level of explicitness of attitudes, rationales and motivations, as well as geographical scale. Furthermore, as examined in the Introduction, the book investigates this topic from a political science perspective (rather than a socio-legal one), with the emphasis being on *why* states behave as they do, rather than on what they *should* be doing. Finally, as noted by Flick (2006:106), the reflexive process of formulating research questions helps 'circumscribe a specific area of a more or less complex field, which you regard as essential'. Indeed, this reflexive approach continued throughout the fieldwork and analytical stages, with the research questions continuing to be developed and refined (Agee, 2009).

The framing exercise also developed a preliminary literature review by incorporating localised literature and interviews with local academics, in order to select and adapt a suitable conceptual framework for the book. As both the framework and research questions were formulated (although not finalised) during this scoping phrase, the research questions could be constructed so they explicitly made links with the theory (Agee, 2009). Moreover, similarly to the reflexive approach used for finalising the research questions, the conceptual framework adopted for the book was also amended during the research process. Specifically, this occurred when the initial data collected indicated that the ideational influence of national governance frameworks in the implementation of reception policies was far greater than initially proposed by Betts and Orchard's (2014) theory of norm implementation. Conversely, this suggested that the role of the global refugee regime on reception policies in Southern Africa was potentially less influential than inferred from the original theory. Lastly, as proposed by Mackenzie et al. (2007), the informal dialogues conducted during the framing exercise were valuable in developing future questions for more structured interviews and drawing attention to new areas for investigation. Thus, the framing exercise itself became an integral part of the research design, with the informal interviews and attendance at key stakeholder symposia forming part of the analysis.

The finalised research design

Based on the framing exercise, an explanatory research design was finalised at the end of the first trip. KIIs were chosen as the main method for collecting data. Two further methods were then selected to augment and triangulate data in conjunction with this dominant approach. Firstly, the relevant national legal and policy documents were examined and secondly 'Informal Interviews and Symposia' were drawn upon. These are examined further below.

KIIs were selected as the main research method for several reasons. First and foremost, during the initial trip to South Africa, only a limited number of legal and policy documents relevant to refugee reception policy were located. During discussions with academics in South Africa and Zambia at this time, it became apparent that there was an assumption (which was subsequently confirmed during the second field trip) that this situation would be replicated in Zambia. Thus, an alternative method of collecting data was required to address the research questions. Interviewing as an approach was selected over other methods (such as surveys and questionnaires) due to its suitability for the explanatory nature of the research questions (Gray, 2013), time constraints and concerns regarding the availability of key decision-makers. In addition, the flexibility inherent to KIIs provided the room to explore and adapt in response to new ideas and concepts emerging from the interviews.

It was also decided that key informant interviews best fitted the state-focused analysis of the macro- and micro-level structures approach taken by the book. As Kumar (1989) observes, KIIs reveal the perspectives and motivations of persons involved with a specific issue or theme. As the information is obtained directly from knowledgeable people, these interviews can provide data that is not possible via other methods. For instance, KIIs can reveal the personal experiences, observations and underlying motivations and attitudes of interviewees (Kumar, 1989). They can show not only what people do but also *why* they do it. This means KIIs have the potential to add new insight into why reception policies at the national and local level are implemented (or contested) – even ones that appear to conflict with national legal frameworks. Thus, this method has the capacity to elicit new insights behind key decisions and actions that are unlikely to be found in the public domain.

The KIIs were then correlated and triangulated with insights gained from informal interviews with local academics and experts on the sub-region, and attendance at symposia, and the review of national legal and policy documents. The two additional methods were embraced to improve the validity and reliability of the overall project. As Kumar (1989) notes, the more that interview findings are correlated and triangulated with data from other sources, the more confidence can be placed on the findings. Finally, these approaches were also used to identify key areas or themes that were not apparent during the early stages of the KIIs.[5]

The data collection stage

This section considers core elements of the data collection stage of a successful research project, which included for this book, deciding who to interview (and who not to interview), the interviews themselves, and more ethnographical approaches, such as attending meetings between civil society and state officials. Data collection was ongoing throughout the three main stays in Southern Africa between 2016 and 2018. However, the

KIIs did not start until the second visit in mid-2017 once the framing exercise had been completed.

Sampling for the key informant interviews

During the framing exercise conducted in 2016, appropriate 'key informant' groupings were identified (for example, 'state officials' and 'civil society'). In line with the overall methodological approach, gaining new insight into refugee reception policies requires input from diverse perspectives (Flick, 2009). Nonetheless, the book adopts a state-focused perspective aimed at understanding how and why host states (and global agencies) respond to refugees in specific ways, and how these approaches shape refugees' attempts at engaging with local communities and markets. As a result, the sampling process for this book was orientated to finding groups of participants whose perspectives on reception would be the most instructive for this form of analysis.[6] Accordingly, the groups of key informants were decided according to which entities were directly involved in reception policies at the international, national and local level. In total, three distinct groups of key informants were identified: Group A: Government Officials (national and local level); Group B: INGO Officials; Group C: Local civil society, refugee/migrant leaders and refugee experts.[7]

Due to the overall state-focused approach taken, it was decided that the involvement of large numbers of refugees was not essential to answering the research questions. The groupings of key informants therefore initially stayed at the level of refugee leaders (or 'above'). An exception was nevertheless made to this approach, with two 'refugee experts' being interviewed in Lusaka, Zambia. This was done due to a lack of street-level organisations and civil societies working on these issues in Zambia. After consultation with other refugee leaders and civil society, two refugees were selected as expert sources of information to discuss how processes work in both the settlements and within urban spaces.[8] Care was taken to not simply ask for their 'stories', but to treat them like any other key informant interviewed on the topic of refugee reception (Reed and Schenck, 2023).

Turning to the sampling of individual participants, key informants from each grouping (A to C) were selected for interview by purposive sampling and snowball sampling. As a first step, purposive sampling was used to select the KIIs, with the key criteria for selection being that they possessed an intimate knowledge of the subject or theme on which they were being questioned. In turn, 'intimate knowledge' was based on the participant's professional expertise or contribution to a specific project or programme relating to refugee reception.[9] To locate these potential interviewees, local and international researchers and academics were consulted via the two affiliations in South Africa and Zambia during the framing exercise. These consultations generated a lengthy list of possible informants for each grouping within each country.

Due to the nature of KIIs, the possibility of additional snowball sampling was also built into the design of the project. Therefore, when key informants suggested other potential participants, there was sufficient time allocated in both locations to conduct additional interviews. Snowballing offers real benefits for locating difficult to reach or hidden populations (Atkinson and Flint, 2001) and this was especially useful for identifying refugee and migrant leaders and civil society in Johannesburg and Lusaka.

In total, sixty-four semi-structured interviews were conducted across the range of groupings identified.[10] The sample ended up being larger than is often recommended in the literature for KIIs (Kumar, 1989; Rudestam and Newton, 2007). In part, this was to avoid selection bias and ensure sample accuracy and precision (Bernard, 2011).[11] In addition, the decision to end the KIIs was taken when no new information was uncovered in each grouping. As Rudestam and Newton (2007) note, this type of sampling is done to saturate a concept. In other words, the interviews continue to the point where the researcher is comfortable that the specific issue (and its relationship with other concepts) has been comprehensively explored so that it becomes theoretically meaningful. However, total saturation may never fully occur because each new participant is likely to have something unique to provide (Josselson and Lieblich, 2003). Therefore, as Rudestam and Newton (2007) suggest, it is vital to collect sufficient data (hence the large sample) to represent the breadth and depth of the concepts being investigated.

The interview process

As most of the participants were high-level bureaucrats or elite members of relevant communities with demanding jobs or roles, there was an expectation of only obtaining one-off interviews with the key informants. Therefore, semi-structured interviews were selected as the most appropriate form of interview-style (Bernard, 2011). This type of interview allows the interviewer to frame open-ended questions around the central theme of the study, whilst also having the flexibility to allow for the conversation to shift to new areas or points of interest (Kvale, 1996).

Separate interview guides were created for each grouping of key informants (Bernard, 2011). These help to produce more systematic, reliable and comparable qualitative data (Sewell, 1998). There was no need, however, to note every item nor specific questions that would be asked in each interview (Sewell, 1998). Indeed, because the intention of KIIs is to investigate key topics in depth, the guides were deliberately concise to avoid the risk of interviews covering too many topics and resulting in superficiality (Kumar, 1989).

Interview questions arose from the interview guides and had a simple structure to them. The questions aimed to elicit detailed information on topics covering the reception of refugees. These included, for example, the role of different actors in the reception offered to refugees and the interaction between refugee movement in-country and state and UN structures. Thus, the questions remained open-ended and were designed to avoid simple yes or no answers. This allowed respondents to explain what they meant in their own words and produced a relaxed conversational flow (Schoenberger, 1991). Follow-up questions were asked to probe further on specific topics or themes.

The interviews were conducted in English and recorded digitally, subject to the interviewees' written permission. In addition, notes were made throughout each interview. These included: (1) recording most answers given to the questions; and (2) any additional insights that occurred to the researcher during the interview (referred to hereafter as 'field notes'). After each interview, field notes were kept separately from the responses of the interviewees and ultimately used as a source of supplementary information, helping shape additional enquiries in future interviews.[12]

KIIs in South Africa were undertaken during the second field trip between June 2017 and November 2017, in Johannesburg and Cape Town. Gaining access to networks of civil society and refugee and migrant groups in South Africa was relatively straightforward. Indeed, most organisations and community groups responded to the first email enquiry. In terms of state entities, city-level departments were interested in participating as well as entities with specific human rights mandates (such as the Human Rights Commission). In contrast, it was extremely difficult to gain access to the Department of Home Affairs, which has the national mandate to deal with refugee matters. After eventually gaining research approval from the department, interviews were able to take place.

A similar situation occurred with UNHCR, with the South African office generally unwilling to speak to academics. For example, after months of emails, a senior protection officer finally agreed to meet. However, upon arriving for the interview, the officer stated they would not answer questions about UNHCR's role in South Africa or its relationship with the host state. This lack of access in and of itself says a great deal about the role of UNHCR in-country and will be examined further in later chapters. Alternative informants were ultimately found to gain an agency perspective – including UNHCR staff from the Southern Africa office.

The third trip involved spending five months in Zambia (from November 2017 to March 2018) based at Southern African Institute for Policy and Research (SAIPAR) in Lusaka. In contrast to South Africa, research looking at migration or refugee movement is relatively sparse in Zambia. Furthermore, civil society is small, especially in terms of migrant and refugee issues. As a result, obtaining interviews with key informants from these groupings was challenging. In part, these dynamics are due to the refugee settlements and their remote locations. However, it was also to do with the ruling political settlement moving towards more of an authoritarian rule, meaning that the political space for civil society and academics was rapidly shrinking.

Conversely, there remains a large network of international NGOs and agencies present in Zambia. These organisations have greater freedom in terms of discussing social and political issues compared with the situation in South Africa. Overall, they also have a good working relationship with the Zambian state. As a result, international organisations were very accommodating in response to interview requests. The major difficulty in obtaining interviews in Zambia arose due to communication issues, with civil society and state officials rarely responding to emails. It became apparent that WhatsApp was the best means of contacting key informants.

Interviews normally lasted between forty-five minutes and one hour, with most interviewees being accommodating and engaging. In rare instances, high-level bureaucrats within UN and state systems were uncooperative during the meetings. In these situations, the purpose of the study was re-emphasised and a commitment to gaining a non-biased and 'complete' understanding of refugee reception was made. On rare occasions (such as the UNHCR interview mentioned above) when all attempts at creating a genuine and open dialogue failed, the interview was ended early.

Legal and policy documents

The second method of data collection was the use of legal and policy documents originating from the selected countries. Due to the framing of the research questions, documents selected for review and analysis were limited to those produced by the national or local level governments. The existence of official documentation was unearthed either by prior desk-based research, through the framing exercise in South Africa in 2016 or via the KIIs. Documents were then obtained via the Internet or official channels. Legal and policy documentation was more accessible in South Africa than in Zambia, because in Zambia a great deal of refugee policy is not recorded publicly.

The obtained texts were utilised to examine the 'status quo' and official policy and procedures at the national level. In addition, they helped develop an understanding of the varying ideational factors that permeate at different government levels. For example, through an examination of the 2016 South African Green Paper on International Migration, it was possible to advance insight into how the Department of Home Affairs conceptualises forms of cross-border migration.[13] To assess biases within the official documents, the authorship and intended readership of the documents was also considered and examined.[14] Finally, other grey literature, such as parliamentary records and media reporting, were consulted to understand particular debates around key legislation and policy documents.

Informal interviews and symposia

This quasi-ethnographic method emerged from the framing exercise conducted in 2016. During this exercise, six informal interviews were carried out with academics and local experts, as well as attendance at numerous state and NGO meetings. This approach was developed and incorporated into the research design, becoming the third source of research data. Thus, during the second and third visits in 2017 and 2018 a further six informal interviews with academics or local experts were conducted. Furthermore, numerous local level and national level meetings between civil society and state officials were attended between 2016 and 2018. These meetings covered key issues relating to state responses to the arrival of refugees in both Zambia and South Africa. For example: the ability to obtain legal papers and negotiate the asylum processes successfully; the ability to move freely within urban areas; and solidarity initiatives with local communities. These events also touched on key material, ideational and institutional factors that were influencing state approaches to reception and were compared to the information obtained from KIIs.

The analysis stage

The analysis stage of qualitative research is traditionally the stage that either receives the least discussion, is left opaque or simply omitted (Nowell et al., 2017; Thorne, 2000). Yet, for qualitative research to be meaningful, *all* stages need to be transparent, rigorous and methodical (Attride-Stirling, 2001). For this book, a form of thematic (or content) analysis was adopted to examine and interpret the data. In essence, this is a method of identifying and analysing themes and patterns within qualitative data (Braun and Clarke, 2006). Under this broad approach, a theoretical thematic examination was adopted rather than a more inductive thematic style. This means that instead of themes emerging solely from the data (that is, purely data-driven or inductive), themes also emerged from the study's overall theoretical stance. Thus, the formation of categories used in the coding of the empirical data emerged during the initial desk-based research, the framing exercise and the crafting of the original research questions.[15] Subsequently, a systematic approach to the analysis was taken, whereby these categories and theoretical ideas were applied to the data gained from the interviews (Becker, 2009). However, the categories and concepts were also continuously assessed in light of the empirical data and modified if deemed appropriate.

The first analytical step was to transcribe all the interviews from the digital recordings. At this point, handwritten notes from the interviews were also reviewed to improve precision. The second step was to code the transcripts via a systematic recording of the data.[16] The coding involved categories (and families of categories) that were devised during the framing exercise, with each interview first being individually analysed (vertical analysis). Coding categories were recorded on the transcripts, with a summary sheet for each interview being completed, which listed the identified categories and corresponding page numbers for that interview. As the interviews progressed and further understanding emerged, so new categories were also introduced, and others amended.

Once all the interviews had been conducted, the transcripts were compared against each other using the finalised categories (horizontal analysis).[17] For a category or theme to be counted, there needed to be several instances of the theme across the data set. Nevertheless, quantity alone did not dictate the theme's relative importance (Braun and Clarke, 2006). Thus, an exact number of instances across a data set was not needed for a theme to be 'counted'. Indeed, the 'keyness' of a theme is not necessarily dependent on quantifiable measures. Rather, based on the researcher's judgement, a theme or category becomes important 'when it captures something important in relation to the overall research question' (Gray, 2013:92).

A core goal of thematic analysis is to reduce the raw data to a manageable level (Flick, 2009). Therefore, once key categories and themes were confirmed, the material was then paraphrased (first reduction) both vertically (within each transcript) and horizontally (across transcripts). Similar paraphrases were then 'bundled' and summarised (second reduction) (Flick, 2009).[18] In this way, at the end of the thematic (content) analysis, the data that emerged was manageable, and related directly to the research questions and themes that originated from the study's overall theoretical stance.[19] Nevertheless, the data sources (in the form of original interview recordings, transcripts and field notes) were continually revisited during the analysis and write-up stages to explore the 'thick' descriptive content. As Richards and Richards (1994) caution, analysis should never entirely depart from the data.[20]

Validity, ethics and reflexivity: conducting field research in Southern Africa

This final section moves to consider the more evaluative and reflexive components intrinsic within a successful research project. The section firstly investigates how to achieve validity and reliability in analysis, before turning to the positionality and the role that timing plays in the collection of data. The chapter ends with an examination of relevant ethical considerations and potential limitations of the methods used for this book.

Validity and reliability

This section outlines the steps taken in the preparation, implementation and analysis stages to ensure scientific rigour, specifically, the measures put in place to safeguard reliability and validity. Reliability in this context refers to the replication of a study under similar circumstances (Rudestam and Newton, 2007). To achieve this, Gray (2013) underlines the importance of providing an audit trail. As such, this chapter has produced a detailed record of the processes involved in conducting the research. This has included explaining the following:

- the configuration and role of the initial framing exercise;
- information on how interview guides were created;
- the format and types of questions asked in the KIIs;
- the use of national and local documentation;
- the additional ethnographic elements of the fieldwork, including the use of informal interviews, field notes and attendance at local workshops, conferences and meetings;
- how the raw data was analysed, as well as the approach taken to coding; and

- the reflexive elements involved, such as the amending of research questions and key themes during the progression of the data collection and analytical stages.

The validity of a specific study is examined in two ways, by looking at internal and external validity. The internal validity of this book (that is, having sufficient evidence to show that the findings are supported by what was observed) is outlined extensively below. In contrast, due to the design and overall approach, the external validity of the study (or the 'generalisability' of the findings) receives less attention.[21] As this is a comparative investigation of two case studies, the book is focused on the context of specific settings (namely South Africa, Zambia and Southern Africa). As Rudestam and Newton (2007:113) argue, 'generalization is the task of the reader rather than the author of qualitative studies'. Thus, any generalisations made to other settings in this book are intentionally modest.

By comparison, significant weight has been attached to demonstrating the internal validity of the book's findings. Put simply, internal validity is a way to measure whether research is rigorous or not. Gray (2013) outlines several techniques, which were followed for this book, to demonstrate internal validity during the analysis and presentation stages. Firstly, the internal validity is enhanced by the time spent in both locations. Indeed, I lived on and off in Southern Africa for over four years during the life of this extended project, which permitted the time and access to check for any distortions in the data and to explore the topic (why states adopt specific reception policies) in sufficient detail (Rudestam and Newton, 2007).

Secondly, to further reduce the risk of confirmation bias and to improve the validity of the study, interpretations of the data were checked with local academics and experts in both countries.[22] To this end, academic meetings and seminars were held in both South Africa and Zambia during the analysis stage. At meetings with local academics (via the two affiliations), initial findings were presented, and discussions ensued in relation to the data collection and data interpretation. In addition, elements of the findings were presented in public seminars at local universities in both Johannesburg and Lusaka. These occurred during the second and third main visits and before the write-up stage of the project began. In these seminars, the research design, the methods and the initial findings were presented. Following the presentation of the research, academics, experts and civil society representatives asked questions, raised critiques and suggested rival explanations for the researcher to consider.

Thus, throughout these stages, the core theoretical assertions made in the book were scrutinised, questioned and explored in the face of divergent ideas from academics and experts.[23]

The final technique used to establish the internal validity of the research project was the use of methodological triangulation.[24] This is achieved by cross-checking and corroborating the data via multiple sources (Rudestam and Newton, 2007). In terms of application, it is important to combine methodological approaches which are distinct in their focus and in the data they provide (Flick, 2009). This was achieved through a varied approach to data collection. Indeed, data was collected from a range of different sources including the perspectives of key informants and academics; primary source documentation set out the official approach of states and observations and impressions gained during public meetings between key informant groupings. Thus, throughout the visits, and during the analysis stage, methodological triangulation was used to cross-check extensive amounts of diverse data.[25]

Positionality

A key issue that pertains to the validity of the data is positionality. When conducting research, it is imperative for the researcher to be aware of how their perspective and interpretations of what is happening can be affected by their own positionality (Clark-Kazak, 2022). As observed by Maher and Tetreault (1994:118), 'knowledge is valid when it includes an acknowledgement of the knower's specific position in any context'. Thus, for this book, it was not possible for me as the researcher to completely separate out my positionality as a white, British male, from the quality and validity of the data.[26] As noted by Kuch (2016), the value system I have internalised from living in London (that can broadly be defined as secular and liberal) impacts on the questions I ask, my perceptions of people and events, and the arguments I develop. Similarly, the interviewee's perceptions about race, gender, Western values or the role of the British in the history of their country/ host country may all influence their attitudes towards me as the researcher.

Substantial time was, therefore, spent reflecting on these complexities, particularly on the positionality of the researcher and the respondents, and the specific power dynamics that could emerge within the interview setting (Fedyuk and Zentai, 2018). When crafting interview questions, consideration was given to how an inquiry might position the researcher in relation to the interviewee, and what the implications of this might be for the interviewee's life (Agee, 2009). In addition, there is a danger when designing and conducting interviews that they merely end up aligning with the individual researcher's interests or preconceived ideas. To reduce this risk, interviews with refugee leaders, experts and civil society representatives were made as relaxed as possible, with participants given sufficient space to raise their own issues in relation to the broader themes of the study.

In actuality, during the interview process identities (ascribed and assumed) were generally fluid rather than fixed. Consequently, the notion that the researcher is always the one in the position of power did not consistently transpire. Depending on the participant, the researcher was perceived in different ways, for instance as an expert, a student, an outsider with little understanding of the local context, a colleague or 'comrade' or as a link to a wider audience. Indeed, during the interviews with refugee leaders and local civil society members, this full spectrum of identities was often observed. Likewise, the interviewees often presented themselves in varied ways within the same interview, for instance as refugee, expert, victim, guest, host and information source.

Research on migration and forced migration also 'takes place in contexts of global inequalities' (Clark-Kazak, 2022:17). I was aware when conducting the research that as a researcher from London with a UK passport, I had access to resources, including time and money. Within this context, charges of extractivism have rightly been levied against researchers from the minority world. Building on this, Bilotta (2020) suggests that when working within related migration fields, the principle of 'do no harm' is not sufficient. I take this to mean that as privileged researchers we need to be doing more, either in terms of contributing to ending suffering (however modest that might be) (Clark-Kazak, 2021), or saying no to conducting certain forms of research (Hagen et al., 2023). These are difficult conversations for the forced migration field, and I do not purport to have the answers. Taking a lead from Mayblin and Turner (2020:36), perhaps a first step is the need to 'sit with the discomfort' of these charges of extractivism, and take them seriously. In an attempt to address some of these concerns (as it is not possible to remove all of them), the intention was always to publish this book with open access. Further, additional time and assistance was given during prolonged visits with refugee groups, and forms of compensation given to refugee experts and groups who offered their time for the interviews. Nevertheless, it is essential this topic remains an ongoing conversation for researchers and the wider field. More collaborative work is needed, with the development of alternative methods and new ways to reduce inequalities within global research agendas (Chatzipanagiotidou and Murphy, 2022; Grabska and Clark-Kazak, 2022).

Timing of the research

The majority of the research for this book was carried out in South Africa and Zambia between 2016 and 2018, which was a particularly notable time to conduct work in this region. During this time, both countries witnessed their ruling political settlements engaging in high-level discussions involving fundamental shifts in the states' response to refugees, while simultaneously dealing with outbreaks of cholera, xenophobic violence and increased influxes of refugees and other forced migrants.

Zambia had recently signed up to the CRRF in 2016, with the now former President Lungu attending UN meetings in New York and committing to *considering* opening up the urban space for refugees. If implemented, this would see a move away from the country's traditional settlement approach to reception. This meant that the issue of refugees was a hotly debated topic within specific government bodies and international NGOs (INGOs). In addition, during the period of interviewing in 2017, two relevant events had recently surfaced and were ongoing. Firstly, renewed unrest in neighbouring DRC meant that considerable numbers of refugees were arriving at the border with Zambia, with emergency transit centres having to be set up. Secondly, an outbreak of cholera was declared on 6 October 2017 in Lusaka. Thus, these events added to the impression that migrant and refugee issues were – at least at that moment – a high priority for international agencies and some government departments.

At the same time, the national government in South Africa was going through the process of publishing the Green and White Papers on International Migration (DHA, 2016a, 2017). These two policy documents set out concrete proposals for moving all asylum-seekers to the processing centres at the border, thereby restricting access to the urban space for forced migrants. These publications generated a great deal of debate between Home Affairs, UNHCR, civil society and academia. Furthermore, after a relatively quiet 2016, incidences of xenophobic attacks on migrants and refugees in large urban areas started to increase throughout 2017 and 2018 (BBC, 2019).

The combination of these varied large-scale events and the high-level policy discussions taking place in both countries indelibly influenced and shaped the context of the conducted research. Inevitably, if the research had been carried out in less fraught times certain interviews might have been less rushed or politically charged. Nevertheless, the timing of the project is ultimately understood as being advantageous (if a little fortuitous). There was sufficient time in both countries to develop key insights into the maintenance of long-term and entrenched approaches to refugee reception as well as an examination of the reasoning behind potential shifts in policy.

Ethical considerations relating to the adopted methods

Research that focuses on migration issues retains specific ethical challenges (Clark-Kazak, 2021). In part, this is because migration, and especially forced migration, can result in unstable or dangerous situations, including precarious or temporary legal status (Anderson, 2010). Equally, migration across the globe is increasingly criminalised and/or vilified by states and local populations (Clark-Kazak, 2021). Thus, projects that engage with these populations need to be held up to relevant ethical principles (Müller-Funk, 2021).

In November 2016, during the first trip to South Africa and following the finalisation of the research design, ethical clearance was gained from the University of London. In addition, the project followed the ethical guidelines for conducting interviews as set out by the Refugee Studies Centre, University of Oxford (Refugee Studies Centre, 2007). These include acknowledging the responsibilities of the researcher towards participants, host communities and governments and the wider society when carrying out research. Furthermore, gaining ethical approval and adhering to guidelines is one part of the responsibility undertaken by a researcher when conducting empirical research. As highlighted below, it is important to consider existing and emerging ethical concerns throughout the entire research process (Miller and Bell, 2002).

Several core ethical considerations relating to refugees and local communities were identified during the design stage and as such were scrutinised and considered throughout the life of the project.[27] Firstly, informed consent is widely seen as the 'cornerstone of ethical practice in research that involves human participants or personal data' (LSE, 2019:1). Following the example of Corti et al. (2000) and Sin (2005), when obtaining informed consent from each participant, several key points were highlighted verbally. These included informing participants that they could terminate the interview or renegotiate consent at any point during the research process, and that they had the opportunity to opt out of the project entirely. The steps taken to ensure confidentiality and anonymity were also made explicit. In addition, before each interview formally started, participants were given a participation form (which set out the goals of the project) and a consent form. On the consent form, participants were asked to agree to the recording of the interview and for the content of the interview to be used in the study. After explaining the content of each form and responding to any queries, each participant was asked to sign to indicate their consent to these arrangements.

Secondly, with regards to confidentiality, the consent form gave participants the option of remaining entirely anonymous or allowing their name to be used in the book. While some participants asked to be named, ultimately, I decided to anonymise all the participants' names.[28] Given this desire for self-determination by certain participants (Clark-Kazak, 2017), this decision, while not taken lightly, was not ideal. The reasoning was based on the tense political climate surrounding refugee and migrant reception within the two countries at the time of the research. Indeed, this has only escalated further in South Africa since the initial collection of data was completed, with renewed xenophobic attacks in cities such as Johannesburg and Cape Town occurring in 2019 (BBC, 2019).

Limitations of the book's research design

Firstly, it can be argued that the use of KIIs risks privileging the perspectives of states and international organisations over other actors such as refugees and civil society. A concerted effort was therefore made to find interviewees from a wide pool of informants in both countries, with the range of KII 'groupings' ultimately including local civil society members and migrant and refugee leaders. Nevertheless, the lack of migrant community groups and civil society members working on migrant issues in Zambia, in contrast to the abundance of international organisations in that state, can be considered a constraint in terms of the final data set.

Following on from this point, the role of refugees and migrants in this research project warrants reflection. Within the academic field, there are ongoing discussions and critical self-reflections surrounding the form and role that refugees and migrants should play in research (Krause, 2017; Hagen et al., 2023). A key outcome of this introspection has centred on the idea of active collaboration and participation with the target population during the design and investigation stages (Fiddian-Qasmiyeh, 2020). Thus, a limitation of this research project is the absence of refugee voices. This is particularly relevant when attempting to gain new understanding of how reception policies may affect this population on the ground.

The lack of refugee participation is a valid constraint and was considered during the design stage. Ultimately it was decided that due to the state focus and ethical concerns, the engagement of large numbers of refugees was not necessary to answer the book's central questions. The primary focus of the project is on key stakeholders at the international, national and local level who are involved in the creation and implementation of reception policies. Due to this approach, it was not seen as justified to request considerable time from populations who are living in precarious situations. As Turner observes, a balance needs to be struck between the value placed on a refugee's time and privacy versus a need to include their views on a given topic (in Hagen et al., 2023). This thinking was further crystallised during the initial period of fieldwork in South Africa, where a general sense of research fatigue was found amongst refugee groups within Johannesburg.[29]

Linked to this overall approach to refugee participation was the decision not to conduct research directly in the two settlements in Zambia. Sufficient data was collected through the interviews with key informants who work in the settlements or who travel there regularly. This information was also supplemented by available existing research that had been conducted within the settlements. As this research did not involve directly interviewing refugees, there were ethical concerns about visiting people's homes and communities in the absence of an obvious immediate benefit of the research for them. The next chapter now turns to present the results of this methodology through the case studies of Zambia and then South Africa.

Notes

1. Exploratory research is conducted when little is known about a phenomenon and the 'problem' is unable to be defined succinctly (Boru, 2018; Saunders et al., 2007).

2. These amounted to what Spradley (1979) sees as ethnographic interviews, whereby they are not formal interviews but are elevated above 'friendly conversations'.

3. Framing or scoping exercises such as informal interviews should be done as part of 'the process of observing a social setting of interest' (Cohen and Crabtree, 2006:331).

4. See Maple (2016).

5. For example, if key informant understandings differed from official documentation or past findings, these disparities raised additional queries as the study progressed.

6. See Flick (2009).

7. Participants from Set C had travel expenses reimbursed and were offered a non-monetary form of thanks, that is, a phone card or lunch. See Bernard (2011).

8. The refugee experts were individuals (female and male) who had lived in Zambia for over five years and had lived for a substantial amount of time in both the settlements and Lusaka.

9. See Kumar (1989).

10. There was a broad balance between the three groups, although as examined below, there were differences and some limitations within each case study.

11. See Atkinson and Flint (2001).

12. See Rudestam and Newton (2007).
13. See DHA (2016a).
14. See Grant (2018).
15. See Flick (2009).
16. See Kumar (1989).
17. Inevitably, these forms of horizontal analysis informally started once interviews began, with connections and contradictions being observed and retained (Spiggle, 1994).
18. Nevertheless, key quotations from transcripts were kept as this process of reduction was carried out.
19. See Braun and Clarke (2006).
20. See also Veroff (2010a, 2010b).
21. See Rudestam and Newton (2007).
22. The findings of the study were also compared to previous literature relating to the reception of refugees (Rudestam and Newton, 2007).
23. See Rudestam and Newton (2007).
24. Not specifically set out by Gray (2013), but by many others (Hentschel, 1998).
25. See Pratt and Loizos (2003).
26. See Kuch (2016).
27. See Pittaway et al. (2010); Mackenzie et al. (2007).
28. Renzetti and Lee (1993); Sin (2005).
29. See Omata (2019).

Chapter 4

Encampment: the maintenance of a camp-based reception in Zambia

Zambia has maintained refugee settlements as the dominant mode of receiving refugees since the 1970s, irrespective of various exhortations by UNHCR and public commitments by present and previous presidents to relax this approach. The overarching aim of this chapter is to investigate the reasoning behind this continued stance. To achieve this, the chapter utilises the book's conceptual framework to appraise key factors found at state and international levels that are influencing, contesting and ultimately maintaining Zambia's national reception policy.

In particular, the case study seeks to move the analysis of camp-based reception policies beyond generalised discussions on 'security' factors and state sovereignty. Indeed, via an examination of the causal mechanisms that are maintaining the national camp policy, the chapter clarifies how complex relationships emerge between the refugee camp and other reception sites in the interior (notably the urban space). Furthermore, the analysis shows how a focus on maintaining stability (or avoiding instability) through controlling and monitoring access to urban spaces (rather than stopping all movement) is driving refugee policy within Zambia, including the maintenance of the overall encampment reception policy. This emphasis on *controlling or managing* movement has unexpected repercussions. Firstly, it helps challenge regional and global trends that frame all refugee movement through a security lens. Secondly, these complex associations between two geographical sites (the refugee camp and the urban space) play a key (if paradoxical) role in the settling of some refugees outside the camp space in Zambia.

The chapter concentrates on the initial arrival of refugees in Zambia. It starts with an examination of the processes and procedures surrounding registration in Zambia. In so doing, it draws out core themes related to conceptualising refugee reception in Southern Africa, such as the conditionality of reception and the position of refugees as long-term guests in the territory. The section also provides context for the second half of the chapter, which analyses the key factors at the different levels of the state (including variations in approaches in border areas) that are ultimately maintaining the encampment approach in Zambia.

The registration of refugees in Zambia

According to national law and policy, the initial welcome and registration of refugees in Zambia involves them being granted a form of legal recognition by the state and then made to reside in a refugee settlement. In many ways, this approach to registration follows the dominant conceptualisation of refugee camps as popularised by academics in the 1990s or 2000s. Indeed, at this initial stage of reception, the emphasis is on the removal of refugees to contained spaces away from citizens and the political life of the state. Yet, in reality the empirical data shows that the maintenance of refugee camps as a national response to new arrivals is far more complex.[1]

Legal framework and registration procedures in Zambia

Zambia has been associated with the global refugee regime for over forty years. In the 1960s, Zambia permitted UNHCR to enter its territory and it acceded to the 1969 OAU Refugee Convention. Zambia is also party to the 1951 Refugee Convention and 1967 Protocol, although it has entered reservations on several key rights and norms contained within the 1951 Refugee Convention, such as freedom of movement and specific employment rights. Moreover, Zambia as a dualist state never incorporated either international treaty into national legislation.[2]

Until 2017, refugee reception and the treatment of refugees in Zambia were governed by the restrictive 1970 Refugee (Control) Act ('the 1970 Refugee Act'). This act required that refugees remain in camps. The purpose of the national legal framework until 2017 was controlling refugee movement via encampment. This means that the procedure adopted to register refugees in Zambia is based entirely on administrative processes designed by governmental departments, with assistance from UNHCR.

This legal-administrative 'gap' is a constant theme in relation to refugee policy in Zambia, which in turn contributes to variations in the treatment and initial welcome received by refugees during registration and beyond. The Refugees Act No.1 of 2017 ('the 2017 Refugee Act') replaced the 1970 Refugee Act. As explained below, it contains several progressive elements, but still grants the state the authority to restrict freedom of movement and demand that refugees remain in refugee settlements.

In terms of registration procedures, refugees are expected to make themselves known to immigration officers and request asylum at official border crossings. In practice there are several different scenarios that can occur. As observed by a UNHCR official, if a refugee has a passport, it is possible for them to travel unimpeded to urban areas such as Lusaka before making themselves known to the authorities.[3] This may also happen if they are not detected at the border (for example when they cross the border informally) and then decide to claim asylum when they reach an urban space. Nevertheless, for the vast majority who enter through a border point:

> they present themselves to immigration or are intercepted by immigration at the entry point and then when they apply for asylum, the application is screened, and they get interviewed.[4]

In all these scenarios, after the request for asylum has been made, applications are screened and refugees are interviewed either by: (1) the National Eligibility Committee (NEC) in Lusaka or (2) the Provincial or District Joint Operations Committees (PJOC and DJOC) in the provinces and by the border.[5] Note that the coming into force of the 2017 Refugee Act changed the semantics of the procedures but not the substance. The provincial system (pre and post 2017) involves the PJOC and DJOC determining refugee claims based on the broader 1969 OAU Refugee Convention definition of a refugee, with recognition being on a *prima facie* basis. In comparison, refugees seeking to make an individualised claim (using the individual limbs in the 1951 Refugee Convention) have their claim ultimately referred to Lusaka and the NEC (both pre- and post-2017).

The NEC in Lusaka encompasses the Commission for Refugees (COR), Department of Immigration, Department of Foreign Affairs, Ministry of Labour and Social Services, Security and Intelligence personnel from the Office of the President and the police and UNHCR.[6] Due to the composition and mandates of the governmental departments involved in the NEC, there is an emphasis on national security within the committee. Decisions are based in part on country-of-origin information and eligibility assessments, with refugees appraised to see if they are combatants and/or a risk to the state.[7] The government ultimately makes the final refugee status determination (RSD) decision. In contrast, officers at the PJOC and DJOC can grant asylum-seekers *prima facie* status based solely on one-to-one interviews. The difference in the attention given to national security concerns between the two decision bodies is therefore salient.

Academics, particularly legal scholars, tend to agree that in principle refugee status granted on a *prima facie* basis is no different from, and carries the same rights as, status based on an individualised claim (Sharpe, 2018). However, in Zambia, refugees' ability to gain access to urban spaces post registration partly depends on the procedure they went through. Refugees in both groups (that is, those granted refugee status from the NEC and those granted status by the PJOC and DJOC) are expected to reside in refugee settlements after their registration has been completed. Yet refugees with individualised status granted by the NEC have an advantage when applying for urban permits post registration. The inference is that refugees granted status by the NEC have already passed rigorous checks as part of this RSD process. Thus, they are not deemed to present the same risk to the urban space as refugees whose status is gained via the provincial procedure.[8]

Initial reception during the registration period

Once refugees have been through either of the registration procedures and the accompanying administrative processes, they are normally moved to one of the two main settlements in Zambia: Mayukwayukwa or Meheba.[9] The Mayukwayukwa Settlement is situated in the Western Province. It was established in 1966, making it one of the oldest refugee settlements in Africa (UNHCR, 2017a). As at 2022 the current population of the settlement stands at over 20,875 refugees, with refugees from Angola, DRC, Rwanda, Burundi and Uganda (UNHCR, 2022). The Meheba settlement was established in 1971 to accommodate refugees fleeing the Angolan War of Independence and the Great Lake War (Stein and Clark, 1990). Located around 75 kilometres from Solwezi, in the North-Western province, it is roughly the size of Singapore, and hosts approximately 34,360 refugees (Thorsen, 2016; UNHCR, 2022). The majority originate from Angola, DRC, Burundi and Rwanda (Thorsen, 2016). Both camps are served by extremely poor infrastructure and, despite their age and large population sizes, have remained underdeveloped remote rural spaces. The state chose to locate the camps far away from urban areas in order to exclude refugees from the political and social aspects of the host state (Bakewell, 2002). Refugees, therefore, need permission to leave the settlements, even for short amounts of time.

Since the 1990s, host states and aid agencies in Africa have traditionally treated and supported refugees as temporary guests for the duration of their stay (Maple, 2016). As Hayden (2006) points out, national legal and policy frameworks are usually based on the premise that refugees want, and will be able, to return to their country of origin as soon as possible. Thus, refugee camps are usually intended as a temporary solution and are designed as such. Their distinct social and geographical set-up is aimed at preventing, rather than creating, opportunities to integrate with the local community (Kibreab, 1989). Yet in reality, despite being treated as temporary guests, refugees often have little choice but to stay in camps long term.

Zambia's approach to encampment differs in certain respects from that used by other countries. For instance, there is an acknowledgement at the national level that refugees are likely to remain in the territory, at least in the short to medium term. This means that there is recognition that the national government must conduct long-term planning to provide for refugees. Indeed, the two main settlements were designed with the intention of becoming self-sustaining, with refugees granted individual plots of land to use for agriculture.[10] Self-reliance, however, has never been fully realised, particularly in the case of Meheba. Instead, as pointed out by an official at the United Nations Children's Fund (UNICEF), most refugees in both settlements remain dependent on assistance from the state and UNHCR.[11]

The initial granting of land attests to the longer-term planning aspects of the Zambian state's approach and indicates its recognition of the likely longevity of the refugee population's stay. It also signifies, at one level of an analysis, a generous form of reception. For example, refugees in Zambia have generally been spared the repeated threats of *refoulement* or forced return as seen across the continent. Nonetheless, forms of reception offered by states to refugees are rarely unqualified. State sovereignty, democratic pressures and key material, ideational and institutional concerns that come with these concepts mean that any form of reception will usually trigger conditional rights and obligations on the visitor.

At the initial registration stage in Zambia, this conditional and often precarious welcome manifests itself in two ways: firstly, through the distinct geographical restrictions inherent to confinement inside the settlements and secondly, through the fact that refugees remain *guests*, even if their stay is likely to be long term. With little chance of gaining a form of citizenship, refugees in the settlements continue to be treated as visitors or outsiders in the territory. Indeed, political rights such as the ability to vote remain inaccessible, meaning that refugees' access to the political space of the state is limited.

It is important to note that not all refugees experience this kind of initial reception stage in Zambia. Instead, many refugees bypass this reception policy altogether and stay with local communities or go into hiding after a negative RSD decision. They may settle informally (in border or urban areas) finding forms of *de facto* acceptance and hospitality within the local communities and/or local government structures.[12] Large numbers of others chose to settle in border areas, often entirely outside the reach of the national government and official reception policies.[13]

The encampment approach in Zambia

Based on previously examined literature, the question of why a state like Zambia maintains an encampment reception approach to refugees, may appear to have a straightforward answer. Indeed, in many respects, Zambia fits within traditional understandings of why refugee camps have remained popular amongst host states on the continent. These include material and ideational factors such as capacity and state security and with them a perceived need to separate refugees from the political life of the state. Yet it is evident that the on-the-ground reality is far more nuanced.

Ideational factor: the historical legacy of the national legal framework

Both the 1970 Refugee Act and the replacement 2017 Refugee Act allow for the creation of refugee camps. For this reason, and from a purely legal perspective, the persistence of refugee settlements in Zambia today can be explained by legal obligations based on compliance and implementation. Nevertheless, the state's motivation for adopting and maintaining this restrictive reception policy is more complex than simply wanting to fulfil its legal commitments. Indeed, the empirical evidence highlights how conflicting ideational and institutional factors (present in different key national institutions) play a prominent role in how the old and the new legal frameworks influence the national-level reception approach in contrasting ways.

In terms of national bodies that respond to refugee arrivals, the COR is primarily responsible for implementing refugee policy for the government of Zambia.[14] COR is situated within the Department of Home Affairs. Other subdivisions of Home Affairs with differing mandates, such as the Department of Immigration, also interact with refugees daily. Numerous other governmental departments and agencies have regular, but varying contact with refugees. For example, the Office of the Vice President supports the settlement of former refugees from Rwanda and Angola and the Ministry of Community Development and Social Services (MCDSS) provides assistance in the two main settlements.[15]

COR, with its specific refugee mandate, faces distinct institutional and ideational pressures and responsibilities that can conflict sharply with those of other government departments. For example, COR retains less of a security focus than the Department of Immigration or the police, who are more concerned with matters of national security surrounding refugee and migrant affairs.[16] For these reasons interpretation and implementation of national refugee policy can vary enormously between different state actors.

Forms of conceptual and ideational contestation between key national entities that engage with refugee issues in Zambia largely stem from the 1970 Refugee Act. The old Act is principally interested in one aspect of refugee reception: refugee movement.[17] The emphasis is on the stopping of movement and hosting refugees in camps (UNHCR, 2017a). In essence, as observed by a refugee leader in Lusaka, the Act conceptualises refugees as guests who should reside in camps where they can be cared for by the international community.[18] This is also the view taken by UNHCR officials, with one noting:

> There is a belief that humanitarian needs [are] to be covered by the international community – it's not something that Zambia has to cover – that is very clear.[19]

The old legal framework therefore set out an understanding of refugee encampment reminiscent of the work that has adopted Agamben's (2005) concept of 'states of exception'. The goal of the legal framework was principally to isolate refugees and keep them away from key political and social space(s). In doing so, the intention was in effect to create distinct reception sites *on* the territory but not *of* the territory.

The old legal framework continues to shape many Zambian national officials' understanding of *who* refugees are and *where* they should be hosted. Indeed, as confirmed by a former senior COR officer, understanding and knowledge of refugees in many departments within Home Affairs comes *entirely* from a strict reading of the 1970 Refugee Act:

> For [the Department of] Immigration and Home Affairs – remember, the knowledge they get about refugees is from the [old] refugee Act.[20]

As a result, many in the national government understand refugees solely within the geographical context of settlements. By extension, this framing means that any movement outside of a settlement is immediately constructed as illicit. This 'illicit' movement has a two-fold effect. Firstly (as examined in the next chapter), it effectively reframes refugees residing outside the settlements in Zambia as illegal migrants. Secondly, it creates a feedback-loop within these government departments whereby the 'illicit' nature of the movement reinforces the perceived need for control and encampment reception policies. For these reasons, compliance with the restrictive reception policy within the national government has now taken on a robust ideational power beyond the simple need to implement 'the law'.

This construction of refugees in Zambia sits in stark contrast to COR's approach to the previous legal framework. COR, in part due to its close partnership with UNHCR, has historically interpreted national refugee law more broadly and progressively than other government departments. Its characteristic approach can be seen in the way UN agency officials discuss their day-to-day interactions with COR. For example, a UNHCR official noted:

> we have a good working relationship with them – whenever they make a decision, they do it . . . in consultation with us. You see in other countries the government just makes a decision without consulting the UN agency but here it is different – they have [been] very collaborative.[21]

The progressive approach of COR can be appreciated in practical terms through the way it focuses on regulating and managing movement into urban areas, rather than attempting to stop all movement or ensuring every refugee resides in a refugee camp. For example, COR has allowed groups of refugees to remain in cities and permitted them to leave the camps for differing periods of time. It has done this either officially or by employing 'a blind eye approach'.[22] Another refugee leader confirmed that this approach was particularly evident during the 1980s and early 1990s, before renewed pressure emanating from other sections of the national government saw refugees returned to the settlements in the late 1990s.[23]

By interpreting the old Act broadly (namely by seeing it as regulating movement via the encampment policy rather than stopping all movement per se), COR stretched its mandate beyond the confines of the old Act. For example, COR has created numerous ad hoc administrative procedures to allow greater movement and access to urban spaces. This includes the granting of gate passes and urban residency permits (URPs).[24] As observed by an ex-manager at COR, these practices were often not even recorded officially:

> even the criteria for deciding whether someone should be inside the camp or outside was not written down or contained in any policy. It was just an agreement agreed by appointment.[25]

In 2017, after years of negotiations with UNHCR and numerous draft bills, the government passed the 2017 Refugee Act. The new Act formalises COR's mandate to deal with refugee matters in Zambia. It also incorporates both the 1951 Refugee Convention refugee definition and the wider 1969 OAU Refugee Convention definition. Importantly, it also explicitly includes, for the first time, several of the fundamental rights contained within these international refugee treaties.[26] The new Act nevertheless falls some way short of incorporating all core global refugee norms into Zambian national legislation. Key to this was the state's refusal to remove the historical restrictions on freedom of movement. Consequently, the responsible minister retains the ability to designate spaces in Zambia for refugee settlements.[27] Thus, COR is still responsible for implementing and enforcing the overall encampment policy.

A manager at an INGO noted that the continued restrictions on freedom of movement and the ability to create specific sites of reception was a disappointment for non-state actors working on refugee protection, noting 'especially I remember for UNHCR'.[28] Indeed, it was particularly frustrating for the UN agency following their years of negotiating for the removal of the restriction. As examined further below, opening up new reception sites for refugees has been the key point on which UNHCR and the state have disagreed, behind the scenes. One official noted, 'the only thing that we are battling with the government of Zambia is freedom of movement'.[29]

Nevertheless, when speaking to UNHCR officials and civil society representatives, it is evident that they ultimately saw the new Act as a progressive step, if not necessarily the ideal outcome. In addition, similarly to previous approaches (set out above), COR is interpreting and implementing the new Act in ways that allow refugees some access to urban spaces. For instance, COR has begun interpreting specific articles relating to self-employment in such a manner that there is the potential for far greater access to urban spaces in the future than has previously been observed.

This more progressive Act has not altered other government departments' approaches, however. UNHCR officials contend that many government officials still take their conceptions of refugees and the spatial dimensions of refugee reception from the old Act. One official noted, 'they are still using the old legal framework of encampment where refugees are put in a certain perimeter of area and they cannot go out, without permission'.[30] By extension, immigration and police officers continue to regularly view all refugees outside of the camp space as illegal immigrants/foreigners.

These opposing constructions of refugees and acceptable reception spaces, through the differing interpretations of the legal framework, produce and sustain institutional confusion and contestation. Consequently, wide variation in the treatment of refugees outside of the settlements was reported. Indeed, refugees in urban spaces still harbour serious concerns about being detained or having bribes extorted from them by law enforcement officers, regardless of reassurances by COR that their stay in these spaces is permitted.

The recent positive developments (in terms of implementation of regime norms) have not helped resolve the ongoing contestation between government departments. This is partly because the new Act only goes so far in relation to the inclusion of global refugee regime norms. Freedom of movement continues to be restricted, and spatial limitations to refugee reception are maintained. This means that convincing other government departments to re-imagine refugees and their movement outside camp spaces is likely to continue to be a difficult endeavour for UNHCR and COR. The old Act has held sway over state bodies' understanding and approach to refugees since the 1970s and remains deeply entrenched within bureaucratic structures and mind-sets. Moreover, recent attempts by COR and UNHCR to facilitate further access to the urban space is based on a liberal interpretation of *one* clause in the new Act. This means that the more open approach to refugee movement outside the dominant reception space is not established in any official government-wide refugee policy document.

Thus, these recent developments related to the new legislation can be viewed as a positive step in improving Zambia's implementation of the global refugee regime. Yet, unless the historical ideational power of the former Act within all relevant branches of the national government is properly addressed, the treatment offered to refugees outside the settlements is likely to remain inconsistent. Indeed, there is a risk that without training to promote the new official guidelines and policy, any additional numbers of refugees in urban spaces may trigger the opposite reaction to that intended by COR and UNHCR. For instance, increased movement into spaces such as Lusaka may create a feedback-loop within government departments, whereby the movement reinforces the perceived need for the overall encampment approach.

Material factor: the capacity to receive and host refugees

The chapter now moves to analysing a key material factor that is influencing the maintenance of Zambia's encampment policy, namely capacity concerns. In the existing literature on refugee camps, material concerns regarding capacity are discussed in the context of two interlinked issues: (1) keeping refugees away from local populations to avoid strain on local infrastructures; and (2) creating sufficient visibility for continued international support. These two issues are studied in the context of Zambia using a multi-scalar lens and illustrate how capacity concerns around the movement of refugees on the territory are highly localised.

The separation of refugees from local populations: capacity concerns in urban spaces

Zambia is a middle-income country, which struggles with high levels of poverty amongst its own nationals. Thus, its ability to absorb and respond to forced migrants, particularly in major urban areas, is a factor that requires consideration. Interestingly, the movement of refugees in small numbers outside of the camp space has always been permitted in Zambia. Many refugees and other migrants stay in border areas before returning to their home countries once the prevailing situation improves. Also, government officials frequently permit (or turn a blind eye to) small refugee communities in urban and peri-urban areas. Yet, the size of the refugee population in urban areas has always been more closely monitored compared to self-settlements in border areas (which will be discussed further below). Indeed, the government's reservations about its capacity to manage large numbers of refugees in urban areas have been a key reason why Zambia has maintained a camp-based reception policy for the last sixty years.

The distinction in terms of capacity concerns in these two different reception sites (urban centres and border areas) is evidenced by the varying degree to which the encampment policy has been implemented over time. Refugee leaders in Lusaka noted that in the 1970s and 1980s, during which time Zambia experienced large economic growth, COR adopted a relaxed approach to the encampment policy.[31] As a result, even though most refugees remained in settlements, many found their way to urban areas, where COR and other government departments would turn a blind eye to their presence.

By the early 1990s, due to increases in refugees *and* internal migrants in urban areas combined with a downturn in economic growth (which started during the 1980s and continued into the 1990s), the national government started to become concerned about instability in the cities. This unease was based on the strain that increased numbers were putting on urban social services and the tension this was creating between host communities and refugees (UNHCR, 1994). These kinds of concerns created negative democratic feedback loops, through which government departments became worried about the number of refugees in large cities and the destabilising effect this might have on the space (due to extra demands on urban services and infrastructure) and on the voting public (due to tensions over scarce resources).

According to a refugee leader in Lusaka, it was these concerns that led the state to attempt to reassert a stricter interpretation of the national legal framework by the end of the 1990s. It did this by removing urban refugees to the refugee settlements and effectively ending urban livelihood programmes.[32] As confirmed by another refugee leader:

> all refugees – [were] told to leave on 21st January [2000] . . . [if] trading in the city markets . . . told to leave the market. I had to sell my shop.[33]

This was also the view of a senior legal officer at COR, who noted that, 'once the social and economic impact was felt, the government had the will to implement the law and enforce its measures'.[34]

Ultimately, this shift in policy led to the creation of the Sub-Committee on Urban Residency in 2000, which began deciding all requests from refugees in camps for urban residency. The new sub-committee made the process of leaving the settlements extremely difficult. Indeed, the refugee leader cited above suggested that by the early 2000s:

> to be in town, refugee must be employed by Zambian employer. And they have to pay [for] a work permit . . . Imagine this in a country like Zambia?[35]

The inference in this quote being that for a country like Zambia, with its reliance on the informal economy, this shift in approach by the state was essentially 'a way of blocking us from being in town'.[36]

Since the early 1990s, the Zambian economy has marginally recovered, yet the broad historical pattern of a renewed relaxation in camp policy in times of increased prosperity has not been entirely replicated. Similar to the dual economy and wealth disparity seen in countries such as Nigeria and South Africa, the market recovery in Zambia is not being translated into socio-economic improvements for residents in urban spaces (UNHCR, 2017a:1). As a result, the informal economy accounted for around 84 per cent of the labour force in 2014, with most refugees in urban areas working in this sector (UNHCR, 2017a). This remains broadly the case today, with a UNHCR official suggesting, 'it's a known fact . . . the vast majority of refugees are engaged in self-employment in the informal sector'.[37] This issue is regularly raised as a major concern by the national government in discussions with UNHCR regarding the removal of freedom of movement restrictions.

Taxation and host capacity are often overlooked by academics when research has promoted the benefits refugees can bring to local economies in Africa (Betts et al., 2017). Yet, the ability to increase revenue for public services via taxation emerges as an important issue when advocates of refugee rights canvass for greater freedom of movement for refugees (IFC, 2018). As observed by refugee networks in Lusaka, with most urban refugees working in the informal sector the number of refugees paying tax is consequently very low. Another refugee leader went further:

> To me it's an issue we are not paying tax . . . I can't at the moment, as I will get taken back to camp. We discussed this with Home Affairs . . . [we could be] an asset.[38]

Regardless of this inability to contribute via taxes, all refugees in urban areas, irrespective of their exact status, in theory at least, have access to free health services and primary and secondary education.[39] Any government struggles to maintain social protection systems if portions of the population are unable to pay into them. The current state of the taxation system in Zambia also faces challenges due to issues such as corruption and social and political barriers impeding nationals from contributing tax (Martini, 2014). This means that the additional strain on social services resulting from increased numbers of refugees in urban areas could have serious ramifications for the local population and ruling political settlement.

The separation of refugees from local populations: *capacity concerns* in border areas

Zambia's borders are notoriously porous, with many refugees and other migrants regularly disregarding the designated entry points. Yet, in contrast to the capacity concerns seen in large urban areas, refugee movement within border areas (including subsequent self-settlement among the local population) is not seen as a pressing issue at the national level. Indeed, most refugees in these areas are simply ignored by national and local government bodies. As a result, transnational historical patterns and customs endure in many border areas, and refugees find alternative forms of reception within communities at the sub-local level, along ethnic and cultural lines. Technically, the national government still considers these self-settled refugees to be breaching reception policy. However, it lacks the capacity or the political inclination to try and uphold the reception policy in these remote areas far from urban centres. Consequently, to many refugees, this behaviour is read as a form of tacit acceptance of their presence in border areas.[40] In reality, as observed by a UNHCR official, there is 'minimal state presence in these areas'.[41] Thus, this lack of 'state' presence is as relevant to the citizens in these spaces as it is to the refugees.

Some capacity concerns were raised by the state in response to the influx of refugees from the DRC into these geographical areas between 2017 and 2019, with aid agencies unsure of the true number of 'new' arrivals.[42] As discussed below, these concerns were connected to security issues brought on by a specific moment of mass influx due to civil unrest. Yet even during these heightened times, many fleeing the violence simply crossed the border and stayed with family or members of their extended social networks and tribes, with whom they already shared similar languages and customs. Indeed, as noted by a UNHCR official, for many refugees, these can be circular movements they have performed many times before, 'particularly [for] the Congolese – they just go to Zambia to wait for the wave to pass'.[43]

With the state absent, local and sub-local actors regulate the reception of refugees and decide on whether refugees have permission to remain. As observed by an INGO officer, the local community or tribal chiefs often give this 'permission':

> Most of the refugees who are here are from DRC or from countries that are culturally similar to Zambians and are connected to them – tribal, cousins or related or you know . . . the way that the borders are drawn . . . they are welcomed. It's not a big deal.[44]

These alternative forms of reception, coupled with the lack of a state presence in border areas, emphasises how capacity concerns connected to refugee movement varies within Zambia depending on the geographical space. In addition, the reality in border areas raises questions about the relevance of the host state and the global refugee regime to the many refugees in these areas. Certainly, these entities can appear like abstract concepts to refugees attempting to locate a welcome and find economic opportunities in border areas.

The separation of refugees from local populations: creating visibility for continued international support

The involvement of international organisations and donors and their willingness to fund the reception of refugees affects states' behaviour towards refugees. Scholars generally argue that international donors have traditionally preferred to support refugee camps over facilitating urban settlement because camps remain visible, with a spatially confined population that is easy to register, monitor and control (Jamal, 2003; Crisp, 2003; FitzGerald, 2019). As a result, host states view refugee camps as a gateway to continued international attention and funding (Stevens, 2006). Zambia appears to contradict these assumptions. It has a reception policy that stipulates that all refugees should be hosted in settlements, yet it receives very little international funding. Indeed, the Zambian case study challenges this 'funding-visibility-sedentariness' nexus as a way of understanding camp-based reception.

Firstly, refugee camps are never completely visible. Indeed, they are normally located in 'out-the-way locations' and permission is needed to access them (Kaiser, 2008; Agier, 2011). Zambia is no exception, with the state establishing the refugee settlements in very remote, underdeveloped areas of the country. In turn, the intention was originally for these sites to become self-sustaining and, thus, not dependent on state or international funding.[45] From their inception, refugees in these settlements were expected to use plots of land for subsistence farming and trade. In reality, subsistence farming has never been fully achieved in the Mayukwayukwa and Meheba settlements. Growing enough food to be self-sufficient has become increasingly difficult over time. As one refugee leader commented, with extreme over-use of the land and a lack of proper fertiliser for the last fifty years, 'what hope have you got now of growing crops?'[46] Due to this inability to become self-sufficient, both settlements require national and international funds to support and sustain their populations. Despite this, Mayukwayukwa and Meheba remain heavily underfunded.

Secondly, a lack of visibility in terms of Zambia as an international actor plays a key role in this dearth of funding. A UNHCR official observed that Zambia is regularly ignored on the international humanitarian and political stage because of being perceived as a peaceful, stable and relatively democratic state. In essence, it is just not very 'interesting' to the international community or donors:

> People have no idea where it is or how to get there . . . very often there's this assumption that it's not a place that people talk about.[47]

As Cheeseman (2017) notes, it is neither the 'clear democratic success story like Ghana or South Africa, nor a case of extreme authoritarian abuse, as in Cote d'Ivoire and Zimbabwe'. Consequently, international priorities lie elsewhere.

The refugee settlements – and the refugee populations within them – are examples of this near invisibility. As explained by an in-country UN official working on refugee issues, 'Zambia is not a priority country for international donors'.[48] Seen as a landlocked and transit country for migrants by regional bodies like the EU, it does not receive the same attention as states such as South Africa, which is viewed as a departure point for migrants travelling to the minority world. In addition, because Zambia has lower numbers of refugees and persons of concern than neighbouring states in East Africa, development and humanitarian actors tend to focus their attention further north.[49] As a result, obtaining international support and funding for the permanent settlements has proven immensely challenging.

To conclude, capacity concerns continue to emerge when UNHCR broaches the topic of improving refugees' access to the interior with the government. These issues have geographical dimensions, with the national government acutely focused on regulating the movement of refugees (and other cross-border migrants) into urban spaces, but less concerned with the movement of refugees in border areas. In essence, managing the number of refugees in urban spaces counter-balances capacity concerns and any resulting political ramifications arising from instability.

Material and ideational factors: security

This section investigates the role of security in the maintenance of the encampment reception policy in Zambia. The discussion is structured using Milner's (2009) distinction between: (1) direct security concerns; (2) indirect security concerns; and (3) securitisation. As highlighted above, during registration security concerns emerge as a factor in how the state receives refugees and the form of immediate welcome offered to them. Yet as examined below, by unpacking security into these three components, a more intricate and context-specific understanding of the relationship between security and the reception of refugees materialises – one that has historical roots and frequently involves concerns around instability.

Direct security concerns

The colonial and post-colonial history of Africa demonstrates that there are genuine direct security concerns in relation to the arrival of refugees. This is particularly pertinent during periods of mass influx, the nature of which can legitimise a state such as Zambia taking security precautions, for instance, by keeping refugees separate from the local population until security checks and registration processes have identified and removed any harmful individuals. At the time the 1970 Refugee Act was enacted, several of Zambia's neighbours were still fighting for their own liberation. As pointed out by a former officer at COR:

> Thirty-four years after we had obtained independence, most of our neighbouring countries were still fighting for their own liberation. So, some at that time were freedom fighters – guerrilla warfare etc. – so there was that security concern. The primary objective of the

Control Act was to control refugee movements in order to monitor the refugees.[50]

In the 1970s and 1980s, large numbers of freedom fighters and refugee warriors from countries such as South Africa, Zimbabwe and Mozambique sought refuge in Zambia (Veroff, 2010a).[51] Consequently, there was a need for the Zambian government to monitor and control who was entering the territory and specifically, who was gaining access to the interior and urban spaces. The same former COR officer noted that the 1970 Refugee Act was the mechanism used to achieve this, namely, to contain refugees and keep them away from densely populated areas in order to keep the local population safe.

Over the last sixty years, Zambia's geographical position in the middle of Southern Africa has also placed the country close to some of the world's largest and longest ongoing refugee situations (Brosché and Nilsson, 2005). The memory of horrific events, such as the civil war in Rwanda in 1990s, remains ever present among many Zambians. In fact, the freedom granted to armed militants from Rwanda in neighbouring countries during the 1980s is regularly seen by civil society and refugee leaders as a key reason Zambia maintains a commitment to camp-based reception policy.

Although the make-up and pattern of refugee movements into Zambia has altered radically over the last sixty years, the overriding reception policy has remained the same. In general, the state no longer receives large movements of refugees fleeing civil war nor faces the risk of armed combatants infiltrating those movements that often accompany them. As a result, some members of civil society (and even some officials in the Department of Home Affairs) consider the nationally run encampment policy to be an historical relic based on past security concerns. A former COR officer illustrated this when they observed that, with the passage of time, the policy and the supporting archaic legal framework 'became the yoke that bound the government'.[52] Legal frameworks and policies were set in place to deal with a specific and genuine security concern and over time there has been little motivation for the state to radically move away from this policy. Levi (1997:252) describes this as path dependency: the 'entrenchment of certain institutional arrangements obstructs an easy reversal of the initial choice'. Indeed, as observed previously, eventually the legal framework has acquired its own ideational authority within core sections of the national government.

Interviews with officials at UNHCR and INGOs at the sub-regional and regional level suggest that in stable times, direct security concerns remain less of a priority to the Zambian government than in neighbouring states in SADC.[53] When state officials and UN agencies brought up security, it tended to be in reference to the movement of refugees within urban areas or to gaining access to urban areas. Yet direct security concerns frequently merged with other indirect security concerns and broader fears over instability in the urban space.

Similar to its limited capacity to regulate the settlement of refugees in border communities, the Zambian government is also less able to respond to any perceived security concerns linked to the regular movement of refugees and migrants within those same areas. As noted above, large numbers of refugees and migrants gain permission at the sub-local level to freely move within border areas without raising security concerns. Yet, it would be disingenuous to suggest that security concerns do not exist at all at the border. The identity of those crossing the border (either via formal checkpoints or through more illicit means) remains a concern for the government. This presents the almost paradoxical situation whereby border areas can be the space where the state is *most* present and *least* present (Hovil, 2016).

As with all nation states, direct security concerns exist in relation to cross-border refugee movement in Zambia. However, these direct concerns remain less of a priority in Zambia than is witnessed in neighbouring states and more broadly on the continent. These findings also go some way to explain how refugee movement in Zambia is not subject to the same intense securitisation seen elsewhere in the region and globally. This observation will be developed further next.

Indirect security concerns

The second material factor influencing states such as Zambia towards maintaining camp-based reception, relates to indirect security concerns. These concerns focus on the potential increases in levels of insecurity and instability within the areas in which refugees settle. These may often manifest as locals' grievances against the refugee population due to a perceived deterioration in local structures (such as social services, crime levels, healthcare and education) seen as a result of the refugee presence (Milner, 2009). In turn, this can inflame tensions within communities, giving rise to increases in xenophobia and ultimately negative repercussions for the ruling political settlement. For these reasons, the settling of refugees and other forced migrants in urban spaces is habitually understood by host states in terms of risk (Loescher, 2003). To alleviate these concerns, refugees are confined to camps, thereby nullifying the threat that this form of 'non-rooted' movement creates for national security and the overall stability of the nation.

These kinds of national-level concerns surrounding capacity, insecurity and stability in urban areas regularly emerge in Zambia. Indeed, they are given as an overriding reason for the continual push back by the state when UNHCR requests Zambia to lift the restrictions on freedom of movement. As stated previously, during the 1990s, when the state became uneasy about the number of refugees in urban areas, it started insisting that refugees move back to the settlements. It cited the limitations of urban social services and the tensions that an increased refugee population might create between local communities and the refugees. State officials viewed these concerns as vindicated by the small pockets of friction that surfaced between local communities and refugees after large numbers of Rwandan and Burundian refugees arrived in the 1990s (UNHCR, 1994).

Little empirical work has been carried out to examine the validity of the claimed causal link between refugee and other migrant movement in and around urban spaces and the increased insecurity and instability of a nation. Research does point to several major risk factors confronting Africa, such as the sheer speed of urbanisation on the continent (including internal and cross-border migration into cities) and the increasingly high proportion of young people with relatively low job prospects (Muggah and Kilcullen, 2016). Yet, with weak data in this area, it is difficult to know exactly whether and how African cities are destabilised by refugee and other forms of migrant mobility. For example, only a few cities report homicide rates (most are in Nigeria, Kenya and South Africa) (Muggah and Kilcullen, 2016). Nevertheless, what is evident from the empirical data highlighted in this section is that concern around the tension caused by competition for scarce resources and jobs, colours the official mind-set in Zambia and the view of refugees in urban spaces.

The construction of refugees as security risks

Security is a factor that interacts with refugee reception on an ideational level, as well as on a material level. While states express legitimate concerns when refugees cross borders, they also regularly label refugees as security concerns to further political agendas. Instead of being discussed in terms of repairing a rupture between an individual and their political, social or economic rights, the movement of refugees is instead 'framed in the language of existential and urgent threat' (Hammerstad, 2012:5).

The construction of the refugee as a security risk helps to explain the continued popularity of refugee camps as a reception policy in Africa. Remote camps provide a way of removing, or containing, the perceived threat. However, the trade-off for protecting the local host population in this way is that key global refugee regime norms (such as freedom of movement and the right to employment) are curtailed for the refugee. This sets up a separation between the movement of 'rooted' people or citizens (seen as a fundamental freedom and entitlement) and the movement of 'non-rooted' guests (seen in terms of risk or instability).

Remarkably, Zambia appears to be bucking regional and global trends by not securitising the cross-border movement of refugees and other African migrants into its territory. It is not engaging in the kinds of securitisation activities commonly seen elsewhere, such as erecting border fences, manning expensive border checkpoints, externalising (outsourcing) and internalising (insourcing) its border controls. It is also not using the language of security when refugees are discussed by state officials. Equally, xenophobic or anti-refugee sentiments were not used by political parties in their 2021 election campaigns (UNHCR, 2021a). The empirical evidence identifies two key explanations for this pattern: the maintenance of a broad, if not strict, encampment policy (particularly at this initial stage of reception), and the size of the refugee population in Zambia.

Regarding the first point, in neighbouring states in Southern and East Africa, the securitisation of outsiders is observed specifically in large urban spaces, with vast differences seen at other scales of the state (Wanjiku Kihato and Landau, 2019; van Noorloos and Kloosterboer, 2018). In contrast, in Zambia security concerns surrounding migration and refugees have not filtered down below the top levels of the line ministries. When discussing the global trend of securitising refugees, a UNHCR official observed, 'if you see an immigration officer [you] won't hear the issue of security as we see in the West'.[54]

The lack of visibility of refugees in urban centres plays an important role in this observed behaviour at all levels of the state. Most refugees remain in the settlements, away from local populations and cities. As such, they are generally not perceived as a threat to local communities, the state or the current government's political power. As a result, beyond the direct and indirect security concerns discussed above, refugee stakeholders (such as UNHCR, implementing partners and refugee community groups) are not witnessing security-framed arguments from state officials, local government departments or bureaucrats. Some refugees are allowed a degree of movement (see Chapter 5), but spaces such as Lusaka have not witnessed the influx of African cross-border migration at the level seen in other cities, such as Johannesburg. The contention is that as the number of refugees and other forced migrants coming into urban spaces is regulated and managed (although not stopped) via the overarching encampment reception policy, there has been little need or desire by the national government to securitise refugee movement.

Regarding the second point, the size of the refugee population plays a role in the lack of securitisation of refugees and refugee movement. The refugee population in Zambia is significantly smaller than in other neighbouring states, such as South Africa.⁵⁵ In addition, Zambia has a comparatively low population density when compared both regionally and globally. Its sizeable land mass and relatively small overall population means that Zambia has large areas of sparsely populated and unpopulated land.⁵⁶ Due to the remote location of most refugees (in the settlements) and the relatively small size of the population, the 'refugee issue' is not seen as a pressing one in urban areas, even in the capital. Indeed, interviewees noted that the influx of refugees in 2017 (as a consequence of the civil unrest in neighbouring DRC) caused little concern within government departments nor local communities, beyond the line ministries affected. This was corroborated anecdotally by the field notes taken from informal interviews with certain academics, policymakers and civil society members in Lusaka who knew very little about the contemporary and large-scale movement of refugees in the border areas between Zambia and the DRC.

For these reasons, the continued monitoring and management of refugee movement into urban spaces has meant that the state and local communities have not felt sufficiently threatened by refugees (or the idea of refugees) to seek greater securitisation measures.⁵⁷ In turn, the presence of *some* refugees and forced migrants in urban spaces (either via official pathways or via more illicit movement that places them outside conventional state reception policies) is not currently perceived as large enough to be a cause for concern for the local communities or the state. In this regard, Zambia starkly deviates from its neighbours in the region, where it is increasingly popular for ruling political and local officials to scapegoat forced migrants (Van Hear, 1998; Bakewell and Jónsson, 2011). In this way, the current relationship between refugee camp and urban spaces is, almost counter-intuitively, allowing geographical and political space for some movement and by extension, for some forms of reception in the urban space.

Securitisation of the 'opposition' in Zambia

The historical variability in national refugee policy in Zambia is an important factor to consider when examining the securitisation of refugees. Policy and practice relevant to hosting refugees have been prone to sudden changes over the past few decades, at all levels of the government system. For example, this was seen in the 1990s with the pushback of many urban refugees to the settlements. This volatile characteristic is relevant to these discussions because of recent shifts seen in the approach of the governing political settlement in Zambia to numerous forms of 'political opposition'. With refugee policy outside of the settlements entirely based on administrative practices and policy, the national government's attitude to refugees and their movement has the potential to be able to shift quickly. This in turn means that the current dynamics and relationship between the two reception spaces remain precarious.

During Zambia's well-documented slide towards a more autocratic rule between 2016 and 2021, securitisation was employed as a tactic against perceived threats to the government. It was deployed against civil society, the national press and opposition political parties (Frontline Defenders, 2018; Siachiwena, 2021a). For example, the former president, Edgar Lungu, pronounced that fires in the Lusaka City market in 2017 were 'acts of sabotage' by opposition leaders, even though no official investigation was conducted. He used this to justify him invoking 'State of Public Threatened Emergency' procedures for three months (Civicus, 2017).[58]

The securitisation of civil society by the Patriotic Front was another attempt by the then ruling party, since the late 1990s, to severely restrict the space available for NGOs. The head of an international aid agency set out the landscape for NGOs in Zambia:

> It's been ongoing, this shrinking space for a decade or so but it has picked up speed . . . it has picked up since elections. So what might happen is if, if they speak up they get arrested.[59]

According to a leader of a refugee women's organisation, the result of the shrinking space has been that assistance provided by NGOs to vulnerable and marginalised groups (in the form of aid or advocacy) is now minimal.[60] With a new government coming into power in 2021, there has been some optimism from civil society and the media that these tactics will be reversed (Siachiwena, 2021b). Yet, at least in the short term, it appears as if the new regime is following similar strategies, with reports of the government increasing censorship on civil society watchdogs and other publications (USDS, 2023).

Given that most refugees stay separated from large urban spaces, it remains unlikely that the state will securitise refugees in the near future. However, these broader political patterns highlight the dangers inherent in relying on the goodwill of ruling parties who continue to suppress democratic ideals. Indeed, time will tell if the election of the UPND will see a realigning of the political settlement in Zambia towards a more democratic one.[61]

Both UNHCR and COR continue to use recent national and global developments in their attempts to improve reception policies for refugees. By deploying a broad interpretation of the new 2017 Refugee Act and building on the international commitments made by the former and current president, these entities are actively pushing for increased access to urban spaces for more refugees. These actions are commendable from the standpoint of a normative and global refugee regime. Nevertheless, with limited political space available for civil society on the ground, the UN and other relevant parties within the international community need to monitor the situation closely. This is especially pertinent if the numbers of refugees in urban areas rise to levels that become perceived as a threat to the security and stability of the state, or if they become such a real concern to the voting public. In these scenarios, the state and Zambians might start viewing refugees in urban and other areas as part of the 'problem'.

The initial stage of reception in Zambia: a case of ongoing negotiations between encampment and urban spaces

Zambia has adopted and maintained an encampment policy to receive refugees for the last sixty years. This chapter has drawn out and appraised the key material, institutional and ideational factors, at the international, national and local levels that continue to influence, contest but ultimately reinforce this policy. In doing so, the analysis offers key observations in relation to the initial stage of reception in Zambia and the two reception sites examined in this book.

Firstly, the national legal framework holds a prominent position in relation to reception policies in Zambia. On one level of analysis, this is a straightforward conclusion, with both the 1970 Refugee Act and the new 2017 Refugee Act permitting the creation of refugee settlements and allowing the state to house refugees in these spaces. Nevertheless, the chapter demonstrates how the influence of the national framework goes far beyond a simple obligation of the state to implement the law. Importantly, this legal framework also shapes the way in which government officials understand refugees and the appropriate policies for managing refugee populations. The old 1970 Refugee Act still retains a great deal of ideational power within key departments of the national government. Even after the new 2017 Refugee Act came into effect and finally incorporated some core global refugee regime norms, government departments (including the Department of Immigration) continue to derive their understanding of refugees and their reception from the old 1970 Refugee Act. As commented on by a former officer in COR, in several ways the archaic legal framework still provides the glue that binds the government's approach. Thus, for many at the national level, refugees are solely understood within the confines of the settlements. This inevitably creates institutional contestation as COR continues to permit refugees to travel between the settlements and urban spaces, and even to settle in cities such as Lusaka. In addition, this has ramifications for urban refugees who see their status continually confused with economic or illegal migrants by state officials.

In contrast, the influence of the global refugee regime (that is, international conventions and UNHCR) on reception in Zambia at the point of registration is less evident. This is not to say that UNHCR is not working behind the scenes. The agency has had some success in adopting a support role to COR over the last few decades; for instance, it was involved in discussions and lobbying around the introduction of the new 2017 Refugee Act. As will be examined in the next chapter, UNHCR has a more prominent role in the settlements, post registration. Yet, with Zambia generally being ignored by international donors, combined with key departments adhering to national law that overlooks regime norms, the influence of the 'global' (at least at this initial stage of reception) appears relatively minor.

The underlying tension between the ideational power of the former Act within key state departments versus the institutional approach of COR (and UNHCR) demonstrates how contestation between different causal mechanisms embedded within state (and international actors') behaviour causes ongoing negotiations (and renegotiations) between key actors and, ultimately, unique outcomes in terms of reception policy. At the initial stage of reception, this results in a precarious situation, whereby while the overall camp-based reception approach is upheld, COR frequently permits some movement and access to urban spaces. This approach, and the additional movement that comes with it, inevitably clashes with broader institutional understandings of what a 'refugee' is and where they should be housed. Eventually this results in the opposite intended effect: namely, confirmation within other government departments of a need for the encampment policy.

Secondly, the chapter proposes that the use of the refugee camp as a reception modality is, remarkably, helping to prevent the emergence of top-down and bottom-up securitisation of refugees in Zambia. This is not to say that the government dismisses security issues arising from the arrival of refugees. Indeed, legitimate security concerns do play a role at this initial stage of reception. Nonetheless, it is apparent that there is not the overriding preoccupation with security that is prevalent in other states in Africa (and more globally). By managing the movement of 'non-rooted' persons into urban spaces, the settlements can be understood as a key reason why refugees and their movement are not currently securitised by either state bodies or local populations.

This finding leads to the contention that a complex association between the camp and urban reception spaces transpires during the initial reception of refugees in Zambia. These spaces are intrinsically linked due to the state's approach to receiving refugees and their initial movement. Indeed, a theme that emerges is the focus on the management of movement into urban space, with movement in the interior being regulated and controlled via the camp policy. The aim of the refugee camp in Zambia appears not to be about stopping *all* movement of refugees, but rather to filter and manage the numbers of refugees in urban spaces. This supports contemporary academic literature from a ground-level perspective that has pushed back against the idea that the camp and urban space are diametrically opposed to each other. In Zambia, the empirical research suggests that the relationship between the two reception spaces is symbiotic, with the actions in one regularly affecting policy and practice in the other. As examined further in the next chapter, this complex association between the two geographical spaces plays a key, if paradoxical, role in the settling of some refugees outside the refugee camp in Zambia. During post-registration, greater movement is permitted between each site by elements of the national government. Thus, as the analysis moves to focus on this second stage of reception, the relationship between the two reception sites can be seen to become even more complex.

Notes

1. Chapters 4, 5, 6 and 7 are drawn from analysis of the empirical data and supplemented by secondary sources. Due to publication requirements, reference to interviews and other quasi-ethnographic methods has been minimalised to key quotes or specific examples.

2. In a dualist state, a piece of domestic law is required to incorporate international law into national law.

3. Zambia INGOs Interviewee 10.

4. Zambia INGOs Interviewee 10.

5. In 1993, UNHCR handed over running of RSD procedures to COR.

6. UNHCR officials, as observers in these committees, share expertise and advice.

7. See also Chitupila (2010); Brosché and Nilsson (2005).

8. Applicants have a right to appeal if their claim is rejected under both RSD procedures (Chitupila, 2010).

9. See Chapter 5 for a discussion of the third settlement – the Mantapala settlement – which was opened in 2018 during the main period of data collection.

10. See also Bakewell (2007).

11. Zambia INGOs Interviewee 14.

12. See also Hansen (1979, 1982, 1990) and Bakewell (2000, 2007).

13. Exact figures involved in self-settlement in Zambia are unknown.

14. The 2017 Refugee Act officially gave COR a mandate to deal with all refugee matters. Prior to 2017, the departments' responsibilities were agreed purely at an administrative level.

15. A 'strategic framework for the local integration of former refugees' from Angola in Zambia was set up in 2014 (UNHCR, 2014b). The aim was to integrate former Angolan refugees with Zambians around the existing refugee settlements by giving them land (Kambela, 2016; Osmers, 2015).

16. COR is part of a larger hierarchical structure and reports to Home Affairs, with its mandate for maintaining internal security.

17. See also Rutinwa (2002).

18. Zambia Civil Society and Refugee Groups Interviewee 12.

19. Zambia INGOs Interviewee 10.

20. Zambia State Entities Interviewee 01.

21. Zambia INGOs Interviewee 06.

22. See also Bakewell (2002).

23. Zambia Civil Society and Refugee Groups Interviewee 13. See also Frischkorn (2015).

24. Official avenues run by COR that allow access to the urban area do have *de jure* and *de facto* restrictions attached to them.

25. Zambia State Entities Interviewee 02.

26. See Part IV of the Act.

27. See Article 10 of the Act.

28. Zambia Civil Society and Refugee Groups Interviewee 05.

29. Zambia INGOs Interviewee 13.

30. Zambia INGOs Interviewee 13.

31. See UNHCR (2017a).

32. Zambia Civil Society and Refugee Groups Interviewee 13. See also Frischkorn (2015).

33. Zambia Civil Society and Refugee Groups Interviewee 10.

34. Zambia State Entities Interviewee 02.

35. Zambia Civil Society and Refugee Groups Interviewee 13.

36. Zambia Civil Society and Refugee Groups Interviewee 13.

37. Zambia INGOs Interviewee 02.

38. Zambia Civil Society and Refugee Groups Interviewee 10.

39. However, refugees face systemic barriers in accessing these services (Donger et al., 2017).

40. See also Bakewell (2000, 2007) and Hansen (1990).

41. Zambia INGOs Interviewee 11.

42. UNHCR estimate that between 2017 and 2020, around 23,000 Congolese arrived in Zambia after renewed waves of conflict (UNHCR, 2021b).

43. Zambia INGOs Interviewee 02.

44. Zambia Civil Society and Refugee Groups Interviewee 05.

45. See also Bakewell (2002).
46. Zambia Civil Society and Refugee Groups Interviewee 10.
47. Zambia INGOs Interviewee 10.
48. Zambia INGOs Interviewee 09.
49. UNHCR's budget for Zambia was USD 20 million in 2015. In 2017, it was 12 million (UNHCR, 2019a).
50. Zambia State Entities Interviewee 02.
51. See also Zolberg et al. (1989).
52. Zolberg et al. (1989).
53. See the security strategies targeting refugees in South Africa (Misago, 2016) and Tanzania (Landau, 2001).
54. Zambia INGOs Interviewee 02.
55. Zambia has 76,027 persons of concern. By contrast, South Africa has 275,377, Tanzania 337,000, and Kenya 490,000 (UNHCR, 2019c).
56. The population of Zambia is around 17 million, with a large landmass of 752,000 sq. km (WorldAtlas, 2019). This is roughly three times the size of the UK, which itself has a population of 66 million.
57. This is with the exception of one incident in 2016. See Chapter 5.
58. These powers further limited political space for other political parties and civil society (Civicus, 2017).
59. Zambia INGOs Interviewee 11.
60. Zambia Civil Society and Refugee Groups Interviewee 02. Non-state assistance comes from international organisations (and their implementing partners), faith-based organisations and refugee networks.
61. See Siachiwena (2021b).

Chapter 5

Encampment: post registration in Zambia

This second chapter on Zambia investigates the behaviour of key actors towards the settlements, once refugees have gained official refugee status and have settled in these sites. At one level of inquiry, the post-registration period in Zambia conforms to the more traditional conceptualisations of the refugee camp. Similar to the registration phase, the post-registration phase in the settlements is characterised by minimal engagement on the part of the national government. This is the case despite self-reliance being extremely difficult to achieve in these locations. Material concerns such as capacity, and the continued ideational power of the national legal framework in framing the spatial and geographical dynamics of reception are key factors in the settlements ostensibly remaining spaces of struggle for many refugees in the long term.

Nonetheless, the post-registration experience in Zambia diverges from more traditional depictions of the refugee camp once the movement of refugees is included in the analysis. According to the prevailing wisdom in the literature, by adopting a camp-based reception policy, *states expect* refugee populations to remain immobile passive victims in the camp space after the initial registration stage. Here, refugees wait to be resettled, or for the situation in their home state to stabilise enough for them to be repatriated. In recent years, academics have added more nuance to these discussions by noting that even where immobile passive waiting is the intention of the dominant national reception policy (something that is questioned in this book), empirical evidence shows that refugee camps are rarely separated entirely from state structures and local communities. Yet, in contrast to the wealth of research from a ground-level perspective, there has been less examination of the long-standing presumptions, aims and intentions of the states that deploy refugee camps. Equally, limited research has examined how the aims of the state may interact with the movement of refugees and the realities of urban spaces.

By taking a state-focused perspective, this chapter analyses the interplay and interaction between the settlements, urban spaces, state structures and international frameworks. A significant proportion of refugees who reside in the settlements regularly find ways to work *within* state systems and structures to move back and forth between the settlements and urban areas. This includes the official pathways out of the settlements that allow refugees to find alternative forms of welcome with local communities and to access labour markets. However, these officially permitted types of movement vary greatly in duration. Some refugees are moving between the different sites daily, while others remain away from the refugee camps for months or even years at a time. This acceptance of some degree of refugee movement into urban spaces by the national government (specifically COR) is nonetheless at odds with the overarching national legal refugee framework. Because of this, it is regularly contested by other state structures. By illuminating these conflicting understandings of refugee reception post registration, a more complex and nuanced depiction of the relationship between refugee camps and urban spaces in Zambia becomes possible.

The chapter starts by setting out an understanding of post-registration reception in Zambia. In doing so, it illustrates the value of framing reception – in the context of a country like Zambia – as more than merely registration or simply removing refugees to a confined reception space. The subsequent section then builds on this by examining reception on the ground in Zambia, post the initial registration phase. This analysis investigates the approach to the refugee camp by key actors, to deepen understanding of how and why this stage of reception has shifted away from the original intentions of the settlement approach. The chapter then shifts to examine the various official pathways that permit refugees to leave the settlements and move back and forth between the camps and urban spaces.

To conclude the analysis on Zambia, the final section considers a recent development in refugee policy: namely the recently opened Mantapala settlement in the north of the country. The Mantapala settlement represents a novel 'whole society' and 'whole of government' approach to reception, one which: (1) reflects attempts to include the local government and the local community in the design and running of a new reception site; and (2) suggests that the state may be willing to move towards a more free-settlement style of reception.

Contextualising post-registration reception in Zambia

For most refugees in Zambia, post-registration involves becoming established in one of the two main settlements and effectively residing in these spaces in the long term. The original intention of the settlements was for refugees to achieve self-sufficiency through agricultural means, within the confines of these designated sites. As examined below, however, self-sufficiency has never in fact been fully achieved; this is due to several material and institutional factors. Refugee leaders noted how this situation has resulted in vast numbers of refugees relying on support from the national government and UNHCR to sustain themselves.

Given this scenario, it can be queried whether the post-registration period in Zambia really constitutes part of 'reception'. Refugees have already registered with the state, are residing in the refugee camps and broadly have access to essential humanitarian goods and services. Certainly, in accordance with some literature, this is where the concept of reception would likely end (Deardorff, 2009). Yet, as contemporary research has shown, the initial welcome that refugees receive in a refugee camp is often only one element of the overall reception they regularly encounter in a host state.

The book's working model of reception proposes that registration is one component of a larger, more comprehensive reception process. Refugee reception also includes how state structures and policies shape newcomers' experiences as they attempt to settle. This framing goes beyond the mere notion of registration. In line with this perspective, interactions between different key actors in different settings all become worthy of study, including responses to refugees in the settlements post registration, state-approved movements between refugee camps and urban and peri-urban areas, and the resultant interactions between refugees and the local communities. In this way, the book's model of reception permits a more nuanced picture of state-run refugee reception in Zambia.

The post-registration stage in Zambia: the role of the national government and UNHCR in settlements

The purpose of this section is to develop an understanding of how the national government and UNHCR conceptualise the refugee camp after initial registration has taken place. The section also studies the ensuing dynamics that have evolved between these entities within the settlements. A feature of this stage of reception is in fact the apparently minimal involvement of both entities. UNHCR handed the overall running of the settlements to the state in 1993 (Chitupila, 2010), yet the government's current engagement (particularly financially) within the settlements remains nominal.[1] Conversely, the UN agency still retains a great deal of influence over policy inside the refugee camps. This is expressed through its ongoing (albeit marginal) financial and operational commitments. There exists a mixture of material, institutional and ideational factors at play, involving different national entities and UNHCR (and its implementation partners) that result in this minimal engagement. These factors interact and contest with each other, but ultimately reinforce the overarching long-term encampment policy.

Material factor: capacity concerns

On a material level, capacity issues post registration remain a dominant factor in the continuance of the encampment reception policy. As discussed below, these concerns appear both at the national and international level. As examined in the previous chapter, government officials cited capacity concerns as a key reason why refugees remain long term in the settlements. These include a lack of funds, as well as the need to prioritise poverty reduction and social protection of the national population. Beyond the initial granting of the land to build the settlements, UN officials confirmed that national funding for the two settlements has remained minimal since their inception.

In interviews, government officials within the MCDSS did show openness to the idea of increasing funding to refugees in the settlements (and beyond). However, any action could only 'take place with the cabinet approval', and with core line ministries having shown little appetite for investing in these spaces over the last sixty years, the likelihood of this happening remains remote.[2] In addition, funding for the humanitarian and development needs of refugees remains understood as an international concern and thus outside the responsibility of the national government. Underscoring this belief is the lack of inclusion of refugees in the government's development planning. For example, regardless of the lobbying by the UN, the Seventh Zambian National Development Plan 2017–2021 made only minor reference to refugees and migrants.[3]

Most of the funding for long-term hosting of refugees in Zambia therefore comes through UNHCR.[4] Indeed, as confirmed by government officials working in the settlements, the funding for government programmes and services ultimately originates from UNHCR and its donors. This also includes the wages of government employees who administer the programmes. Thus, the conditions and quality of the overall reception granted to refugees post registration in Zambia are directly connected to the levels of funding from the international level, rather than from the government.

Significantly, the bulk of the funding allocated to refugee matters is confined to the settlements. UNHCR officials cited capacity as the reason for this spatial focus. For example, UNHCR's budget in Zambia was decreased by a third in 2018. An official confirmed:

> The priority is to reach the most people possible – in the settlement we invest our funds in services provision. We reach more people than if we invest our money cash assistance for individuals in Lusaka where cost of living is much higher.[5]

The reduced funding is therefore earmarked for immediate goods and services and essential farming equipment. Once refugees are registered, they are given plots of land within the settlements and offered specific non-food items such as farming equipment, for instance ploughs and spades, and domestic essentials, including blankets and kitchen utensils. All refugees in the settlements have access to rudimentary services, such as health and education provisions, as well as banking and financial services. In addition, via the MCDSS, UNHCR has implemented other projects, such as a Cash Based Intervention (CBI). This involves giving new arrivals K100 (US$10) per month.[6]

The CBI and the handing out of essential equipment and food demonstrate the presence of the global refugee regime *within* the camp space. In contrast, these services are generally not provided to urban refugees. During 2017, there were a few notable exceptions, for example, Caritas Zambia (an implementing partner of the UN agency at the time) maintained a network of outreach centres and programmes focused on self-reliance for urban refugees in Lusaka. However, due to funding gaps, UNHCR urban livelihood programming in Zambia ended in 2018 (UNHCR, 2021b). Significantly, this type of initiative outside the refugee camp demonstrates that the national government is not actively preventing the UN agency working in urban areas.[7] Indeed, when speaking to UNHCR officials in 2017, the reason given for the emphasis inside the settlements was not the national camp reception policy per se, but rather capacity concerns. The same official stressed, 'but by and large we have limited resources in assisting in Lusaka and it would only be a pull factor'.[8]

There is an element of logic to confining implementation of the refugee regime to a designated area when factoring in the above-mentioned capacity concerns. By restricting the regime to the refugee camp, limited funds can be used in an efficient way to reach large numbers of people, particularly those deemed to be in vulnerable situations. Nevertheless, refugees are effectively faced with a fait accompli, whereby to gain access to the protections of the regime they are required to give up their freedom of movement. In many ways, this approach is more in keeping with care and maintenance models of the past than with recent pushes by the UN agency to focus on urban settlement.[9]

The proclivity to fall back on concepts from historic care and maintenance models by UNHCR Zambia is illustrated by the agency's response in 2016 to one of the only major recent incidents of xenophobic violence seen in Lusaka. The outbreak of violence lasted forty-eight hours and caused many refugees to flee to churches in the city to find safety.[10] UNHCR's reaction was to arrange for the refugees to be moved to one of the main settlements. A refugee expert, who was caught up in the violence, commented:

> UNHCR sent us to the church and then a bus came and took us to the Mayukwayukwa camp . . . I stayed two/three months in the camp . . . before getting a new gate pass and returning [to Lusaka].[11]

The type of circular movement between the camp and urban space illustrated in this quote will be examined further below. For this point in the discussion, it is telling that when faced with protection issues in an urban area, the response by the UN agency was to move refugees to the camp or 'regime' space. During this unprecedented time of unrest, and with limited funds, the response seemed sensible to many in INGOs. Nonetheless, it does aptly illustrate how UNHCR continues to act within countries such as Zambia. The agency relies on historical institutional understandings of 'protection', with refugee camps (rather than urban areas) seen as the most appropriate location for providing safety and security to refugees.

Finally, the capacity issues within the settlements also create a temporal component to the humanitarian assistance offered. Food and cash hand-outs generally end after the first year of residence in the camps. The underlying expectation is that refugees will be able to grow their own food and sustain themselves after this point. This was described succinctly by a refugee expert who has resided spasmodically in the Mayukwayukwa camp for the past five years:

> First they give you a chicken, knife, vegetables etc., blanket, bucket, socks etc. K100. Take you to camp. For a year – then . . . self-sufficient.[12]

In addition, discrepancies and variations in the implementation of these programmes are widespread. The same refugee expert noted that implementation was 'not always the same', and that it was typical to not receive any money for a while and then 'get K300 [Zambian Kwacha] after three months'.[13]

This time-related aspect to the provision of essential commodities for refugees conforms with the framing of the settlements as development sites. By giving refugees farming equipment and land (albeit limited in nature), they are expected to become self-sufficient within a year. Nevertheless, with no genuine development assistance or investment seen for decades, the settlements have largely failed to evolve beyond long-term humanitarian sites (or permanent reception sites). As a result, the temporal restrictions to goods and services add an extra level of unease to the conditional form of reception afforded to refugees in the settlements in Zambia. This, in turn, intensifies the precarious and paradoxical nature of the reception offered, whereby refugees are allowed to settle in these sites long term but remain as permanent guests.

Ideational factor: the 'regime refugee'

The modern system of states is premised on the idea of 'sovereign' states, whereby membership of a state is needed in order to demand rights and protection (Arendt, 1951). Persons outside of this system of states – such as refugees – are viewed as 'helpless objects of pity who must be assigned to some political community in order to have an identity at all' (Aleinikoff, 1995:267). In the majority world, UNHCR and the humanitarian machinery that has emerged to support the regime over the last sixty years, has regularly worked within this ideational framing of the refugee. Refugee camps are set up and maintained to offer immediate protection to a group perceived as homogeneous, sedentary victims (Daley, 2013). Through this depoliticised humanitarian lens, containment approaches for refugees can be justified. In this way, the global refugee regime empowers host states more than refugees.[14]

The legal framework in Zambia has always limited the spatial dimensions of refugee reception, with the hosting of refugees officially restricted to the designated settlements. Yet the original intention for the settlements was different to this framing of refugees as victims in need of protection. As set out previously, the initial aim was for refugees to become self-sufficient within the settlements. Nevertheless, a lack of investment by the state and international agencies, overuse of the land for farming and the isolation of the settlements (sited away from large urban areas) have permanently stalled this objective. When discussing the settlements, refugee experts and leaders were adamant that the development strategy had failed. One refugee expert commented, 'you can't stay there . . . the life in [the] camp is very difficult'.[15] Another interviewee, a refugee leader, saw the current situation as an 'archaic system of looking after refugees'.[16]

Indeed, with desolate living conditions in the camps, most refugees who remain immobile in these spaces are reliant on hand-outs from UNHCR's implementing partners to survive – particularly for the first few years they are there.

The inherent construction of refugees within the global refugee regime as victims in need of protection has continued to empower states to adopt reception approaches that contain refugees and restrict movement. In the context of Zambia, by focusing its work within the settlements, UNHCR is essentially confining the global refugee regime to these spaces and in doing so it is undermining its ongoing negotiations with the national government to loosen freedom of movement restrictions. The reception of refugees, and by extension the construction of a refugee, remains framed by the spatial confines of the refugee camp.

This analysis of the 'regime refugee' in Zambia also shows how refugee movement is often distinguishable from other types of migrant movement and, as such, is easier to regulate, manage and control. Refugee movement is potentially less threatening due to the intrinsic protector/ protectee relationship between the refugee and the host state. As observed previously, all forms of cross-border movement are commonly framed via a security lens and therefore seen as a risk to the stability of the nation state. Nevertheless, approaches to regulate movement (such as refugee camps) are easier to justify via this 'protection' lens – in comparison, for example, to the long-term detention of migrants in immigration centres. In addition, the official policy, and the continued framing of refugees in this manner means that refugees in urban areas can be returned to the camps at any time, for instance, if their numbers increase to the point that they are deemed to be a destabilising presence.

Institutional and ideational factors: divergence and contestation in approaches to the settlements

The final subsection on factors that are maintaining the encampment reception approach post registration examines the ideational and institutional contestation at the national and international level that relates to the overall framing of these long-term reception spaces. As examined above, UNHCR's overall approach to refugee reception in Zambia is reinforcing a camp-based policy. In turn, this approach also shapes and fortifies the state's understanding of the settlements as fundamentally being long-term humanitarian sites. In contrast, the empirical evidence also highlights opposing ideational and institutional structures within UNHCR and other UN in-country agencies, which still regularly frame the settlements as development sites (in keeping with their original purpose).

The state's ideational approach to the settlements

At the national level, the refugee settlements are generally now understood as: (1) fundamentally humanitarian in nature; and (2) the responsibility of the international community. Furthermore, the original aim of enabling refugees to become self-sufficient in the settlements (that is, a development approach) has largely been ignored, with participation from the state predominantly focused on initial humanitarian concerns.

The main ministry that works in the settlements, the MCDSS, understands its mandate as looking after the 'vulnerable'. Officials certainly took this view, as can be seen from the comments made by a high-ranking official in the department:

> So the ministry is there to receive them, to provide the basic necessities of food, of clothing, of shelter, whatever form of assistance they usually give.[17]

Another official within the same department suggested that refugees have 'everything they need' in the settlements.[18] This official used the building of schools and hospitals in the settlements as examples of meeting the 'needs' of the population.

By conceptualising post-registration reception as a humanitarian endeavour, the national government maintains this idea of refugees in Zambia as apolitical, sedentary victims. It also reinforces, within many parts of the government, the notion that refugees are long-term guests being offered a conditional form of reception. Within the confines of the settlements, they are given immediate help and assistance, but no access to sustainable, long-term employment opportunities beyond subsistence farming.

Contestation in UNHCR's approach to the settlements

This framing of the settlements at the national level is supported and strengthened by the international response. As examined above, in terms of concrete responses to refugees, UNHCR is working within a broad humanitarian remit, with activities inside the settlements post registration focused on the handing out of food and services. Consequently, the approach by UNHCR and donors in Zambia shares a number of similarities with previous care and maintenance humanitarian models. These principal actions by the UN agency and national government nevertheless conflict with other ideational and institutional factors within the in-country office of UNHCR and the UN system more broadly. Specifically, on an operational and discursive level, UNHCR and other UN agencies still see the settlements as fundamentally development projects. Indeed, international organisations operating in Zambia today are geared towards development rather than humanitarian interventions.

For UNHCR, this focus on development is largely due to the changing patterns and demographics of refugee movement into Zambia over the last sixty years. Firstly, before the influxes of refugees from the DRC in 2017, the number of refugees had been declining steadily, with numbers of new arrivals being relatively small over the last few decades (Darwin, 2005). Secondly, large portions of the Angolan and Rwandan refugee populations, who have been in Zambia for decades, have refused to return to their country of origin despite UNHCR suggesting repatriation as a durable solution (Chiasson, 2015). These changing patterns of cross-border movement and the long-term hosting of specific populations are part of the reason why the composition of aid organisations and of international funding in-country has shifted over time. Indeed, Zambia is now seen as 'purely [a] development context' and a 'development country'.[19]

Furthermore, framing responses to the long-term refugee situation in Zambia in terms of development rather than humanitarian responses is in line with contemporary approaches towards protracted situations of displacement. As noted by a UNHCR official, once emergency humanitarian phases come to an end, UNHCR and its international partners will ideally attempt a slow retreat from the settlements.[20] In parallel with this withdrawal, the intention is to gradually increase engagement in the day-to-day running of the camps by the different development organisations, NGOs – and ultimately government departments. The final aim is to fully hand over the running of the camps to the state. This has been the approach in Zambia – confirmed by an official – at least on an operational and discursive level:

> we have already reached a point in the settlement . . . just typical phases . . . you have an emergency, you have international NGOs that come, then slowly you engage the national NGOs and then eventually shift over to government departments. So in both settlements we are already at the stage where we work with government – we don't fund INGOs anymore.[21]

This overall push towards development projects in the settlements can be seen in the policy decisions of UNHCR. Firstly, the UN agency has reduced its presence in the settlements substantially. Indeed, UNHCR is no longer based permanently in the settlements and the closest UNHCR office to the Meheba settlement is now 60km away in Solwezi. A refugee leader highlighted the inherent problem with this, from a refugee perspective:

> ... so not easy to speak to them. 1hr 30min from UNHCR to the settlements. 10 to 12 dollars to get there – how do refugees speak to them?
>
> Interviewer: *I understand they go twice a week?*
>
> Refugee leader: Sometimes they go there randomly but not regularly.[22]

State officials and UNHCR officers confirmed that officers visit the settlements and suggested that these visits were regular and weekly. However, there are no fixed times or days when refugees know they can speak to a protection officer. Secondly, as noted above, UNHCR and the government generally do not provide food or cash payments via the CBI scheme after a year following their arrival.[23] Thus, this broad approach can be seen as an attempt to return to the original intention of the settlements when they were set up as sites of self-sufficiency.

As detailed throughout this chapter, the framing of Meheba and Mayukwayukwa settlements as sites of development is nevertheless not replicated on the ground. Indeed, the broad developmental approach is not supported by any genuine engagement by UN agencies within the two main settlements (beyond the humanitarian assistance detailed above). The sheer lack of investment in terms of infrastructure in the settlements is surprising when you consider the number of UN agencies who have been involved with the settlements (including UNHCR, UNICEF, UNDP and UNCDF).

In conclusion, on an institutional and ideational level, UNHCR's approach towards the settlements is continuously contested due to opposing internal approaches. The funding allocated to the settlements by the UN agency, including the wages of specific government departments and hand-outs for refugees, is geared towards humanitarian aid. In contrast, the parallel slow retreat from the refugee camps by UNHCR (at least at an operational and discursive level) and the time-limited nature of the material assistance provided, can be seen as attempts to return the spaces to their originally intended function.

This overall inconsistency in approach by UNHCR, coupled with little state buy-in, means that a shift back to the original intention of the settlements is unlikely to be successful in the long term. Instead, the result of this contestation concerning approaches to the long-term encampment reception policy has been to arrive at a halfway house. The two settlements are neither emergency refugee camps nor long-term development projects. In fact, in contrast to their original aims, in many ways they resemble a more traditional long-term form of closed encampment.[24] Refugees continue to be expected to reside in spaces of exception, away from the interior of the host state, living off hand-outs and with very few opportunities for becoming self-reliant.

The first part of this chapter has set out how key actors understand and engage with the settlements following initial registration. In contrast to registration (and in opposition to their intention to withdraw further from these reception spaces) UNHCR emerges as the dominant actor in terms of how, and in what form, reception is extended to refugees. As a result, the state, by choice, very much occupies a subordinate role. A key reason for this shift in responsibility post registration is the continued perception of refugees as 'regime refugees' by departments of the national government. The combination of the ideational power of the old 1970 Refugee Act and the spatial restrictions given to the global refuge regime shapes the handling of reception at different phases of the process. National security concerns emerge at the initial reception phase (that is, who is coming into the state), but by the time refugees have been registered the national government is less interested in them and deems this population to be the responsibility of the international community, thus, determinedly limiting any perceived financial and material burden on the Zambian state. In contrast, within the context of these designated humanitarian spaces, refugees are understood as victims and gain protection and financial and material assistance from the international community.

Official access to the urban space: pathways out of the settlements post registration

The focus of the first half of this chapter has remained predominantly inside the refugee camp at the later stage of reception. Yet, this does not give the complete picture of refugee reception in Zambia. State-sanctioned pathways out of the settlements, namely gate passes and urban residence permits (URPs), provide formal avenues for exiting the settlements. These allow refugees the opportunity to interact, trade and work with the local communities that are in close proximity to these reception sites. Giving access to the local economic life of the state in this way is essential to many, given the limiting conditions and limited services offered within the confines of the settlements.[25]

In addition, these pathways also regularly connect the settlements with the urban space. In particular, the URPs (and to a lesser extent the gate passes) allow refugees to travel and remain (although not indefinitely) in large urban centres such as Lusaka and Kitwe. Consequently, this section develops further understanding of the connection between the refugee camp and the urban space. This is achieved by an examination of the institutional and ideational factors involved at the national level that have created and shaped these approaches, as well as contributing to the ongoing confusion and contestation at various levels of the state concerning the movement of refugees outside of the spatial confines of a refugee camp.

Gate passes and urban residence permits

Post registration, official opportunities to leave the refugee camp remain restricted in Zambia. This means, as one might expect, that the overarching approach by the state broadly conforms to the national legal framework, with refugees expected to remain in the settlements. Nevertheless, COR has a long history of adopting approaches that allow for some movement between the camp and urban space, which suggests a 'soft' application of the legal framework by the government department. Currently, URPs and gate passes are the only official ways for refugees to leave the two main settlements once they enter the post-registration stage of reception. Both permit refugees to travel to other areas in the state and by doing so enable them to engage with local communities and government structures outside of the refugee camps. The two procedures share several commonalities relating to their overall ephemeral nature and the dominant focus on control and regulation of movement. Nevertheless, they diverge sharply in terms of the length of time granted in urban spaces.

In terms of gaining access to gate passes or URPs, the processes for obtaining both are ostensibly open to all recognised refugees in the settlements. Yet both official pathways have numerous barriers that are either built into the procedure itself or have emerged due to bureaucratic and institutional contestation. The consequence of these obstacles is that the numbers of permits and passes handed out are consistently limited.

The procedure for URPs is, at least on the surface, well organised. In addition, as a former COR officer confirmed, the number of rejected applications by the sub-committee remains low, indeed, 'not more than 20 per cent would be rejected'.[26] In practice, however, there are several material and institutional barriers blocking access for most refugees. These include security concerns, associated costs and the bureaucratic complexities involved with making an application. For example, with the urban permit allowing refugees to live outside of the camps for one to two years (which is also renewable), there are security checks completed at the decision-making stage. Depending on the specific reason for the permit request, refugees may also have to go through different government offices and undergo complex processes to obtain the required forms and/or visa. Even though the cost of visas and permits (for instance, for education, employment or self-employment purposes) are provided at a reduced rate for refugees, the price remains prohibitive for the majority of refugees in the settlements (Ochieng, 2023). For example, a refugee leader in Lusaka observed, 'the self-employment permit is . . . , it's like basically an investor's permit for any other foreigner and that's very prohibitory for regular refugees'.[27] Consequently, while the exact number of refugees in Zambia with residence permits is unknown publicly, civil society actors suggested that the number remains low.

The process for obtaining the gate pass is less rigorous than for URPs, in part due to the shorter length of time it permits outside of the camp (usually one to two months and renewable). In addition, refugee leaders commented that the gate pass system is generally accessible for most refugees in the settlements. A COR official went further, asserting, 'the gate pass – you [are] asked where you going, how long you going for, what is the reason. They will always get it.'[28] This concurs with previous research, with Jacobsen (2005) noting that gate passes are open to all – indeed she suggests this means that refugees in Zambia have freedom of movement.[29] The real level of access to spaces outside of the settlements is disputed by civil society and community leaders. Refugee leaders suggested that ingenuity was often necessary on the part of the individual refugee because the shared impression within refugee communities is that decisions to grant the passes are often arbitrary or ad hoc. Indeed, the same COR official later in their interview accepted that there is a great deal of disparity in how the policy is implemented across the settlements.[30]

UNHCR has been working with COR to systematise the gate pass procedure. Yet, as explained by an ex-COR officer, 'the problem is that every refugee officer [has] his [or her] own interpretation on the gate pass'.[31] Finally, there is a general impression that gate passes are not granted to new arrivals nor immediately post initial registration. This was reinforced by a refugee expert who, when requesting a gate pass soon after arriving, was told, 'no – expect to stay here one year'.[32]

These numerous bureaucratic hurdles and security measures inevitably add an element of control and screening to the process of gaining access to urban spaces. Ultimately these procedures (and the variations seen in their implementation) have the effect of restricting and regulating the number of successful applicants of both forms of 'travel pass', especially during the first year of arrival.

The management of movement

Both formal pathways were created as a response to perceived increases of uncontrolled refugee movement into urban areas. Firstly, URPs were introduced into the formal reception policy of Zambia in 2000, as part of an overall approach to reinstate the camp-based reception policy (UNHCR, 2012). This shift in strategy was due to overcrowding and instability concerns in urban areas. Permits were seen as an attempt to regulate the movement of refugees outside the camps. As observed by a UNHCR official, this was particularly the case for large urban spaces such as Lusaka.[33] Gate passes were also introduced as a subsidiary element of the overarching refugee reception policy of Zambia. Again, the aim of the passes was to regulate or manage the number of refugees in urban spaces. As explained by senior UNHCR and COR officers, the original intention was that passes would allow the agency and the state to document people who had legitimate reasons for being outside of the refugee camp.

As examined in the previous chapter, during the early 2000s many in the national government became concerned about the number of refugees informally settling in urban spaces due to the destabilising effect this might have on the space and on the voting public. These increased numbers were, in large part, due to a broad relaxation of the encampment reception policy by COR. By allowing formal avenues of access to urban centres, the intention was to bring more control and regulation to this form of 'non-rooted' movement into the interior. At the same time, these processes were also designed to aid better implementation of the overarching encampment policy. Consequently, there was an acknowledgement that stopping all movement between the settlements and urban spaces was unrealistic.

This almost paradoxical approach to regulating movement by opening new official opportunities *for* movement builds on previous analysis in relation to states' understanding of the movement of 'non-rooted' persons and state stability. No country interprets freedom of movement as the unchecked or unconditional movement of all persons on their territory. Thus, political settlements today are in many ways regimes of movement. In essence, the modern state is 'a system of regulating, ordering, and disciplining bodies (and other objects) in motion' (Kotef, 2015:6). By understanding movement in this way, encampment reception policies in

Southern Africa can be seen in part as a system of regulating and managing particular visitors (or 'non-rooted' persons). States such as Zambia do not have the capacity of minority world states when it comes to adopting increasingly sophisticated approaches to regulating borders and managing movement. As an alternative, the refugee camp (which is often funded by international donors) can perform part of this function by filtering the movement of refugees into the interior and the urban spaces. Therefore, the regulating of refugee movement in Zambia through the refugee camp allows for the possibility of *some* movement into urban spaces. Given that an aim of the encampment policy in Zambia is to regulate or control the movement of refugees into urban spaces, obtaining permission to leave the settlements is inevitably heavily restricted.

The temporality of access to the urban space

The adoption of settlements as the main reception policy frames refugees as guests on the territory. Their stay in Zambia has little to no official permanence, with routes to citizenship extremely difficult.[34] Accordingly, they remain visitors beholden to a specific and conditional form of reception by the host country. Nevertheless, since the inception of the settlements in Zambia, there has been an acknowledgement that hosting refugees is unlikely to be short term in nature. Indeed, as an officer at COR confirmed, COR and other elements of the national government appreciate that large portions of refugee communities will remain long term or simply never return to their countries of origin.[35]

In contrast to this acceptance of the long-term nature of hosting refugees via the dominant encampment reception approach, both official pathways out of the settlements are characterised by their temporality. Residential permits are issued for a maximum of one to two years, depending on the specific grounds, with costs often accruing throughout the process. When they expire, the holder is expected to go through a process of renewal, which can incur additional costs or mean being returned to the settlements. Gate passes are granted for much shorter time frames, usually one to three months, with refugees historically expected to return to the settlement before the pass expires.[36]

The temporariness of these options that allow movement outside of the official reception site causes regular circular movements between the camps and urban spaces, with refugees returning to renew their permits/passes. Refugee leaders and experts noted examples of refugees living in Lusaka for years who continue to return to the settlement regularly to renew the gate pass. In many cases, this can be 'every three months – go back to camp for two weeks then come back'.[37]

In interviews, refugee leaders reported a sense of uneasiness surrounding refugees who held either valid gate passes or residential permits. As one refugee leader with a gate pass observed, she has a pass, but she 'is not free'.[38] Leaders of a refugee association echoed this feeling by emphasising how passes and permits inevitably expire (whether it is in a month or a year). This means concerns over renewal decisions, additional costs and the possibility of uprooting a family from the urban space, are never far away. Thus, the forms of reception that these two pathways open up at the local and sub-local level, which grant refugees access to local communities and the local economy in urban spaces, are equally affected by a sense of impermanence.

Alternatively, if a refugee remains in the urban space with an expired gate pass or permit, they run a higher risk of being arrested or, more commonly, forced to pay a bribe to enforcement officers. This was discussed by a former COR officer:

> Yes – they turned a 'blind eye'. It comes at a cost – on the migrant. Because they know if they say they are a refugee or asylum-seeker they are expected to have specific documentation that would allow you to be outside camp. So if you don't have them, shouldn't be there . . . you would have to pay a bribe.[39]

The difference between the permanent/temporary dynamics at the national level in relation to refugee camp vs. urban spaces is an important feature of reception in Zambia. Official pathways out of the settlements connect and develop relationships between these two sites of reception. Yet the ideational understanding of the 'temporariness' of hosting refugees in these spaces differs considerably. There is an acceptance of the long-term presence of refugees in the settlements. In contrast, numerous barriers halt the permanent settlement of refugees in urban spaces. An eventual consequence of the temporariness of the official status granted to refugees in urban areas sees the dominance of the encampment approach to reception reinforced within government departments.

Refugees in both reception spaces though remain inherently as guests throughout their stay in Zambia. As examined in the previous chapter, refugees in the settlements are accepted as long-term visitors, giving the reception afforded to them a quality of permanent temporariness. This is appreciably different from the uneasiness felt by refugees who move and attempt to settle within urban spaces on short-term permits or passes. Nonetheless, both distinct forms of reception have a sense of impermanence to them, which means that they remain entirely conditional. As such, movement can change the form of reception received but, in and of itself, it does not appear to end the reception process.

Institutional and ideational factors: contestation and the conceptualisation of refugee movement

This section examines the differing institutional and ideational factors surrounding the implementation of these official pathways and how different stakeholders conceptualise refugee movement and reception in the urban space. Policies that permit refugees to leave the settlements post registration have remained outside the scope of the 1970 Refugee Act and as such – up until 2017 – were not covered by the national legal framework for refugees in Zambia.[40] This has resulted in COR (with input from UNHCR) creating ad hoc procedures to deal with all refugee matters that do not specifically relate to hosting refugees in refugee camps. At the institutional level, this has created the scope for COR to slowly bring in specific facets of the global refugee regime (including key regime norms) to the broader national reception policy.[41] Nevertheless, the lack of a legal framework, or even at times any policy in writing, to support these administrative practices has created a great deal of inter-governmental contestation. This contestation within the national government concerning differing conceptualisations of refugees and their reception is further complicated by UNHCR's overarching approach to urban refugees in Zambia.

Line ministries

At the level of line ministries, the Department of Immigration and other law enforcement agencies have traditionally responded to refugee movement via a construction of refugees based on the old 1970 Refugee Act. Refugees are viewed spatially in terms of the confines of the settlements. In addition, the Department of Immigration is mandated to implement the Immigration and Deportation Act (2010), which has little commonality or convergence with the 1970 Refugee Act or the new 2017 Refugee Act. Put succinctly by a former COR officer:

> Immigration implementing the Immigration Act and the Commission for Refugees implementing the Refugee Act. There is no overlap, either you are a refugee or you are a migrant.[42]

Furthermore, as shown in the following response by a UNHCR implementing partner, there are clear ideational differences in how the departments understand refugees in Zambia – especially those present outside of the refugee camp. These differences arise from contrasting mandates and over forty years of differing interpretations and understandings of reception stemming from the 1970 Refugee Act:

> And then you have also the Department of Immigration which is powerful and much bigger, and their perspective is that we are here to primarily protect our citizens. That's fine that you're a refugee but . . . after all you are a foreigner. For COR, refugees are Zambians.[43]

Consequently, immigration officers regularly approach all non-nationals on the territory in the same way: namely, as 'foreigners'.

When these ideational and institutional factors are combined (that is, the spatial construction of refugees as essentially immobile bodies residing in a refugee camp, little overlap between the two main national acts focused on the movement of non-nationals, and sharply opposing ideational approaches by government bodies), the result is that all migrants, including refugees outside the settlements, are seen by the Department of Immigration and other law enforcement agencies as under the purview of immigration law. This was certainly the view of a former COR officer who noted that this has caused the line between refugees and economic migrants 'to be quite blurred'.[44] Indeed, once refugees have travelled across the country to get to Lusaka, it can be very difficult to distinguish them from other migrants wanting to regularise their stay in the country. This contestation and confusion at the national level have seen urban refugees frequently deemed as illegal migrants by government departments. As examined next, this creates a situation whereby urban refugees are regularly shifted from a global protection regime to a national immigration regime.

UNHCR and its implementing partners

Reception policies that constrict some of the key regime norms but simultaneously offer others within the confines of the refugee camp have the effect of constraining the global refugee regime spatially. Refugees are expected to give up key regime norms such as freedom of movement to gain access to the basic protections that the regime can offer within a refugee camp. This is particularly noticeable at the post-registration stage in Zambia when refugees utilise the official pathways out of the settlements. For UNHCR and its implementing partners, by choosing to leave the camp (either via legal or illicit channels) urban refugees are signalling that they can be independent and are no longer in need of protection or assistance.

Capacity and ideational factors are behind this broad institutional approach. Currently UNHCR have almost no resources for assisting in urban areas and as noted above, they are concerned that further assistance in urban spaces would act as 'a pull factor' and stimulate additional movement into cities. Indeed, an official went further, stating, 'you live outside [the camps] if you are self-sufficient'.[45] Significantly, the national government shares these conceptualisations of assistance/protection in the urban space. For example, at the sub-committee stage of an application for a URP, there is an implied requirement that the refugee is self-sufficient. Equally, with a URP based on health requirements, indirect security concerns are often raised regarding how the refugee will not become a burden on the state. The rationale for these arguments is based on the premise that assistance is offered in the settlements, so if you choose to live outside this space, 'you can fight for yourself'.[46]

A consequence of this approach by UNHCR (in conjunction with the government tactics set out previously) is that urban refugees in Zambia are being removed from the global refugee regime and potentially even from the refugee label. Framed by Betts (2009a, 2013b) as 'regime shifting', refugees in urban spaces in Zambia are in effect being shifted from one regime to an alternative parallel immigration regime.[47] Betts (2009a) suggests that states frequently attempt to move the 'problem' in this way because their aim is to relocate the politics of a given issue/area from one regime to another. By effectively redefining the criteria for being a refugee in Zambia as remaining in the camp space, UNHCR and the Zambian government appear to be de-linking urban refugees from the global refugee regime. In doing so, these refugees are being shifted away from the refugee label towards a generic (and often illegal) migrant label and hence into the national immigration regime.

Commissioner for Refugees, Zambian government

COR has continued to maintain a general commitment to the dominant camp-based reception policy, as set out in the national legal framework for refugees. Equally, COR preserves a good reputation amongst relevant non-governmental stakeholders in Zambia, including refugee leaders, community groups, UNHCR and its implementing partners (UNHCR, 2021b). This has been achieved by the Commission's role (in collaboration with UNHCR) as the main driving force behind opening up access to the urban space and creating stronger connections between these disparate sites of reception. Equally, there has been a historical willingness on the part of COR to listen to ideas, engage in projects that pilot refugee integration, and maintain a relatively relaxed view of the imposed restrictions on freedom of movement for refugees.

This reputation was reinforced and enhanced with the appointment of Abdon Mawere, who took charge of the department in 2016. This was affirmed by a COR officer, who noted how his progressive approach to refugee regime norms sits in stark contrast to other departments in Home Affairs:

> [In] Home Affairs, there is the Commissioner for Refugees and the Immigration, Department of Immigration. So they are supposed to be one family but they go directly against one another because the Commissioner for Refugees is refugee trained. He's very understanding (and his whole office) and if it was his will, people will be moving forward doing their businesses and being integrated in the society.[48]

Firstly, the Commissioner worked closely with the former President of Zambia on the implementation of the new 'development-style' Mantapala refugee settlement (see the next section). Secondly, he was an important catalyst for the new 2017 Refugee Act finally coming into force. In turn, he pushed for new policy documents to ensure that the Act would be implemented progressively. For example, he took the lead in interpreting the new legislation in a way that would mean more refugees are able to leave the settlements and access urban areas in a semi-permanent manner.[49]

At the institutional level, the role of personality in the implementation and interpretation of refugee reception policy in Africa has been noted in the literature (Albert, 2010; Schmidt, 2014). In Zambia, the progressive steps taken by an energetic Commissioner have further softened COR's interpretation of the national legal framework. As such, movement outside of settlements and by extension access to urban spaces has increasingly been incorporated into post-registration reception. The extent to which this is happening, at least within the confines of COR, is illustrated by a high-ranking officer in COR suggesting that refugees actually *have freedom of movement* in Zambia: 'they just need to ask for it'.[50]

It will take time to see if these shifts in ideational and institutional approach to refugees and the urban space within COR can be translated into permanent practice on the ground. On one hand, these developments bring optimism for improved implementation of the fundamental regime norm of freedom of movement and with it a shift from the spatial confinement of refugee reception seen in Zambia since the 1960s. On the other hand, Zambia has witnessed relaxation in the overall understanding of the encampment policy in the past, only for it then to be reversed when numbers of refugees in urban areas increased to levels perceived as unstable. Changes in policy on the ground have traditionally remained discursive and self-contained within the COR. As the 2017 outbreak of violence in the DRC illustrated, this more liberal approach to refugee movement by the Commission is especially vulnerable to geopolitical events. At that time, the influx of refugees at the border led to COR and UNHCR abandoning plans to draft policy guidelines on the new Act, which would have allowed more access to urban areas. As noted by a UNHCR official, during a heightened time of unrest at the border, it did not make sense strategically to continue these negotiations with other line ministries.[51]

To conclude this section, until COR's more 'open' approach to movement outside of the settlements is seen in official policy documents, if not the legal framework, and gains cross-departmental agreement and understanding, then confusion and contestation between national departments is likely to remain. For example, it is evident that the interpretation of the new Act, that allows more access to the urban space, is currently confined to COR and UNHCR. Equally, regardless of the accuracy of the statement, the idea that refugees do have freedom of movement in Zambia ('*they just have to ask*') is not shared more broadly within the national government or even by UNHCR.

This national-level institutional contestation means a great deal of policy relating to refugee movement outside of the settlements is contested and/or left to individual interpretation. This feeds into wider issues of miscommunication and confusion relating to the procedures for obtaining and renewing official permission for accessing urban spaces. This in turn causes further mistrust between the refugee and the state.[52] The progress started by Abdon Mawere in slowly opening up urban spaces to refugees at the post-registration stage is good news for advocates wishing to see Zambia implement more core norms of the global regime. Nonetheless, with large discrepancies in approach at the national level remaining, the contestation within the government ultimately reinforces the perceived need for the dominant reception approach in Zambia. Refugees moving around the territory are seen by government agencies as being outside of the national refugee legal framework. Consequently, external to COR, the adoption of these strategies for facilitating refugee movement has also had the effect of further criminalising and reframing (or regime shifting) urban refugees as irregular or illegal economic migrants.

Contemporary shifts in refugee policy at the local level: the Mantapala settlement

In interviews with state and (some) INGO informants, the opening of the 'whole of society' and 'whole of government' Mantapala settlement in the north of the country in 2017 was heralded as a new approach to receiving refugees. With an emphasis on the integration of refugees with local communities and the inclusion of the local government, this venture gives an indication of the further relaxation of the encampment policy in Zambia. This section probes whether this approach, with its emphasis on the local level, has the long-term potential to resist the key material, institutional and ideational factors that have dominated national-level refugee policy in Zambia since independence and ultimately reinforced the perceived need for a camp-based reception policy.

Additionally, this section develops a line of argument, based on Milner's (2009) work on the 'democracy-asylum' nexus, which suggests an association between increased democratisation and more restrictive forms of asylum. Using the logic of Milner's work, but turning it in the opposite direction, this section asks whether a shift from a competitive/democratic political settlement to a more authoritarian-style political settlement, allows for the possibility of improved reception conditions for refugees? Political scientists such as Khan (2010) and Letvisky and Way (2010) have suggested that when a political settlement moves towards an authoritarian style of governance, *long-term* programming/projects can more easily be implemented if they align with the interests and ideologies of the incumbent president. This is because the ruling party becomes less worried about democratic systems and short-term concerns such as losing re-election.

As noted previously, before Edgar Lungu unexpectedly lost the national election in 2021, power in Zambia was increasingly being retained by a president who had an ideological commitment to pan-Africanism. Thus, the argument is that as a government such as Zambia's moves towards a more authoritarian political settlement, they become less concerned about the concomitant short-term political risks of integrating refugees into communities than neighbouring states with more clearly defined democratic structures. Hence, the political space emerged for the creation of the Mantapala settlement and its 'whole of society' and 'whole of government' approach.

Mantapala: a 'whole of society' approach to refugee reception?

Incremental shifts in approach and attitude towards the reception of refugees in Zambia (particularly post registration) by the now former president and COR have been discussed previously. These have included Edgar Lungu making public international commitments relating to the New York Declaration / the CRRF and the Global Compact on Refugees. As part of these broad international commitments, a form of 'whole of society' and 'whole of government' approach was adopted in the design and implementation of the Mantapala settlement in the Nchelenge district in the Luapula Province.

The settlement was designed to embody a more inclusive development approach to refugee reception in Zambia. In contrast to the two existing settlements, arrivals from the DRC are given plots of land alongside Zambian nationals. A UNHCR official who had been working on the project since inception gave an account of the approach:

> It's about 6000 hectares plus. It is a type of settlement for refugees. Settlement in that the refugees will be supplied with plants to sustain themselves and also the host community there will not be displaced. The new concept is that the host community lives alongside the refugees. The local community will also have access to the services. Health, schools and boreholes will all be new and available to local community. We are also building the roads and the schools and the health centres.[53]

As part of this 'whole of government' approach, there has been buy-in from key ministries and departments involved in the project, including those working in the areas of employment, health and education. In addition, there is participation and engagement by local-level government departments and officials. Also, District Joint Operation Committees were set up, which run monthly meetings as part of strategic responses to assist with new arrivals.

There has also been a concerted effort to embrace the CRRF and include partners not just focused on immediate humanitarian concerns. During interviews, UNHCR officials described the approach as a new way of working: 'trying to bring in solutions and long-term solutions from the start, trying to bring in diversified partners including development partners from the start'.[54] With meaningful engagement by development agencies and the ability of refugees to easily interact with local communities, the hope is that lessons have been learnt from the experiences of the previous settlements and that this time refugees will have a realistic chance at 'self-reliance and access to livelihood opportunities'.[55]

Certainly, the inclusion of local communities alongside multiple government departments (including local government) in the designing and implementation of the settlement represents a key operational shift by the state in its approach to the reception of refugees. This is particularly striking given that the Mayukwayukwa and Meheba settlements have been neglected by the Zambian state (and arguably UN agencies) for decades. Nevertheless, it will take time to see if this approach is deemed successful long term for all stakeholders. At present, it remains unclear whether this project heralds a more permanent shift away from the current camp-based reception policy in Zambia or not.

Early warning signs: material and ideational contestation

When speaking to key stakeholders about the execution and development of the project, the responses were not entirely promising. As hinted at by a UNHCR officer, 'it's an ongoing process but it can be slow'.[56] Indeed, several key material, institutional and ideational factors that influence the maintenance of the dominant camp policy reappeared when interviews turned to the topic of the new settlement.

A familiar material factor that emerged was capacity and funding levels. In fact, concerns were raised around funding issues at three levels of state analysis: international, national and local. Firstly, INGOs noted how gaps in international funding (in contrast to the commitments made by donors) started to appear immediately. As one INGO worker observed, from its inception donors almost instantly switched attention to other ongoing global refugee situations, where the number of affected refugees were higher.[57] This tendency has only increased since the launch of the settlement, with the national government in 2019 publicly expressing frustration at the lack of international support (UNHCR, 2019c). Secondly, at the national level, from the start concerns were expressed around the lack of infrastructure and genuine engagement by key departments (such as health and education).

Thirdly, during the time of the interviews, key stakeholders were unsure about the exact role of local authorities. It was evident that there was interest at this level of government (and the provincial level) in being involved in the running and implementation of the project. Yet it was not entirely clear how much power would be decentralised down to the local level. To many, local government in the country is ill-equipped to function properly. Thus, without the re-allocation of funds, it is unlikely that local authorities will have the political and economic power to really influence the development of the settlement and surrounding areas.

Capacity issues also had a role to play in the location of the new project. Rather than selecting land that was close to significant urban settlements (with the accompanying existing networks and infrastructure to draw on), the space chosen was located in the second poorest province in Zambia. It is situated in the far north of the country and is over 1000km away from the capital, Lusaka. Furthermore, over 80 per cent of the population of that area live in poverty. When discussing the site, a UNHCR official noted:

> It is an area that [is] basically the middle of a forest, it will also encourage all humanitarian and development actors to bring in essential services such as education and health. They will benefit both the local population and the refugee population and promote peaceful coexistence.[58]

On a positive note, it is evident from this quote that the choice of land to host refugees means that any new development will also greatly assist a particularly poor area of the country and its locals. Yet equally, it underlines concerns surrounding the ability of a medium-income state to respond to new arrivals when the area selected for reception is already a precarious space for nationals.

The same UNHCR official confirmed this point later in the interview:

> it is already a crisis area in itself – then you add traumatised highly malnourished displaced persons arriving that are in need of a lot of care and you have a major crisis because there is no safety net that is existing for the local population, let alone for the refugees.[59]

Thus, before refugees could even be transported there, urgent international support was required. This took the form of essential infrastructure, schools, health services and other key services and provisions.

When you consider these capacity issues at each level of analysis, as well as the geographical location of the camp, troubling parallels start to emerge in relation to the existing settlements in Zambia. A project that starts out as an innovative development scheme can quickly transform into a halfway house between an emergency refugee camp and a development project: in essence, a humanitarian-style camp space.

Conceptualising refugees and refugee reception outside of the camp setting: a step too far?

A key ideational factor observed throughout the past two chapters has been the construction of reception sites for refugees in Zambia. By broadly maintaining a conceptualisation of refugees and their reception being within the confines of a camp space, refugee movement outside of that space is heavily controlled and regularly deemed as illicit by many within the government. The empirical evidence suggests that this framing of refugees as 'regime refugees' has carried over into the design and realisation of the Mantapala settlement.

The new settlement was established at a time when commitments were made by the former president at the international level to consider relaxing freedom of movement restrictions. In addition, the design of the settlement involves plots of land being given to both refugees and local citizens. Nevertheless, Mantapala remains a *gated* camp for the refugee inhabitants, whereby they need to request permission to leave for a designated period of time.⁶⁰ A UNHCR official framed the situation as a positive for refugee protection:

> [It's] sort of a loose gate pass. It's more meant to protect refugees . . . if they need to be outside the settlement – so they have papers accepted by immigration they can show they left the settlement with permission.⁶¹

In contrast, another UNHCR officer expanded on this by noting that the passes were only issued for a maximum of one week and refugees needed to give clear justification for leaving the settlement.⁶² Irrespective of the exact motivation for the gate passes, this 'new', 'whole of government' and 'whole of society' approach to reception and reception spaces retains the same relationship with refugee movement as the two existing settlements, whereby pathways out of the site are still heavily monitored and restricted. It also suggests a general unwillingness to conceptualise refugees entirely outside of a camp-based setting.

To conclude this section, the establishment of the Mantapala settlement points to the national government being open to relaxing certain elements of the dominant reception policy, particularly around: (1) conceding some power to lower levels of government; and (2) the integration of refugees with local communities. Furthermore, the gradual decline in the quality of democracy, and with it the slow shifting of executive power to the Office of the President, paradoxically created the political space for these positive advances in refugee reception. Nevertheless, while the former president created the impetus for these developments, the above subsections question whether implementation over the long term will measurably improve refugee reception. Indeed, this initial investigation suggests that reservations held at the national level around truly relaxing spatial restrictions for refugees in Zambia continue to dominate reception policies.

Based on these findings and Chapter 4, the overriding concern that emerges is that the new settlement may simply turn into another halfway house, sitting somewhere between an emergency humanitarian space and a truly inclusive development project. Without international support in the form of actual investment on the ground, the goodwill and long-term planning of the former president and COR are only likely to be able to take the new initiative so far.

Post registration in Zambia: a global regime and the 'regime refugee' confined to the camp space

A dynamic combination of inter-related ideational, material and institutional factors at the national and international level work together to maintain the camp-based reception policy in Zambia, post registration. Nevertheless, a more holistic understanding of state-based reception in Zambia emerges when analysis is broadened to investigate the ways in which the refugee camp is regularly connected to the urban space. Indeed, certain institutional and ideational factors (largely stemming from COR) frequently contest and even on occasions constrain these 'dominant' factors. This results in some officially sanctioned movement between the refugee camp and urban space, and the settling of refugees in cities such as Lusaka on a temporary basis.

UNHCR emerges as the main actor within the established refugee camps in Zambia at the post-registration stage (particularly in terms of decision-making and funding), even though the agency is attempting to implement a 'slow retreat' from the settlements. Conflicting material, ideational and institutional factors emanating from the UN agency have resulted in a halfway house whereby, due to capacity concerns, UNHCR mostly works and offers humanitarian assistance within the confines of the camps in Zambia, although at the same time the agency continues to frame these spaces as development sites which should eventually transfer entirely over to development actors.

The result of this contestation between factors is that the global refugee regime is essentially confined to the settlements. For many refugees, there is little choice but to give up certain key rights and freedoms to gain access to essential humanitarian services. For others, the spatial dimensions of the refugee regime, in conjunction with state-imposed restrictions on pathways out of the camp space, results in a great deal of refugee movement within Zambia being circular (for example, between the settlements, nearby local communities and more built-up urban centres like Lusaka). Ultimately, the UN agency is reinforcing the idea of the 'regime refugee', with refugees' reception and long-term presence being understood within the spatial/geographical confines of the settlements. Moreover, this dominant in-country approach is undermining the agency's diplomatic efforts with the ruling political settlement to relax restrictions on freedom of movement.

Nevertheless, almost paradoxically, the adoption of camp-based reception creates sufficient stability for some movement of refugees to occur. In this way, the refugee camp regulates the numbers of refugees in the urban space. Yet, the spatial aspects to how refugees (and their reception) are constructed, shape how those who move between the camp and urban space can access local networks and economies. Their journeys and attempts to pursue their own personal and economic aims move them outside of the conventional understanding of a 'refugee' within large parts of the government and UNHCR. Urban refugees are expected to be entirely self-sufficient and are seen as fundamentally distinct from 'regime refugees' in the settlements. In this way, refugees in the urban space are being shifted from a refugee label (and therefore from the global refugee regime that attaches to that) to one of being a migrant, or illegal migrant, which moves them into the remit of the national immigration regime.

Finally, the current implementation of the Mantapala settlement reaffirms underlying assumptions about refugee reception within key elements of the national government. The recent initiatives at the international level and the former president's public commitment to consider relaxing the camp-based policy do not satisfactorily tackle the underlying ideational factors leading to refugees being conceptualised by many government bodies as existing solely within confined reception sites. Thus, without addressing the dominant factors detailed in the previous two chapters, any major increases in the movement of refugees on the territory – particularly within major urban spaces – would be likely to be perceived as a destabilising event that needs to be managed. The result would be a likely crackdown on refugees in urban spaces and a renewed focus on the refugee camp as the dominant reception policy. Equally, without tackling these entrenched conceptualisations of refugees and their reception, contemporary attempts at relaxing the refugee reception policy by specific government bodies and UNHCR may in fact be inadvertently reinforcing the generally perceived need for the refugee camp in the eyes of many within the government.

This concludes the Zambia case study and the book now turns to examine state-based refugee reception in the second Southern African case study: South Africa. In line with the dual geographical focus of the project, attention now moves from the refugee camp to the urban space as a major reception site for refugees. Building on the findings that ideational, material and institutional factors interconnect, reinforce and/or contest each other to produce unique reception policies, the following two chapters will identify and analyse the factors behind why South Africa continues to reject the regionally popular encampment reception policy of its close neighbour.

Notes

1. In sharp contrast to national-level engagement once refugees are allowed out of the settlements and they attempt to settle in urban spaces.
2. Zambia State Entities Interviewee 07.
3. See 7NDP (2018). The latest National Development Plan (8NDP, 2022) makes no reference to refugees.
4. See also Bakewell (2002).
5. Zambia INGOs Interviewee 10.
6. See UNCDF (2018).
7. There are state-led restrictions as to who can access these services, for example, they are only available for officially recognised refugees.
8. Zambia INGOs Interviewee 10.
9. See Verdirame and Harrell-Bond (2005); Long (2014).
10. This occurred in 2016 after a small number of shops and homes were looted and destroyed.
11. Zambia Civil Society and Refugee Groups Interviewee 09.
12. Zambia Civil Society and Refugee Groups Interviewee 11. The CBI is available longer term for refugees seen as particularly vulnerable.
13. Zambia Civil Society and Refugee Groups Interviewee 11.
14. These ideas were developed with Professor Loren Landau.
15. Zambia Civil Society and Refugee Groups Interviewee 11.
16. Zambia Civil Society and Refugee Groups Interviewee 13.
17. Zambia State Entities Interviewee 04.
18. Zambia State Entities Interviewee 07.
19. Zambia INGOs Interviewee 02.
20. Zambia INGOs Interviewee 10.
21. Zambia INGOs Interviewee 10.
22. Zambia Civil Society and Refugee Groups Interviewee 10.
23. See UNHCR (2017a). Although when refugees have serious problems, they are often given extra food and the cash payment.
24. Many refugees do however find ways of leaving the settlements on a daily basis to conduct piecemeal work.
25. See Neto (2019); Bakewell (2002).
26. Zambia State Entities Interviewee 02.
27. Zambia Civil Society and Refugee Groups Interviewee 05.
28. Zambia State Entities Interviewee 06.
29. This is an extremely generous interpretation of freedom of movement.
30. Zambia State Entities Interviewee 06.
31. Zambia State Entities Interviewee 06.
32. Zambia Civil Society and Refugee Groups Interviewee 11.
33. Zambia INGOs Interviewee 02.

34. The state has on multiple occasions committed to integrating *former* refugees. In 2014, the Strategic Framework for the Local Integration of Former Refugees aimed to regularise former Angolan and Rwandan refugees (Maple, 2018). In 2019, the state again committed to the integration of former refugees from these two countries (World Vision et al., 2019); and in 2022, the state committed to *considering* the 'significant permanent solution to local integration of former refugees' (Republic of Zambia, 2022).

35. Zambia State Entities Interviewee 05.

36. COR now has a system that allows refugees to renew gate passes in Lusaka.

37. Zambia Civil Society and Refugee Groups Interviewee 11.

38. Zambia Civil Society and Refugee Groups Interviewee 11.

39. Zambia State Entities Interviewee 01.

40. The 2017 Refugee Act does allow for new forms of urban permit – although the Act at the time of writing had not been transferred into a set of practice and procedure rules.

41. In 2002, the Zambia Initiative was a 'Development through Local Integration project that focused on the needs of host communities in the Western Province and included the refugees in the Mayukwayukwa and Nangweshi settlements' (DTS, 2014). Another example includes the Comprehensive Strategy 2009, which focused on Angolan refugees (UNHCR, 2012).

42. Zambia State Entities Interviewee 02.

43. Zambia Civil Society and Refugee Groups Interviewee 05.

44. Zambia State Entities Interviewee 02.

45. Zambia INGOs Interviewee 10.

46. Zambia INGOs Interviewee 10.

47. This follows global trends, see Mourad and Norman (2019).

48. Zambia Civil Society and Refugee Groups Interviewee 05.

49. Article 42 is being interpreted by COR and UNHCR as allowing certain refugees the right to work in urban areas (in the informal sector) without the need to apply for visas.

50. Zambia State Entities Interviewee 05.

51. Zambia INGOs Interviewee 10.

52. This leaves refugees outside of the settlements vulnerable to extortion and bribes.

53. Zambia INGOs Interviewee 06.

54. Zambia INGOs Interviewee 10.

55. Zambia INGOs Interviewee 10.

56. Zambia INGOs Interviewee 06.

57. Zambia INGOs Interviewee 14.

58. Zambia INGOs Interviewee 10.

59. Zambia INGOs Interviewee 10.

60. Citizens in the new settlement have no restrictions on their movement.

61. Zambia INGOs Interviewee 10.

62. Zambia INGOs Interviewee 06.

Chapter 6

Free settlement: the maintenance of a free-settlement reception in South Africa

Post-apartheid South Africa has maintained a generous 'open door' policy to refugees from neighbouring states. By implementing a free-settlement approach, the host state grants refugees permission to move freely within the territory and settle anywhere. This approach remarkably stands as an outlier in Southern Africa, where most states restrict and manage access to their interiors by adopting encampment reception policies. The aim of this chapter is to investigate the continued implementation of the free-settlement approach to refugee reception in South Africa, through an analysis of the behaviour of state bodies and UNHCR. Specifically, the chapter interrogates the question of why South Africa has maintained this method and how this translates into policy and practice during initial registration.[1]

The chapter highlights how, even at the initial point of registration, two levels of reception emerge. At the national level, the granting of freedom of movement within the national refugee framework, coupled with a policy of non-interference, can be understood as its own form of reception. This means that the initial welcome granted to refugees, at least in law, comes with no spatial restrictions, allowing refugees to freely move and access networks and economies in cities and towns. In addition, by permitting refugees these freedoms within urban spaces, the free-settlement approach also encourages refugees to find their own forms of reception at the local and sub-local level.

The national-level policy of non-interference post the initial registration procedures is nonetheless regularly contested and altered by numerous material, institutional and ideational factors operating at different levels of the state and at the international level. Indeed, through an examination of the key causal mechanisms that are influencing the implementation of the national-level policy, the chapter explains the rapid shift seen in how refugees are received by the South African state over the last twelve years. Ultimately, the unrestricted movement of refugees and other migrants has resulted in perceived instability in the urban space, an increased securitisation of all forms of cross-border African migration, and the shrinking of the overall asylum space. The government is now aggressively adopting *de jure* and *de facto* policies and practices that restrict access for refugees to urban spaces.

These issues are examined through the lens of initial registration, with the next chapter turning to look more broadly at post-registration reception. Nevertheless, due to the inherent 'messiness' surrounding urban displacement, the registration phase can continue long term. Indeed, for many refugees and asylum-seekers in urban spaces in South Africa, a post-registration stage never fully materialises. Instead, many remain stuck in limbo at the registration stage while they wait indefinitely for an RSD or appeal procedure at a Refugee Reception Office (RRO). As a result, either they remain engaged with state structures by regularly renewing temporary documentation or simply avoid the state entirely (skipping this element of reception) and instead attempt forms of 'urban citizenship' at the sub-local level. Nonetheless, there is analytical value in separating out these stages of reception. As observed in the next chapter, this conceptual separation allows for an examination of how the host state's and global refugee regime's responses in urban spaces shape and interact with refugee movement, beyond initial registration processes.

The chapter starts with an explanation of the initial welcome and registration of refugees in South Africa, with an emphasis on the urban space. This opening section serves to contextualise the subsequent sections, which will go on to examine why the state has broadly maintained the free-settlement approach to reception. Utilising the book's conceptual framework, the chapter draws out key ideational, material and institutional factors influencing this approach, including the ideational power and authority stemming from the national legal framework relating to refugees. The chapter concludes by investigating the regressive changes seen since 2011 in national policy towards refugees at the point of registration. Recent proposals to construct camp-like reception (or processing) centres at the border – thereby removing asylum-seekers (and potentially refugees) entirely from urban centres – appear to be the culmination of these policy shifts.

The registration stage in South Africa

Historically, South Africa has generally maintained an 'open door' policy to refugees. Yet, in terms of contemporary history, it was not until the post-apartheid period that the country effectively transformed from being a sending state to a receiving one in relation to refugee movements (Landau and Segatti, 2009). Due to the modern geopolitical shifts, from apartheid rule to the coming into power of the ANC, the state's official involvement with the global refugee regime has been relatively short. A commitment to international cooperation in relation to refugees started in 1991 when South Africa signed an agreement with UNHCR. This allowed UN field officers to assist with the repatriation of exiles wishing to return to South Africa, following the beginning of the dismantlement of the apartheid regime (Khan and Lee, 2018). In 1993, this was extended to allow UNHCR an active presence in the country to assist with Mozambican refugees (Polzer, 2007). In terms of international conventions, the government signed the 1969 OAU Refugee Convention in 1994 and signed the 1951 Refugee Convention in 1996. To implement the international regime in the national context, the Refugee Act came into force in 1998 (1998 Refugee Act).[2]

Legal framework and registration procedures

The 1998 Refugee Act set out a national-level approach for the first time – at least in terms of procedural requirements – towards the initial reception of refugees.[3] Since its inception, the Act has received international praise and is regularly held up by UNHCR as a model of how to receive refugees on the African continent.[4] Some academics and commentators have gone so far as to suggest that the Act is a beacon of progressive African-centric legal frameworks, moving refugee law (particularly the refugee definition) beyond the European-centric 1951 Refugee Convention (Smith, 2003). For example, the Act incorporates the 1969 OAU Refugee Convention 1(2) definition and includes an expanded definition of *non-refoulement*. In addition, the existence of a nationally run and individualised RSD procedure combined with a strong judiciary brings further credibility to these assertions (Johnson, 2015). Although, as explored later, this idea of an example of progressive national refugee governance was significantly weakened in 2020 with the entering into force of the Refugees Amendment Act 33 of 2008 (RAA 2008) in 2020, which itself triggered the coming into force of the Refugees Amendment Act 12 of 2011 (RAA 2011) and of the Refugees Amendment Act 11 of 2017 (RAA 2017). These acts and their accompanying regulations reduce access to the asylum system and deny asylum-seekers rights that they formerly held (Ziegler, 2020).

The final component of the legal framework relating to refugee reception is the National Constitution of South Africa. This sets the legal requirements for all national legislation and the key underlying values that should be applied when interpreting legislation (Klinck, 2009). The Bill of Rights specifically grants rights to *all* people *in* the state and affirms 'the democratic values of human dignity, equality and freedom'.[5] By viewing the Refugee Act through this constitutional lens, it 'points towards an interpretive approach which gives effect to South Africa's constitutional and international human rights commitments' (Klinck, 2009:655). Civil society confirmed this constitutional focus in relation to refugee's rights, with a human rights lawyer noting, 'in our submissions we start with constitutional law. This gets more traction'.[6]

In terms of the procedural implementation of the national legal framework at initial registration, the process starts (at least theoretically) when an asylum-seeker makes her/himself known at the point of entry and requests asylum. At this point they receives an asylum transit visa, which allows them to proceed to one of the RROs to deliver the application in person (Vigneswaran, 2008). Alternatively, many forced migrants make their way to urban spaces without being detected via the porous borders. They then decide to either make themselves known to the authorities or remain hidden.[7]

The 1998 Refugee Act establishes the RSD procedure; consequently, once the claim has been lodged, refugees will undergo an RSD interview at an RRO.[8] Throughout the registration process, refugees receive a temporary asylum-seeker permit from an RRO, which regularises their stay and allows free movement within the state until the claim is decided (Vigneswaran, 2008). Regular trips back to the RROs are needed to renew the permits, which are usually granted and extended from one to six months.

The initial reception at the point of registration

The RSD process and the administrative issues and procedures that stem from it dominate the initial registration period. Beyond these procedures, the approach by the government and UNHCR towards refugees at this initial stage of reception can be considered non-interventionist. In contrast to the provisions provided in refugee camps, there is no guarantee of immediate assistance or provision of services by the state or UNHCR. Consequently, even at this initial point of reception, there is very limited access to the global refugee regime in urban areas.[9] Indeed, at its core, beyond procedures aimed at legal registration, state-run reception in South Africa is purposefully hands-off. Nevertheless, the non-action of the state and UN agency within this free-settlement approach to reception does create its own form of welcome. This is to say, it allows refugees to move around the territory and in doing so creates the room for refugees to find political space and other forms of reception at the local and sub-local level.

As confirmed in interviews, and by numerous Department of Home Affairs officials in public events with civil society and academia, South Africa does not have an integration policy – rather it has a policy of 'self-integration'.[10] In many respects, this national approach to reception creates many freedoms (or at least a *sense of* freedom) for refugees in urban spaces. For example, refugees are technically permitted to settle anywhere. Yet as discussed below, the lack of assistance during registration and beyond, coupled with the ability of substantial numbers of migrants to move freely in these spaces, results in this form of 'non-rooted' movement being continually contested by material and ideational factors within state bodies. Chief among these are democratic pressures. Many in civil society see this central element of the national approach to reception as a major failing:

> I think one of the biggest gaps or failures by the state [is] that there is no – as far as I can understand – from a national level, an active and clear coordinated coherent policy, to achieve some kind of social integration.[11]

Due to this policy of non-intervention, refugees generally have to rely on finding reception and ultimately acceptance at the local and sub-local level within local networks and communities, rather than through state structures. In urban areas, refugees 'join the ranks of the urban poor and other migrants (citizens and non-citizens alike)' (Sarkar, 2017:1).[12] These self-adopted approaches to protection and acceptance are nevertheless *de facto* solutions and exist outside of the national legal framework and the global refugee regime.[13] This is the same for refugees with official documentation and others living in these spaces more illicitly.

From this preliminary analysis of the registration stage, two levels of reception emerge. At the national and international level, the government's dominant free-settlement approach (and by extension the global refugee regime) permits refugees a good deal of autonomy. Thus, due to a broadly liberal legal refugee framework that grants key norms of the global regime, refugees are free to move and settle with local communities in urban spaces. Nonetheless (as examined further below) with the requirement to regularly visit RROs to renew permits, constraints on geographical space emerge immediately for refugees during this initial reception.

At the local or sub-local level, refugees are forced to locate forms of localised reception. This is due to the lack of assistance from higher levels of the state, although avoiding state and UN agency structures is often also an active choice. These local forms of reception retain a precarious quality, with the risk of exploitation by state actors (such as immigration officials, police) and other actors (such as a hostile local community) ever present.[14]

Both levels of reception open up some access to the political realm, although this is constantly contested at both the local and national level. As underscored throughout this chapter and the next, there are several key reasons for this restricted access to the political space, including the multitude of exclusion mechanisms at the local and national level that prevent access to services.[15] Another reason is the quality of temporariness attached to refugee status at the national level. According to civil society activists, the idea that refugee reception is intrinsically short term is deeply entrenched within elements of the Department of Home Affairs:

> [There is] a dogmatic view of refugee status [as] inherently temporary. Refugees remain permanent guests on the territory.[16]

As a result, refugees face real difficulties accessing pathways to obtaining permanent status in South Africa (Landau, 2011; Landau et al., 2018): indeed 'you can't become a permanent resident . . . you can get this idea of long-term residence but not permanent, you cannot become a citizen'.[17] Finally, due to the numerous exclusion mechanisms, refugees in cities in South Africa are regularly confined to specific areas of the urban space. Indeed, they have little choice but to live in enclaves of the city, such as informal or illegal settlements and townships (Landau and Freemantle, 2017; Chekero, 2023). Civil society activists and leaders certainly took this view, with a prominent human rights lawyer in Cape Town noting that these enclaves are 'pretty much . . . the only place that asylum-seekers and refugees can get reasonable accommodation – where they can afford to live is in poor communities'.[18]

The free-settlement approach in South Africa

This section considers how the initial registration of refugees in urban spaces in South Africa has traditionally been implemented, and how it shapes refugees' attempts to pursue their own personal and economic aims. Utilising these findings, it examines why the host state: (1) implemented the free-settlement approach in the early 1990s; and (2) has generally maintained the same approach during the period since. It is evident from the empirical data that the motivations behind the adoption and implementation of a free-settlement reception policy are more complex than simply deriving from a sense of obligation to the legal commitments set out in national and international law. Indeed, the reception policy at the national level is heavily influenced by numerous key material and ideational factors originating from various levels of analysis (regional, sub-regional, national and local).

Material factor: contemporary movements into South Africa

The character and make-up of cross-border movement into post-apartheid South Africa has been one of the factors that has enabled the maintenance of a free-settlement reception approach. Specifically, the state has not experienced the levels of influx of refugees seen in other states on the continent, where refugee camps have been set up to respond to a large-scale emergency. Certainly, in Africa, the adoption of encampment policies remains a popular approach to receiving large numbers of refugees simultaneously (Crisp, 2003; Schmidt, 2003).

During deliberations surrounding the drafting of the 1998 Refugee Act, refugee camps were considered as the model for South Africa, but it was agreed that they would only be deployed in times of mass influx (Jenkins and de la Hunt, 2011).[19] This option for setting up camps and restricting movement in times of emergency or mass influx is common in national refugee legislation on the continent (Maple, 2016). As examined in Chapter 2, long-term refugee camps often start life as a short-term humanitarian response to a mass influx of refugees. Over time, with return deemed unrealistic, such emergency camps often then transform into protracted encampment situations. Moreover, once this new form of reception is in place, the official or dominant state reception policy often switches to upholding encampment as the model for all future refugees (regardless of the nature and make-up of the movement).[20]

The last forty years have witnessed numerous examples of a mass exodus in Africa. This includes (but is not limited to) the hundreds of thousands leaving for Sudan and Somalia during the Ethiopian famine of 1983–5, the hundreds of thousands of Hutu refugees fleeing Burundi in 1993 (ICG, 1999), and the millions fleeing South Sudan in 2016. At the sub-regional level, however, Southern Africa has not seen the levels of mass expulsion or exodus observed in neighbouring sub-regions, such as central and eastern Africa. For this reason, it is debatable – with the possible exception of the arrival of refugees from Mozambique during the 1980s – whether South Africa has experienced what would amount to a contemporary understanding of a mass influx of refugees (Jenkins and de la Hunt, 2011).

The movement of refugees and other forced migrants into South Africa has naturally fluctuated since the adoption of the global refugee regime into the national legal framework (Segatti, 2011). Nonetheless, patterns of refugee movement, while certainly increasing substantially at times, have not turned into urgent mass movements unfolding over short periods of time as seen elsewhere on the continent. This is due to a number of key reasons: (1) South Africa's geographical location; (2) its willingness to grant freedom of movement, coupled with perceived economic opportunities; (3) the political and economic reasons fuelling the large exodus of Zimbabweans over the last twenty years to neighbouring countries; and (4) the lack of any major incidences of unrest caused by genocide, war or extreme climatic events in immediate neighbouring states since the late 1990s.

This analysis is borne out in the limited data available on asylum applications in South Africa, which shows that the majority of refugees in the state (if we set aside Zimbabwe for the moment) come from the Horn of Africa, the Great Lakes and a small but significant number from South Asian countries (World Bank, 2018a).[21] The available data suggests that refugees who reach South Africa regularly travel long distances and pass through numerous countries before reaching the territory (World Bank, 2018a). For these reasons, the movement of refugees and forced migrations into South Africa has effectively been held in check since the introduction of the global refugee regime and its core norms into the state. That is to say, refugee movement into the state has been curbed by external geopolitical factors in the sub-region and continent. As a result, there has not been (at least until recently) a pressing need to consider an alternative reception approach aimed at substantially managing or controlling refugee movement into the interior, and by extension into the urban space.

It would be disingenuous to say, however, that patterns of refugee and forced migration movement into South Africa have not altered considerably over the last twenty years. Since the early 2000s, the country has witnessed the in-migration of hundreds of thousands of Zimbabweans (Betts, 2013a, 2014; Thebe, 2017). For example, persons applying for asylum in South Africa rose from 4,860 in 2001 to 364,638 in 2009 (Landau et al., 2011). In 2009, South Africa received the most asylum applications globally (at over 300,000) (Carciotto, 2018). Deemed as a crisis, these numbers elicited a reaction, with the state offering around 200,000 Zimbabweans the option of applying for a four-year Zimbabwean Dispensation Permit (ZDP) (Carciotto, 2018). Asylum figures increased further in the following years, with UNHCR reporting that Zimbabweans accounted for over half of the 778,600 new asylum applications in South Africa between 2008 and 2012 (UNHCR, 2015a).[22]

Yet, broadly speaking these movements over the past two decades, reflecting the long-term economic upheaval and political unrest in Zimbabwe, have been sporadic (if substantial), rather than urgent and sudden as seen in neighbouring countries when large populations flee violence or civil war. For example, by 2018 a human rights lawyer based in Musina (a major border post between South Africa and Zimbabwe) observed that the movement of migrants from Zimbabwe had almost stopped:

> The majority of Zimbabweans aren't coming through because there is a new government there, so there is a feeling and understanding that the political situation is becoming stable.[23]

Yet, by 2019, with little sign of the economy improving under the new government in Zimbabwe the numbers had again increased. This continuing fluctuation in refugee and migrant flows between the two countries over the past twenty years aptly illustrates how the types of migration events triggered by the situation in Zimbabwe typically result in slower patterns and lower numbers of movement (while still considerable) than those consequent to sudden outbreaks of civil unrest.[24]

These dispersed movements into South Africa from Zimbabwe have undeniably put huge pressure onto the national asylum system (Amit, 2011). Nevertheless, ultimately these movements have not threatened the maintenance of the free-settlement approach, with high-level ministerial discussions about the adoption of camp policies remaining in the background. This is particularly important combined with the practical reality, and the political perception, that urban spaces such as Johannesburg and Cape Town are equipped to be able to absorb large numbers of new migrants. Simply put, at least up until 2011, the movement of refugees and other migrants into urban spaces was generally not seen as a destabilising threat to either cities or to the nation.

In addition, direct security concerns relating to the cross-border movement from Zimbabwe are not deemed as an urgent priority due to the make-up of the incoming population. Most forced migrants coming into South Africa from its immediate neighbour have been due to individual persecution based on political beliefs and increasingly also for a mixture of socio-economic reasons. This was the impression given by a human rights lawyer in Cape Town: 'while we saw persecution and beatings in 2007, [it] is not what we see now, it's more of an economic issue in Zimbabwe'.[25] As a consequence, there has been little risk of armed elements infiltrating the forced migrant population. Thus, during the early 2000s, there were no urgent calls to contain the whole population of incomers at the border.

In summary, the geopolitical situation in Southern Africa (and further afield on the continent) has acted as a restraint on the movement of refugees into South Africa. Large amounts of unchecked movement, particularly into urban spaces, is always likely to elicit a national reaction. Until very recently, the make-up and patterns of movement into South Africa have not necessitated additional externally imposed control. Indeed, even the number of migrants and refugees from Zimbabwe, while considerable, have been steady rather than urgent and sudden.

Nevertheless, over the last few decades, with numbers in urban spaces continuing to increase in South Africa, the government has felt the need to react in stronger terms to regulate this movement. Indeed, the numbers have continued to grow to levels now deemed a threat to the stability of the nation (Amit, 2015). Over the last twelve years, refugees and other forced migrants in South Africa are being seen almost exclusively through a security lens, with the urban space being slowly restricted as a site of reception.

Ideational and institutional factors: the lack of international involvement in the initial stage of refugee reception in South Africa

In 1996, South Africa became a member state of the global refugee regime and, unlike many of its neighbours who had adopted encampment reception policies around that time, it elected not to place any restrictions on the right to freedom of movement. In maintaining this commitment over subsequent years, the state has permitted increasing numbers of refugees and asylum-seekers to access densely populated urban spaces. As a result, the state has had to establish, fund and staff numerous RROs in major urban hubs to deal with the various bureaucratic procedures surrounding the registration of increasing numbers of asylum applications.

States in Africa regularly rely on the global refugee regime (via its key actor, UNHCR) to assist with capacity issues relating to the hosting of refugees. Yet membership of the global regime has not been matched by an increased involvement of UN agencies in South Africa. Indeed, the empirical evidence reveals a strained relationship between the state and UNHCR, which has resulted in a lack of substantive involvement by UN agencies at this initial stage of reception. In particular, since the late 2000s, UNHCR has largely been reduced to a capacity building and public education role.[26] At one level of analysis, as noted by a former employee at the Department of Home Affairs, this is a logical step:

In a place like South Africa where we have a functioning democratic government or functioning government, then the organisation's role . . . so they take a step back not dealing with half of the issues – that is not their role in an urban situation.[27]

The assumption that the agency does not have a role in urban spaces in South Africa, as held by elements within the Department of Home Affairs (and indeed by some high-ranking officials in UNHCR South Africa), will be analysed further in Chapter 7. The notion that UNHCR takes a step back and that a democratic host state should be running (and be entirely responsible for) its own reception policy, including an individualised RSD procedure, is rational and consistent with international norms (Maple et al., 2023). However, it is equally apparent that this reduced role for UNHCR was not a decision made entirely by the UN agency itself. Rather, as confirmed by a UNHCR officer, it was a decision by the South African government, steered by the ANC's habitual insistence on keeping UN agencies and other international organisations very much at arm's length.[28]

The reluctance by the state to permit international agencies a more prominent role within the territory stems from historical ideational structures in place since the old apartheid regime. Indeed, there remains a general sense of mistrust by political elites inside the ruling political settlement concerning international organisations, particularly those within the UN structure. This has its roots in the perception of inactivity and lack of support during the ANC's struggles against the former apartheid government.[29] As a result, since the dismantling of the old regime, there has been a general unwillingness to listen to advice or accept assistance on the territory from UN agencies.

By not permitting UNHCR and other UN bodies greater influence within the national refugee framework, it means that any shift of refugee reception policy (to, say, an encampment policy) could potentially fall entirely on the state to fund and implement. This contrasts sharply with neighbouring states who already house refugees in refugee camps, as they generally see these populations as the responsibility of the international community. For South Africa to switch from the current system (where refugees are expected to fend for themselves as soon as they cross the border) to an encampment policy (where refugees are often entirely reliant on aid), would require a great deal more state investment. It would also entail a far greater presence and influence of UN agencies on the territory, which is something that the political elites in South Africa, at least in recent history, seem unwilling to accept.

In the context of post-apartheid South Africa, and considering the average length of displacement seen globally today, the current free-settlement approach to refugee reception remains less of a strain on national resources than an alternative encampment policy.[30] This is a powerful argument when other factors are taken into consideration, such as (1) the lack of engagement by the state in refugees' lives beyond the registration process at the RROs, and (2) a current national registration system that is failing to function properly, in large part due to a lack of adequate funding and resources by the government.[31] This lack of engagement and resources would be harder to justify within the distinct spatial and visual boundaries of the refugee camp. In sharp contrast to this, refugees and asylum-seekers in the urban space regularly merge (and/or 'disappear') into larger poor neighbourhoods.

This stance by South Africa towards UN institutions brings mixed responses from UNHCR. There is understandable gratitude from within UNHCR for the state's reception approach and its refusal, to date, to switch to an encampment policy. Yet, the attitude at the national level towards the presence of UN agencies on the territory has resulted in what can best be described as a tense working relationship between the state and UNHCR. Consequently, there is marked frustration within UNHCR South Africa and UNHCR Southern Africa about the way the state has kept international organisations at arm's length. A prominent human rights lawyer in Pretoria suggested that the agency had effectively been 'shut out' by the government.[32]

As examined below, the recent regressive changes in refugee reception policy in the urban space in South Africa have drawn little in the way of public discourse by UNHCR.[33] This diplomatic approach is in part understandable. As Forsythe (2001:34) notes, the agency regularly has the delicate task of engaging with the political process of influencing governments to make appropriate choices, without running the risk of being 'charged with political interference in the domestic affairs of states'.[34] Equally, the contemporary historical background and the ideational factors that this fraught history has generated within sections of the ruling political settlement in South Africa adds additional layers of complexity for the UN agency to navigate.

Many within civil society and academia nevertheless feel that the recent 'backward' shift in relation to the reception of refugees in South Africa needs a stronger reaction from the agency. Below is a representative response from an NGO official when asked about UNHCR in South Africa:

> UNHCR . . . has been fairly disappointing and whenever we have asked them to take a stand – a stronger position with the

government, the response that we received is that 'we are a guest of the government, we are here to assist the government and we cannot take on an aggressive approach' – which you know, their job is to protect refugees and they do not seem to be doing a fantastic job of that.[35]

Finally, state engagement with the 2018 Global Compact on Refugees had hinted at a change in approach, with the Department of Home Affairs appearing to show a renewed willingness to engage with UNHCR. For example, the state made a pledge at the Global Refugee Forum in 2019, to reduce the number of outstanding national asylum claims. From this, the 'Backlog Project' was created, with Home Affairs and UNHCR signing an agreement in March 2021 (PMG, 2021), which committed the department to spend USD 2.6 million and UNHCR USD 7 million on the project (UNHCR, 2021a). However, as of 2023, little government money had been spent. In turn, the restrictive amendments to the 1998 Refugee Act which came into force after the pledges were made severely undermine these international commitments (Khan and Rayner, 2020).

In conclusion, the combination of historical and ideational factors that have kept the UN at arm's length in-country, and the continued institutional contestation between government departments and UNHCR, has left the agency little to do in terms of refugee reception in South Africa.[36] This 'shutting out' of the agency has left key informants remarking that it is 'unclear at the moment the role UNHCR is playing, if any'.[37] This complex and strained relationship re-emphasises the dominant role the government has in setting and implementing policy on refugee and forced migrant reception. Thus capacity concerns, combined with limited interest in increasing the involvement of UN agencies on the territory, create powerful motivations for maintaining the self-settlement approach (rather than a more resource-heavy and visible camp-based approach).

Ideational factors: the process of nation-building

In analysing the maintenance of a free-settlement approach to refugee reception in South Africa, this final section concentrates on key ideational factors that permeate throughout government departments at the national level. These include the ideational importance of the National Constitution, comparisons between creating refugee camps and the previous actions of the apartheid regime, and the continued (if strained) relevance of pan-Africanism. Grouped together, these factors can be understood as part of the process of nation-building and of the ANC's vision of post-apartheid South Africa.

Taking these factors in turn, the National Constitution in South Africa retains notable standing amongst government officials, with its commitment to human rights and regional cooperation. As Landau and Segatti (2009) note, the preamble explicitly promises that 'South Africa belongs to all who live in it'. By making no reference to citizenship status, the Constitution grants rights for all persons on the territory. Indeed, as previously noted, the Bill of Rights has been a powerful tool for advocates of refugee rights, including the right to work. Thus, any attempt by the government to implement refugee camps, given the severe restriction on human rights that this would entail, would sit in stark contrast to the legal and ideational aspirations committed to at the beginning of post-apartheid South Africa. For example, in relation to the current proposal for processing centres at the border, civil society actors were quick to mention the constitutional fight that would ensue.

> The constitution talks about freedom of movement for everyone . . . it will end up being litigation I'm sure. In terms of the constitution, they will have to argue why . . . you are limiting a right for everyone – a constitutional right.[38]

Complications and contestation do nevertheless arise when attempting to implement particular obligations contained within the Constitution (such as access to health) for refugees and other migrants. This is because many guaranteed rights are not accessible to most nationals (Misago, 2016). Equally, as made evident by the high-level discussions over the border processing centres, an ideational commitment to granting key rights to asylum-seekers and refugees is far from ubiquitous within national-level state entities that deal with refugees. As discussed next, contestation between conflicting ideational approaches regularly occurs within the government.

Turning to the second ideational factor, there are some within the Department of Home Affairs who see uncomfortable parallels between the creation and use of refugee camps and the old apartheid regime. Specifically, the idea of moving African brothers and sisters into confined spaces is reminiscent of the legacy of segregation during the apartheid era. Many ANC members were placed in 'homelands' which were areas designated for black South Africans and organised along ethnic lines during the first half of the last century, as well as forced relocation to these areas in the 1960s from other areas of the state.[39] Thus, many feel that any move towards encampment would be a dangerous backwards step.

Interviewees noted, however, that these views were not universal within government departments. There are many key officials in the government, particularly in the Department of Home Affairs, who were moved into 'resettlement' or 'relocation' camps in the homelands during the apartheid regime. Their attitude now is that if they went through it and survived, 'why can't others?' Thus, discrepancies and contradictory approaches exist at the institutional level, with security and stability-focused views held in the Department of Home Affairs conflicting with more historical and normative-based sentiments. High-level officials concerned by the perceived insecurity and instability caused by the increase in the movement of people into urban areas are behind recent pushes for camp-based reception policies for refugees at the border.

The final ideational factor is the role of pan-Africanism in the development and maintenance of the current reception policies in South Africa. Traditionally states in Africa were generous in hosting refugees, with neighbours fleeing colonial oppression readily welcomed due to feelings of solidarity. This approach was common on the continent until the 1990s when a broad shift to democracy occurred. Since then, feelings of pan-Africanism have decreased significantly, in part because refugee movements are no longer due to violence stemming from liberation struggles from colonial rule and white minority government repression (Rutinwa, 1999). South Africa has broadly followed these trends, with pan-Africanism slowly being replaced with nationalistic and xenophobic views within state bodies and the wider voting population (Palmary, 2002; Misago, 2016; Misago, et al., 2010). As explained via the 'democracy-asylum' nexus, the trend for democratic structures to accompany increased anti-migrant feelings among local populations (particularly in urban conurbations where there is competition for scarce social goods such as housing and employment) has meant reception policies have become markedly less generous (Crisp, 2000). Indeed, the increase of refugee and other migrant movements into South Africa has created negative democratic loops, whereby the state is politically motivated to move away from ideals based on solidarity and pan-Africanism to ones framing migrants as a 'problem'.[40]

Nevertheless, in post-apartheid South Africa, there have been some instances when the national approach has bucked this regional trend,[41] and officials within international agencies still regard South Africa as broadly welcoming to its African sisters and brothers who arrive as refugees from neighbouring states. To some commentators, the state has even gone beyond its commitments under the global refugee regime by stretching the key regime norm of *non-refoulement* to include forced migrants from Zimbabwe who may not strictly fall under the 1951 Refugee Convention or the 1969 OAU Refugee Convention refugee definitions (Betts and Kaytaz, 2009; Betts, 2013a).

For example, as introduced above, in 2009, the state offered around 200,000 Zimbabweans who were living in South Africa the option of applying for a four-year exemption permit: the ZDP. Since then, the permits have been extended – broadly speaking – every four years, with the original permits replaced by the Zimbabwean Special Dispensation Permit (ZSP) and then the Zimbabwean Exemption Permit (ZEP) (Maple, 2023). During interviews with civil society actors, the topic of these temporary visas gave rise to the rare occasions when the Department of Home Affairs was praised. Many (albeit reluctantly) conceded that these policies were a 'good thing' in relation to the ongoing protection of forced migrants.

A form of legal protection offered by a host state is certainly better than no protection at all. Indeed, without the permits, individuals who refused to leave South Africa would be forced to live deeply precarious lives without legal status. Consequently, to some observers, the ZDPs show how the state is prepared to sometimes stretch its welcome to include broad groups of migrants from neighbouring states (Betts, 2013a).[42] An alternative view, however, is that rather than this being an example of a state 'stretching' key refugee regime norms, the permits are an attempt at 'regime shifting' (Carciotto, 2018): through this process, South Africa has effectively shifted refugees from one mobility regime (the national refugee regime) to another (the national immigration regime). As a result, the migrants lose the potential human rights attached to the global refugee regime (Carciotto, 2018; Maple, 2023).

Regardless of how one views the exact motives of the state, this alternative hospitality towards forced migrants from Zimbabwe is, however, still a form of *extended reception* and thus remains conditional and temporary in nature. The permits are inherently short term, meaning that when they expire (every three to four years), migrants will face renewed anxiety about their continued presence on the territory.[43] For many, the renewal in 2017 was the third time the temporary permits had been renewed without the opportunity of alternative pathways to accessing permanent residency.[44] Thus, this prolonged form of reception is framed by some as 'frozen futures' (*Daily Maverick*, 2020a).[45]

In conclusion, within the government, ideational importance is placed on being a beacon for human rights and democratic values on the continent. This framing stems from the post-apartheid nation-building, reconciliation and unity processes instigated by the ANC (Abrahams, 2016), the aim of which was to create a cosmopolitan and inclusive democracy

(Polzer and Segatti, 2011). Within this context, the suggestion of containing refugees and forced migrants in refugee camps naturally evokes painful comparisons with the previous apartheid regime. Yet equally, these are far from universally shared beliefs within national-level structures. Indeed, almost paradoxically, these ideational factors are regularly contested by opposing democratic pressures within the government systems. The pressures against are motivated by a voting public, opposition political parties and media, who are now moving away from the ideals based on pan-Africanism and universal human rights in the face of rising poverty and inequality (Segatti, 2011). Certainly, the profound contradiction of pan-Africanism in South Africa today is the growth of xenophobic violence (African Arguments, 2015).

The first half of this chapter has brought together analysis on why South Africa chooses a free-settlement approach to the reception of refugees and why this has been maintained, even though the refugee camp remains the dominant reception approach in the sub-region. Nevertheless, an examination of key material, ideational and ideational factors has also highlighted ongoing tensions and contestation at the national level in relation to how refugees are received. The next section develops the analysis further by investigating major shifts in policy seen during the initial registration period of reception, since 2011.

Reframing free-settlement reception: South Africa 2011 to present

Based on the empirical data collected and contemporary primary source policy papers, it is evident that refugee reception within South Africa has been undergoing a radical reframing over the last twelve years.[46] This has seen reception slowly move away from ideals based on universal human rights when the 1998 Refugee Act was first drafted, to a more migration management approach, grounded in security and in/stability concerns (Moyo, Sebba and Zanker, 2021; Amit, 2012; Carciotto and Mavura, 2022). Indeed, a reimagining of *all* African migrants in South Africa (with the exception of highly skilled workers) as illegal aliens, coupled with small but incremental regressive legal and policy moves at the national and local level, are having a profound effect on the reception afforded to refugees at this initial stage of reception. As a human rights lawyer in Cape Town noted, this has been a slow but deliberate attempt to frustrate, create barriers and ultimately shrink the asylum space.[47] This shift in policy is naturally shaping how refugees settle and engage with local communities and markets – particularly within major urban spaces. Furthermore, this reframing through shifts in policy and practice is now feeding back up to the legislative branch of the government.

Material and institutional factors affecting the shift in refugee policy

This section investigates the interconnected material and institutional factors that have created a situation whereby shifts in policy towards a more restrictive approach to refugee reception have been made possible. These include material concerns over capacity, institutional contestation between different governmental departments at the national level and increased security concerns that arise with increased movement on the territory. Each element represents a legitimate concern for the state, but also intersects with other factors (discussed below), including the increased securitisation of all immigrant movement in South Africa and overarching concerns about in/stability. When combined, they accentuate a dysfunctional national refugee reception policy and, in turn, a constantly shifting reception for refugees on the ground in South Africa.

Firstly, on a material level, the Department of Home Affairs has consistently struggled with capacity issues (in terms of resources and funding) when responding to the needs and demands of asylum-seekers and refugees during registration in South Africa. A senior barrister in Cape Town, when talking about the registration process, observed: 'it's very hit or miss and I think that's got to do with . . . capacity and management of Home Affairs . . . it's a capacity issue'.[48] The exact number of forced migrants in South Africa is unknown and regularly contested (Mthembu-Salter et al., 2014). Nevertheless, it is evident that the population of all types of forced migrants is at a sizeable level.[49] In addition, since the early 2000s, the number of asylum-seeker claims in South Africa has increased markedly. The sheer quantity of asylum applications, in conjunction with a general lack of government resources at the state and local level, and poor management within the Department of Home Affairs, has produced extensive (and now infamous) backlogs in asylum claims.[50] As observed by a civil society leader:

> The problem is the department [Home Affairs] is so far behind. There [is] such a large backlog, people are waiting for years and years for the adjudication. Therefore the system is broken down at the moment.[51]

The lack of capacity and training also contributes to poor quality decisions and corruption (Mfubu, 2018).[52] A manager of an implementing partner of

UNHCR confirmed: 'look, there is corruption in the system . . . even the Department of Home Affairs acknowledges that'.[53] In fact, many key members of civil society see the registration procedures as entirely broken. Interviews with civil society and refugee groups noted numerous examples of a dysfunctional system. These included vast delays for applicants, a general lack of information given by officials, lost paperwork and people needing to continually reapply for status or claims due to bureaucratic errors or failings. These kinds of delays result in most applicants waiting on decisions well beyond the designated response time of six months, with some waiting years or decades before a decision is made.

Stemming from the capacity issues within the Department of Home Affairs, there are stark differences in the implementation of refugee policy at the RROs. These include variations in information given to asylum-seekers and refugees by officials and differences in understanding relating to correct documentation and procedure. A human rights lawyer suggested there is 'no standard operating procedure at Home Affairs'.[54] The same lawyer observed that 'people will go down there and be refused, but you don't get anything in writing as to why they were refused. Largely up to the manager at the time it seems like'.[55] A refugee community leader explained that because of the constant alterations to the policy on documentation, they must update their clients daily via WhatsApp:

> The biggest issue is lack of information on the ground . . . coming from the Department of Home Affairs . . . because the policy of documentation is changing every day . . . when you meet one official and they say 'x' and then you meet another Home Affairs official and they say 'y'.[56]

This experience of idiosyncratic and arbitrary decision-making, and conflicting information, highlights how reception in the urban space is imbued with a sense of temporariness for refugees. As examined further in the next chapter, the reception offered to refugees reflects ongoing processes of negotiation and renegotiation between various key actors. During these 'negotiations', different factors interact, reinforce and/or contest with each other to create a given response, with refugees remaining as temporary guests within these volatile political spaces.

Secondly, connected to this capacity issue is the increased institutional friction between the national refugee framework and the national immigration framework. Since the introduction of the global refugee regime into national law in South Africa, tensions and contestation have existed between the two systems.[57] These pressures have never been satisfactorily resolved, indeed they have increased in the last decade, with increasing numbers of migrants using the national refugee framework to regularise their stay on the territory.

This national refugee/migration nexus was made explicit with the introduction of the Immigration Act (No. 11) 2002 ('2002 Immigration Act') and its accompanying regulations. These legal instruments created a restrictive immigration regime that assisted highly skilled immigrants but closed immigration to most – if not all – 'low skilled' workers (Johnson, 2015).[58] A glaring imbalance was therefore created between the 'restrictive immigration framework and the liberal refugee protection framework' (Johnson and Carciotto, 2018). Indeed, a former manager in the Department of Home Affairs believes the current failings in the system can, at least in part, be put down to a sub-regional 'migrant issue' rather than a 'refugee problem':

> It's a need to regulate mixed migration . . . many of them don't necessarily have asylum claims but they want to be documented . . . and because the asylum permit gives them the right to work, it is the easiest way to be documented. The alternative is a convoluted visa application process that you probably wouldn't qualify for anyway.[59]

In a sub-region with substantial numbers of all forms of cross-border movement, the huge disparity between the different governance frameworks (for example, in terms of access at the point of initial registration) has left certain groups of migrants with little option. Thus, many migrants and forced migrants use the refugee national framework as an access point to the interior (Moyo and Zanker, 2020). Nevertheless, the narrative used to explain these issues, as illustrated in the above quote, remains problematic, albeit popular. For example, when asked about the current problems with the asylum system, a high-ranking official in UNHCR South Africa observed:

> The regime in South Africa has been very good. Regrettably this situation has been abused by many people.[60]

This prevalent explanation engages with the issues but frames the migrant *her/himself* as the source of the issue, rather than the underlying material, institutional and ideational problems within the two migration systems.

The third material factor that has created a shift in policy relates to security issues. Since the early 2000s, the increasing numbers of refugees and forced migrants coming into the state, coupled with a non-functioning registration process and the granting of freedom of movement and the right to work to all asylum-seekers, have inevitably heightened national security concerns. These include direct and indirect security issues, for example, fears over who exactly is coming into the state and applying for asylum. One civil society leader commented: 'anyone can apply for asylum, we don't know who they are, you don't need passports or papers'.[61] In addition, indirect security issues also emerge in urban spaces due to insecurity caused by large numbers of new cross-border migrants moving into cities with scarce resources (WEF, 2017).

Legitimate security and capacity concerns in South Africa stem in large part from the two entirely dysfunctional national frameworks related to migrant reception. Yet, irrespective of these facts, as the numbers of migrants continue to increase in urban spaces, the arrival and movement of all international migrants are beginning to be seen predominantly through a security lens.[62]

Ideational factor affecting the shift in refugee policy: the increased securitisation of refugees in South Africa

In combination with the salient material and institutional factors set out above, there has been a marked ideational shift within key elements of the Department of Home Affairs and other branches of the government on how to approach the reception of refugees.[63] Specifically, the language of security is now filtering into all aspects of national policy surrounding refugee matters. This has culminated in the ruling party, and major opposition political parties in South Africa, essentially framing all refugee and African migrant movement as a security issue.

Post-apartheid South Africa continues to try and distance itself from the errors of the past, with a commitment to democracy and universal human rights. Nevertheless, the present government still takes several cues in relation to foreign policy, and in particular immigration matters, from the former apartheid regime. As Musuva (2015) and Vale (2002) both examine, the current national discourse on security (as set out below) can be traced to the former apartheid regime with its emphasis on control and surveillance. Both authors suggest this is still seen as the best policy option in dealing with the migration 'problem' (Musuva, 2015).

The current approach to refugees by the Department of Home Affairs has been built from this powerful historical legacy. Yet, the increased movement of refugees into South Africa, in combination with the factors set out in the previous section, has intensified and developed this security lens further still. The department, over the last twelve years, has adopted an increasingly reductive discourse in relation to the asylum-seeker and refugee 'problem'. Building on the narrative of 'people abusing the system' set out above, this discourse goes further by essentially conceptualising all 'individuals in the asylum system as illegitimate claimants without protection needs' (Johnson and Carciotto, 2018:169).

This framing is repeated in the 2016 Green Paper on International Migration (DHA, 2016a). Sections of the policy paper that refer to refugees and asylum-seekers are continually framed by the statistic that 90 per cent of asylum-seekers who apply for asylum do not qualify, the inference being that most asylum-seekers are economic migrants or criminals infiltrating the system. Indeed, there are continued references to criminal syndicates from Africa and Asia coming into the country, with no supporting statistics or evidence.[64] As a result of these 'bogus' claims, 'real' refugees are being stopped from gaining access to protection.[65]

The adoption of this cognitive framework in the Green Paper and other policy documents also implies a consensus within the political space regarding these issues.[66] Accordingly, there is no room for debate over the 'truths' being asserted – even though the empirical evidence set out above shows ongoing contestation taking place inside the government over the correct form of reception given to refugees. This 'fallacy of division' results in statements such as 'massive abuses within the system mean "genuine refugees" are unable to gain access to protection' being made as fundamental truths.[67]

These 'truths' have either informed policy or have merged with policy to the point where many key informants suggest there is now a deliberate policy within Home Affairs to automatically reject asylum applications at the first stage. As a human rights lawyer suggested, the high rejection rates are now reinforcing and confirming this 'truth'.[68] This 'manufacture of illegality' (Essed and Wesenbeek, 2004:68) via high levels of rejection of asylum claims and the construction of forced migrants as illegal migrants, can be understood as an attempt by the Department of Home Affairs to detach refugees from global and national refugee frameworks, and in doing so shrink the asylum space.

This reframing of refugees as illegal migrants or criminals has spread well beyond key elements of the government. Indeed, the ruling political settlement has almost universal approval for a securitisation-style approach to immigration:

> Here there isn't that kind of friction around migration. So there isn't a political party whose constituency advocates for the migrant . . . so even with many of the amendments they just rubber-stamp it to run through Parliament because nobody even in opposition looks at it quite critically.[69]

The data presented suggests that the motivation for the increasingly widespread use of a security lens stems from the belief that the number of refugees and international migrants in urban spaces is reaching unstable levels. As set out above, the current ruling political settlement essentially inherited a security lens for understanding migration from the old apartheid regime. Since the 1990s however, the motivation for using the lens has shifted from apparent direct security concerns to a broader preoccupation around maintaining stability. Analysis in this chapter has continued to emphasise how the state has become increasingly concerned with the perceived instability that migrant movement is bringing into the urban space. This instability emerges from concerns relating to capacity and insecurity (for example, strains on services and labour markets), as well as more democratic fears about the growing tensions within the voting public.[70]

Thus, the 'problem' of refugees and low skilled migrants, particularly in urban spaces, can be understood conceptually as instability. This in turn suggests that securitisation is a *localised process*, which is prone to change and realignment over time (Donnelly, 2017). Motivations for adopting the lens will evolve given the specific context and contemporary factors. However, regardless of the reason for the increased securitisation of refugee movement, the result is typically the same for the refugee: a progressively hostile reception and a shrinking asylum space.

Exclusion from the urban space

The previous subsections have demonstrated that a combination of material and institutional factors as well as ideational and discursive approaches based on security and stability concerns, are producing key policy changes. These in turn are fundamentally reframing refugee reception in South Africa. As changes in policy and practice increase and work their way into the national legal framework, a new form of conditional reception is emerging which includes increased checks and restraints on movement – particularly in relation to access to urban spaces. Indeed, the reception of refugees in South Africa is slowly shifting away from a free-settlement policy towards something resembling encampment.

One of the key provisions of the 1998 Refugee Act was the creation of Refugee Reception Offices (RROs) (Khan and Lee, 2018). These have traditionally been in large urban centres such as Johannesburg, Pretoria, Cape Town, Durban and Port Elizabeth (Moyo and Botha, 2022). By granting freedom of movement to refugees, and by extension access to the urban space, the primary point of contact between refugees and the state during the registration and post-registration stages occurs at these RROs (Johnson and Carciotto, 2018). Certainly, the centres, which are run by the Department of Home Affairs, are the main entry point for accessing the refugee regime, regularising refugees' status and legitimising their presence in an urban space.

The renewal time frames for asylum permits were created when the drafters of the legislation 'envisioned that the application process would finally be adjudicated within 180 days of the application being made' (Khan and Lee, 2018:1269). In reality, the asylum process (and by extension the registration stage of reception) can often take years, with refugees still expected to visit an RRO every one to six months to renew their temporary permits. As such, the urban RROs are 'essential to the functioning of the system and for accessing the protection it affords' (Khan and Lee, 2018:1271). Therefore, any restrictions on accessing the RROs – particularly in urban areas – fundamentally alters the spatial dimensions of refugee reception and the ability of refugees to pursue their own personal and economic aims.

Since 2011, the Department of Home Affairs has closed the RROs in Cape Town, Johannesburg and Port Elizabeth. Moreover, between 2011 and 2020 only three RROs were operating correctly, with others either closed or partly closed (Moyo, Sebba and Zanker, 2021). This occurred despite there being a need for offices in large urban centres. Judicial court orders from the high courts and the Supreme Court of Appeals demanding the reopening of centres have regularly been ignored. Indeed, even a Constitutional Court order to reopen the centres went unheeded (Crush et al., 2017).[71] The result of the closures has meant that asylum-seekers are forced to choose between moving closer to the remaining RROs (far from key urban areas), allowing their documentation to expire or repeatedly travelling long distances to register and receive assistance.[72]

> Where you're closing offices left, right and centre, you're funnelling people into having an out of dated permit . . . if I have to travel up to Durban, to get my permit every three to six months . . . [is your] employer going to allow you to, to take that much leave given it's every three months?[73]

The policy of closing key urban centres ultimately means refugees' ability to freely move around the interior is seriously curtailed. Specifically, due to the often overwhelming practical and material implications of repeated long journeys to the remaining centres, access to specific key urban spaces has been severely reduced. This is seen by civil society leaders as a deliberate attempt to keep refugees out of 'crowded' cities like Johannesburg and Cape Town. As one civil society leader noted, 'this was an attempt to limit freedom of movement. Reducing access to the interior ... [based on a] security argument to keep people at the borders'.[74] In addition, a human rights advisor commented, 'there was no real reason to close the Johannesburg office, it was operating quite fine ... the only reason to really close it was to fit into this plan'.[75]

Finally, this reframing through ideational shifts and changes in policy and practice is ultimately feeding up to the legislative branch of the government. New amendments to the national legal refugee framework (as introduced above), which came into force in January 2020, will restrict the asylum space further and reduce access to the urban space (Ziegler, 2020). For example, the new proposed asylum-seeker registration forms ask questions about asylum-seekers' bank accounts, wage slips and employment history. This information should be immaterial to RSD proceedings. In fact, these questions are more suited to visa applications for labour migration and fit with broader themes of national interest. Furthermore, the 2017 Refugee Amendment Bill amends Section 1 of the Refugee Act to change the definition of an 'asylum-seeker permit' to include the term 'visa' in order 'to align it with the Immigration Act 13 of 2002, as amended'.[76]

The Amendment Bill also removes the right to seek and attain employment for asylum-seekers. Key informants saw these amendments as 'a direct response to get lower numbers of asylum-seekers',[77] or the shrinking of the asylum space. These amendments will especially affect asylum-seekers at the point of registration. With no state-run assistance programmes and now no legal way of earning money, these individuals will need to rely on the informal economy, local networks, civil society and faith-based organisations to locate immediate shelter and basic necessities.

Leading figures in civil society see the ultimate objective of these incremental changes (or as one leader coined it, 'the deterioration of asylum') as the removal of asylum-seekers from the urban space to the border areas.[78] Indeed, this overarching change to the spatial dynamics of reception in South Africa is explicitly set out in the Green Paper, with the proposed creation of processing centres at the border. Under these proposals, asylum-seekers would be processed at the point of entry in shorter timeframes, with refugees then given access to the interior (and granted key norms within the regime).[79] If implemented correctly, the processing centres are therefore unlikely to break international or national law. Yet, as noted by a prominent human rights lawyer, in proposing this approach, the Department of Home Affairs is presuming a level of efficiency they have not been able to deliver in the last thirty years.[80] Without additional investment by the state and the international community, there is a high risk that all refugees under this proposal could remain indefinitely in encampment-like situations or informal townships near the border.

The initial stage of reception in South Africa: a slow decline to a conditional and restrictive approach

In terms of initial welcome in South Africa, refugees have traditionally been permitted to move freely around the country almost immediately from the point of registration. The initial reception granted to refugees via the free-settlement approach, while remaining conditional in many regards, can therefore be seen within the context of the sub-region as generous. In addition, non-interventionist approaches taken by the government and UNHCR at the level of the city creates the space for (while equally *requiring*) other forms of reception at local and sub-local levels outside of the national legal framework. Nevertheless, with the recent restrictive responses to the increased movement of all migrants into urban spaces, new precarious forms of reception are emerging at all levels of the state. Indeed, the initial welcome offered to refugees by the state is shifting dramatically away from a generous approach (in terms of the freedoms allowed) towards a new form of conditional and restrictive approach. In turn, with ideals based on pan-Africanism being slowly replaced by nationalism and xenophobia at all levels of the state, refugees and other forced migrants are regularly finding that alternative forms of reception at the local and sub-local level are becoming equally obstructive and hostile. Thus, refugee reception becomes an ongoing long-term process of negotiation, with the forms of reception offered to these perpetual guests liable to sudden or incremental change.

Turning specifically to the underlying causal mechanisms that are triggering these shifts in policy, the chapter shows how the implementation of the free-settlement reception policy is more complex than simply deriving from a sense of obligation to the legal commitments set out in national and international law. Indeed, the preceding sections were able to separate out and individually analyse key material, ideational and institutional causal mechanisms at play in refugee reception in South Africa at the initial registration stage. Furthermore, these factors at the domestic and international level are interacting (either by reinforcing each other or via contestation) to create shifts in policy, while also broadly maintaining the regionally unique reception policy.

A key factor that emerged is the ideational power of the national legal refugee framework/regime and its ties to nation-building. The empirical evidence emphasises the important roles that the 1998 Refugee Act and the National Constitution have had in conceptualising refugees on the territory. The ideational factors behind the creation of the legal framework, such as pan-Africanism and notions of fairness (stemming from the need to create a distance from the old apartheid regime) are deeply entrenched within the make-up of the modern-day state. These factors historically played a role in helping to shape an understanding of refugees as African brothers and sisters who should be treated with dignity. For these reasons, the state has resisted regional trends of turning to the use of encampment as the dominant reception approach. Taking regional patterns seen in the 1990s as a guide, democratic pressures and structural concerns relating to instability and insecurity would typically see a state adopt a reception approach more focused on controlling/constraining refugee movement.

In contrast to the influence of the national framework, the global refugee regime is ostensibly held at arm's length by the ruling political settlement. Academics from the majority world and international organisations continually praise the 1998 Refugee Act for incorporating key global regime norms. However, national advocates tend to understand the Act through a national constitutional lens, particularly when speaking to state officials or when making legal submissions. In addition, the Act is widely seen within state bodies as replicating ideals aligned with the post-apartheid move to democracy, rather than with international norms.

Yet these findings certainly do not mean that the maintenance of a free-settlement approach to reception is immune from institutional and material contestation. Several intersecting factors are challenging the overall reception policy. Material concerns about capacity and institutional contestation between different governmental departments at the national level are combining to accentuate an increasingly dysfunctional national refugee reception policy. In addition, the unrestricted movement of 'nonrooted' persons on the territory is feeding into the recent policy shifts. At this initial registration stage, ideational concerns around security and instability emerge as dominant factors with regard to the reception of refugees. The cumulative effect of the increased securitisation of refugees and migrants has been the attempts by the Department of Home Affairs and other national-level state bodies to shrink the asylum space and move most forced migrants outside of the legal refugee framework. As will be examined in the next chapter, with boundaries between the national refugee framework and the national labour immigration framework constantly blurred, refugees are slowly being detached from the refugee label (and the global refugee regime). This inevitably has serious implications for how refugees experience forms of post-registration reception in urban spaces in South Africa.

Notes

1. Of the six states in Southern Africa that host large numbers of refugees, only South Africa has an entirely non-camp-based reception policy (UNHCR, 2017b).
2. See also Klinck (2009); Smith (2003).
3. Chapters 7 and 8 have been written with the understanding that the new amendments to the Refugee Act, which came into force in 2020, will potentially change some key elements of national refugee policy. At the time of writing, the exact changes remain unknown, and the new amendments have not been widely implemented.
4. For example, in October 2019, UNHCR publicly praised South Africa for its response to refugees (UNHCR, 2019d).
5. The Bill of Rights is in the second chapter of the South African Constitution, which sets out the civil, political and socio-economic rights of all persons in South Africa. See also Klinck (2009).
6. South Africa Civil Society and Refugee Groups Interviewee 01.
7. Under the RAA 2017, asylum-seekers must hold an asylum transit visa before they can apply for asylum, which is valid for five days.
8. Appeals are allowed after a claim is denied in the first instance. This can be done via an appeal hearing (for unfounded rejections) or via written representations before the rejection is reviewed (for manifestly unfounded rejections) (Johnson and Carciotto, 2018).
9. Access is only available to the most vulnerable, via UNHCR implementing partners.
10. Confirmed in numerous public meetings and events attended between 2017 and 2019.
11. South Africa Civil Society and Refugee Groups Interviewee 11.
12. See Zetter and Deikun (2010).
13. See Landau (2018a).
14. Also see Chekero (2023).
15. Also see Landau (2011); Zetter and Ruaudel (2016).
16. South Africa Civil Society and Refugee Groups Interviewee 13.
17. South Africa State Entities Interviewee 02.
18. South Africa Civil Society and Refugee Groups Interviewee 11.
19. Commentators interpret the final version of the Refugee Act as reflecting this policy (Jenkins and de la Hunt, 2011).
20. See Maple (2016); Cannon and Fujibayashi (2018).
21. In 2009, there were estimates that 17,000–20,000 'mixed' migrants from these countries were travelling through Southern Africa to get to South Africa each year (Horwood, 2009). Estimates in 2017 suggested that around 13,000–14,050 migrants per year were doing a similar journey (World Bank, 2018a).
22. Large numbers of Zimbabweans enter South Africa via its porous borders and may not make themselves known to authorities.
23. South Africa Civil Society and Refugee Groups Interviewee 16.
24. In 2010 about 300 Zimbabweans arrived daily at the South African border town of Musina seeking asylum (ReliefWeb, 2010). Compare this to the 2,400 daily arrivals into Uganda during 2016 due to the conflict in South Sudan (UNHCR, 2016b).
25. South Africa Civil Society and Refugee Groups Interviewee 11.

26. The agency was very active during the late 1990s and early 2000s with the drafting and implementation of the 1998 Refugee Act (Smith, 2003). See also Klaaren et al. (2008); Handmaker et al. (2008).

27. South Africa State Entities Interviewee 02.

28. South Africa INGOs Interviewee 01.

29. Apartheid South Africa became the 'pariah' of the international community and was prevented post 1974 from taking its seat at the UN GA (Vale and Taylor, 1999).

30. The average length of protracted situations globally is twenty-six years (UNHCR, 2015b).

31. See Amit (2015); Long and Crisp (2011).

32. South Africa Civil Society and Refugee Groups Interviewee 02.

33. The agency still attempts to work behind the scenes with the government.

34. See also Loescher et al. (2008); Zolberg et al. (1989).

35. South Africa Civil Society and Refugee Groups Interviewee 17.

36. Material factors at the international level that play a role in the lack of engagement by UNHCR in the urban space post registration will be discussed in Chapter 7.

37. South Africa Civil Society and Refugee Groups Interviewee 01.

38. South Africa Civil Society and Refugee Groups Interviewee 11.

39. These homelands or 'Bantustan' were mainly in provinces such as Eastern Cape, KwaZulu-Natal and Limpopo (World Bank, 2018b). In addition, many refugees currently in South Africa originate from countries that hosted ANC members during the apartheid era.

40. See also Crisp (2000).

41. From 2013 to 2015, 2,049 two-year temporary residency visas were issued to former Angolan refugees after the state announced the cessation of their refugee status. After several renewals and court cases, in 2021, the latest iteration of the visa was announced and finally came with permanent residency and no expiry date (Scalabrini, 2021).

42. It is unclear how many of these individuals would gain refugee status if given the opportunity.

43. See also Moyo and Zanker (2020); Carciotto (2018); Thebe (2017).

44. As of mid-2023, the status of the ZEP remains in flux, with the Pretoria High Court declaring a recent Home Affairs decision to end ZEPs unconstitutional and invalid (*The Herald*, 2023).

45. See also Moyo (2018).

46. 2011 was the point at which new policies were introduced (Johnson and Carciotto, 2018).

47. South Africa Civil Society and Refugee Groups Interviewee 11.

48. South Africa Civil Society and Refugee Groups Interviewee 12. See also Amit (2012); Vigneswaran (2008).

49. In 2016, South Africa received a large number of new asylum claims (35,400) (UNHCR, 2017b).

50. In 2015, there were 381,754 pending asylum claims (UNHCR, 2016a; DHA, 2016b). See also Landau (2007).

51. South Africa Civil Society and Refugee Groups Interviewee 01. The state has publicly committed to reducing the backlog with the 'Backlog Project' in 2021.

52. See also Amit (2015).
53. South Africa Civil Society and Refugee Groups Interviewee 03.
54. South Africa Civil Society and Refugee Groups Interviewee 13.
55. South Africa Civil Society and Refugee Groups Interviewee 13.
56. South Africa Civil Society and Refugee Groups Interviewee 15.
57. See also Johnson (2015); Segatti (2013).
58. Equally, the Immigration Act inherited these principals of exclusion and control from the previous (and now repealed) Alien Controls Act (No 96) of 1991 (Johnson and Carciotto, 2018).
59. South Africa State Entities Interviewee 02.
60. South Africa INGOs Interviewee 01.
61. South Africa Civil Society and Refugee Groups Interviewee 01.
62. Equally, the geopolitical factors in the region examined above are no longer acting as a suitable filter of these types of movement.
63. This change has come about over time (that is, a cumulative effect) rather than being a sudden change of heart.
64. See sections 13, 34, 38, 63 and 64 (DHA, 2016a).
65. See section entitled 'Management of Refugees and Asylum-Seekers' in DHA (2016a:79).
66. See Fairclough (2013).
67. Fairclough (2013).
68. South Africa Civil Society and Refugee Groups Interviewee 11.
69. South Africa Civil Society and Refugee Groups Interviewee 11.
70. For example, increases in xenophobic violence against refugees combined with a lack of perceived protection, accumulated in hundreds of refugees amassing in Cape Town's Greenmarket Square in late 2019, demanding resettlement (*Mail and Guardian*, 2020:1).
71. In 2019, the Port Elizabeth RRO reopened. In June 2023, after an eleven-year legal battle, the Cape Town RRO also reopened.
72. See also Amit (2012).
73. South Africa Civil Society and Refugee Groups Interviewee 11.
74. South Africa Civil Society and Refugee Groups Interviewee 01.
75. South Africa Civil Society and Refugee Groups Interviewee 17.
76. Refugees Amendment Bill [B12-2016].
77. South Africa Civil Society and Refugee Groups Interviewee 13.
78. South Africa Civil Society and Refugee Groups Interviewee 17.
79. Processing centres have been discussed for a long time within Home Affairs.
80. South Africa Civil Society and Refugee Groups Interviewee 17.

Chapter 7

The urban space: post registration in South Africa

This chapter investigates the self-settlement reception policy in South Africa in the period following initial registration. Specifically, it examines the behaviour of state bodies and UNHCR concerning the longer-term reception of refugees in cities such as Johannesburg and Cape Town. There has been limited research examining the role of the national government and UNHCR in the reception of refugees in urban spaces in Africa (Maple et al., 2023). When research has adopted a state-focused lens, discussions on the reception or initial welcome of refugees have predominantly emphasised the procedures involved in (and difficulties surrounding) registration. As a result, analysis of national and local-level structures that influence state and UNHCR responses to refugees in urban spaces, beyond access to legal documentation, remain under-researched.

By utilising the book's understanding of reception, this chapter looks beyond initial registration procedures to gain a more nuanced conceptualisation of refugee reception in the urban space in South Africa. This framing of reception permits the inclusion of analysis on how the state's policies and structures at different levels influence the refugee's ability to move within the city and access labour markets. In doing so, this research builds on existing ground-level literature, which has looked at the role of the individual and communities in locating forms of 'localised citizenship', to generate a more holistic picture of refugee reception in cities in Southern Africa.

Post-registration in large cities in South Africa is reliant on the movement and agency of the individual refugee. At the level of the urban space, the national government and the global refugee regime regards refugees as having sufficient agency to find their own forms of acceptance at the local and sub-local level. Indeed, there are no nationally run integration programmes for refugees in cities such as Johannesburg or Cape Town. For refugees in urban spaces, this non-interference by the government creates the need to continue finding alternative forms of reception at the local and sub-local level. The understanding (at the level of the city) of urban refugees having sufficient agency to be self-reliant conflicts sharply with the security lens approach through which movement of refugees into urban spaces has increasingly been viewed at the national level post 2011. The chapter examines these conflicting understandings, observing how reception policies in the urban space are prone to contestation and change and ultimately reflect processes of negotiation and renegotiation between different institutional actors.

The chapter starts with an analysis of why South Africa has maintained this hands-off approach to refugees in the urban space. The lack of engagement by the state and UNHCR post initial registration has a profound impact on the implementation of the global refugee regime and its core regime norms, such as non-discrimination and access to public education, housing and employment. The chapter analyses the democratic structures and material, ideational and institutional factors involved at the national level that are affecting this inertia towards refugees. The second half of the chapter then switches to examine the role of the local government in the reception of refugees post registration, using the City of Johannesburg as a case study. In doing so it continues a theme running through this book, of probing potential variations in reception at the local level. Specifically, it asks whether it is possible to witness the appearance of regime norms and improved reception policies within local municipality structures, through the emergence of potentially unique causal mechanisms at this level of the state.

The national government and UNHCR in urban spaces post registration

This first section examines key material and ideational factors that are influencing the national level and UNHCR's approaches to the mid- to long-term reception of refugees in the urban space. These factors help develop further insights into how host states and the global refugee regime's key actor view and respond to urban refugees in South Africa. Due to the overarching free-settlement approach to reception, refugees are granted a great deal of autonomy in South Africa. Nevertheless, at the centre of this conditional form of reception remains a fragile relationship between the host state and the 'temporary' guest.

Material factor: state capacity concerns in urban spaces

A key material factor influencing the hands-off approach to post-registration is simply a lack of resources and capacity. Local integration and assistance programmes for refugees are costly both in terms of resources and manpower (OECD, 2017). Furthermore, as set out below, when a country has a multitude of structural issues relating to poverty and inequality within its own voting population, these material factors combine with democratic pressures and national interests, making a potent mix.

South Africa is a dual economy, with nearly half of its population classified as chronically poor (World Bank, 2018a).[1] The World Bank reported extremely high formal unemployment rates of 26.7 per cent at the end of 2017, with the unemployment rate for youths even higher, at around 50 per cent (World Bank, 2018a). The state also has one of the highest inequality rates in the world (World Bank, 2018b). This sees the poorest 20 per cent of the South African population consuming less than 3 per cent of total expenditure, while the wealthiest 20 per cent consume 65 per cent (World Bank, 2018a). This wealth disparity is due to an 'enduring legacy of apartheid' (World Bank, 2018b) resulting from a history of labour exploitation and privilege built through that exploitation (Ballard et al., 2017).

At the municipality level, it is a similar picture. Johannesburg in the Gauteng province is South Africa's largest city with more than 4.4 million residents (City of Johannesburg, 2013). The local economy has increased since the early 2000s, with the Gauteng province being the most industrialised and economically diverse region of South Africa and having the lowest poverty rate (19 per cent in 2015) in the country (Parilla and Trujillo, 2015). Nonetheless, around 20 per cent of its residents are still not in formal housing (de Wet et al., 2011). Similar structural problems persist in gaining access to quality health services for large portions of the local population (Vearey, 2017).

South Africa has attempted to respond to these disparities in socio-economic standards by running fairly generous social assistance programmes for low-income citizens. For example, in 2010 'one in every two households had a social assistance beneficiary, and the budget had doubled since 1994 to over 3.5% of GDP' (Barrientos and Pellissery, 2012). One key motivation for a political settlement (such as the ANC in South Africa) to maintain and expand social protection programmes is as a means of 'securing the acquiescence of groups that might otherwise threaten political stability and economic growth in the future or to undermine political opponents' (Lavers and Hickey, 2015). In this way, the political elites adopt generous social assistance programmes as compensation for the 'capital-intensive growth strategy' that has created and sustained these high levels of inequality and unemployment seen in South Africa (Seekings and Nattrass, 2005).

By comparison, motivation for the ruling political settlement to use scarce resources on a comparatively small proportion of the urban population (namely refugees) who cannot vote, and who are often unable to contribute via taxes, remains low. Firstly, since the end of the apartheid system, all forms of international migration into South Africa have continued to increase, with urban areas such as Johannesburg being a main destination for migrants and refugees from across the continent (Landau, 2007). Consequently, the number of economic immigrants, asylum-seekers and refugees in South Africa is significant.[2] Yet, the total number in urban spaces is relatively small when compared to the number of internal migrants regularly moving to the city. For example, in 2011 nearly one-third of Johannesburg residents were born elsewhere in South Africa (and can vote), compared to around 13 per cent who were born outside the country (Vearey et al., 2017).[3] Secondly, it has become increasingly difficult for refugees and other groups of African migrants to gain permanent residency, let alone citizenship. This means that voting rights remain a remote possibility as permanent residency status does not bring with it the right to vote in South Africa.

Thirdly, refugees and other international migrants in South Africa contribute to the local economy in numerous ways, including through employing nationals and paying some forms of tax (such as value-added taxation), which results in immigration having a positive effect on the gross domestic product (GDP) per capita (OECD, 2017). Yet, due to issues relating to the accessibility of correct documentation and the non-functional registration system, most refugees and asylum-seekers in the urban space find it virtually impossible to obtain work in the formal sector. A government official at the city level argued that this means refugees are forced to work in the informal market and/or become self-employed:

> They can't apply for jobs in private sector. So self-employed. So move around looking for better opportunities ... Some stay more though, especially in the informal sector.[4]

The national government, therefore, does not see much in the way of direct revenue from urban refugees, with numerous *de jure* and *de facto* barriers preventing refugees from paying national-level taxes.

In turn, by limiting refugees and other forced migrants to the informal economy, patterns of short-term residency and onward and circular movement between different urban settlements appear. As confirmed by the same government official, individuals have to continually 'move on' to find better opportunities:

> In and out movement – temporary stay for migrants. Data on migration – hard to track. One day is different to the other. Not even sure how long they will stay.[5]

Comparable observations were made by civil society actors in both Johannesburg and Cape Town, with one NGO employee noting that many refugees and other forced migrants do not see the city as a long-term home; instead, 'a lot of people come to Cape Town with the idea of just being a midway point to somewhere else'.[6] From a national governance point of view, the temporary and cyclical nature of the movement in and out of urban areas makes it hard to monitor and plan for this highly mobile population (Landau, 2006). It also heightens varied barriers to access to public services and tax systems.

Ultimately, capacity issues are helping frame refugees and other forced migrants as low priorities for the democratically elected government. Certainly, the ruling political settlement is more interested in assisting the large sections of their voting public who are themselves unable to access essential rights or fundamental freedoms. Nevertheless, the lack of any discernible investment in the mid- to long-term reception of refugees contributes to the broader issues faced by the government in terms of cross-border migration into urban spaces. The absence of post-registration assistance directly impacts the number of asylum-seekers, refugees and forced migrants who work in the informal sector as well as those who are obliged to regularly move between different urban spaces in South Africa in search of work and opportunities. This movement has the potential to create additional tension and instability within state structures at the local and national level, while at the same time resulting in losses in revenue from taxes.

Material factor: the capacity of UNHCR and the global refugee regime in urban spaces

Capacity issues, including a scarcity of resources, are not exclusively a state issue. This section examines the limited financial capacity of UNHCR to engage with the reception of refugees post registration in urban spaces. In 2018, UNHCR estimated its funding gap at USD 4.5 billion (UNHCR, 2018a). The budget for UNHCR Southern Africa followed this broad trend with large reductions occurring between 2012 and 2016.[7] The shortfall globally means that most funding received is used to respond to emergencies. The 'refugee situation' in South Africa is not categorised as an emergency and as such has witnessed large budget cuts. For example, a 52 per cent gap in the funding was reported in 2015 (UNHCR, 2016a). With refugees permitted, at least in policy if not always in practice, to access economic opportunities in the territory, South Africa is seen as less of a priority to the global refugee regime than other states. Providing humanitarian assistance to large, diverse and mobile populations is extremely challenging in an urban environment (HPN/ODI, 2018). Thus, these financial restraints play a key role in dictating the type of work that UNHCR, and its implementing partners, can conduct in urban spaces in South Africa.

Partly because of these funding deficits, UNHCR in-country work is now mainly focused on educational initiatives, capacity building and hosting forums. For example, the agency runs a Protection Working Group (PWG), which is a semi-regular forum including government bodies and civil society, that meets to discuss protection issues.[8] Yet, with little funding available and the options for formal resettlement limited, the scope and effectiveness of the Working Group was heavily criticised by civil society.

In addition, a small number of implementing partners have a mandate from UNHCR to run its social assistance policy, which includes emergency social assistance relating to food, access to healthcare and education in large urban areas. As a manager of a key implementing partner explained, funds are minimal:

> to give you an example, I have funding to assist with rent and food for seven families and seven individuals, that's not even a drop in the ocean.[9]

Furthermore, due to cuts, implementing partners have had to reserve their remaining funds and resources for new arrivals (that is, a focus on initial registration) and the most 'vulnerable' in the urban space. The same manager commented:

> with UN funding, we can assist people who have been in the country for less than two years. So it's basically, I think that [it's] newcomers and vulnerable groups – as funding gets more restricted going forward. The newcomers will drop out and we'll only have funding to assist people with disabilities . . . and unaccompanied minors.[10]

As a result, most refugees and other forced migrants in South Africa are unable to access any assistance from UNHCR, or the global refugee regime, post the initial welcome and registration phase.[11]

Ideational factor: a 'generous reception' in urban spaces

This section now switches to examining an ideational factor operating at the national level that influences the policy of non-interference with refugees and forced migrants after the initial registration period of reception, specifically, the notion within relevant government departments that the form of reception already offered to refugees in South Africa is in actuality very generous.

A particular form of conditional mid- to long-term reception exists in urban spaces in South Africa. During public events and closed meetings with civil society, high-ranking officials within Home Affairs regularly commented on the gracious hospitality afforded to refugees by the state. This often came up in the context of comparing South Africa's 'generous' free-settlement approach to reception with the more restrictive approaches seen in neighbouring SADC states. Civil society actors confirmed this framing by high-up officials within government departments who see the maintenance of the 'open door' policy, in combination with no refugee camps on the territory, as being highly praise-worthy and generous.

This conceptualisation of reception in South Africa as being expansive and magnanimous is also reinforced at the international level. Following numerous public statements of praise, a high-ranking UNHCR official in the in-country office stressed the generosity of the state (and frequently expressed gratitude to the government) in their interview:[12]

> The regime in South Africa has been very good . . . Soon as you come and claim asylum in South Africa, you are permitted to work, permitted to go to school.[13]

This generosity lens has fed down to the local and sub-local level and into the narratives of refugee and migrant groups in South Africa. Groups representing these categories of migrants regularly adopt varying approaches based on a theme of the 'good migrant'. Repeatedly in interviews and workshops, refugee and migrant leaders expressed their gratitude for the welcome of the host state. In addition, they demanded (at least in public and in interviews) that their fellow refugees and migrants learn to abide by the laws and find ways to integrate and become useful members of the community.

In contrast, demands for the state to offer services beyond registration or better access to rights contained within the global refugee regime were kept to a minimum – even in private and anonymised interviews. As an example, during an annual meeting of refugee and migrant groups in Johannesburg in 2017, the greater part of the meeting was spent discussing how to stop refugees working in informal markets, rather than engaging in pressing issues around a lack of rights or protection.

The notion that refugees should be grateful for the reception they receive (regardless of how conditional and temporary it is) is not a new phenomenon. Nevertheless, specific to South Africa, this perception of magnanimous reception sees the state as only obliged to allow refugees onto the territory and grant freedom of movement. These acts alone should make the refugees grateful and accommodating guests. In this way a delicate relationship forms, whereby obligations within the urban space fall mainly on the guest. The state has completed its side of the 'bargain' at the point of registration, by allowing the refugee onto the territory and granting access to registration procedures. In return, as reception moves to post-registration, the refugee agrees to essentially become an 'invisible' guest removed (at least to a certain extent) from the political life of the state.

In the context of South Africa, historical ideational factors add a further layer of conditionality to the mid- to long-term reception of refugees and migrants. As Landau and Freemantle (2017:291) argue, with the continued suffering of black South Africans post apartheid, foreigners are often framed solely as either helping or hindering the goal of 'economic freedom and transformation for South Africans'. Again, here refugees are constructed entirely as guests whose stay is seen as conditional rather than as equal to nationals (regardless of the time spent in urban spaces). In fact, the reception offered remains dependent upon refugees performing a useful purpose in the urban space. This seemingly one-sided relationship has only been heightened since the recent policy shifts post 2011, with new draft asylum-seeker forms making explicit reference to the potential economic contribution of the asylum-seeker:[14]

> you can see lots of places where *'refugees are useful to us'* ... The claim is not dependent on persecution, rather who are valuable. In the draft of the form it asks questions on bank account, money, wage slips, all sorts of things that are irrelevant or should be irrelevant. [It's about] issues of national interest.[15]

In conclusion, this framing of refugees as useful and grateful guests removes many obligations and responsibilities from the state, particularly pertaining to protection issues. In its place, a delicate if contested relationship emerges in the urban space between host and guest, whereby obligations fall mainly on the visitor. Refugees are being essentially commodified, whereby their status is more focused on their duties *to* the state rather than a set of rights or obligations owed to them *by* the state.[16] As examined further below, this delicate relationship between refugees and state bodies in urban spaces is contested further still, if the number of refugees in those spaces increases to levels perceived to cause instability.

Ideational factor: the global refugee regime and urban refugees in South Africa

The section now investigates how the construction of the urban refugee by UNHCR guides the agency's response to – and informs the national government's conceptualisation of – refugees in these reception sites beyond initial registration procedures. As introduced previously, the global refugee regime in Southern Africa regularly equates the 'refugee' in urban spaces with independence and self-reliance. In doing so, once a refugee arrives in an urban area there is an assumption that there is little need for protection or assistance.

This framing is based on the premise that if a refugee manages to make it to an urban area in Southern Africa, then implicitly they will have the necessary skills and agency to survive on their own. There is a logic to certain aspects of this, albeit state-centric, interpretation of cross-border/continental movement. If a refugee reaches an urban centre in Southern Africa from ongoing conflicts in East Africa or the Horn of Africa, then at this point in their journey the likelihood of needing immediate humanitarian protection is greatly reduced. Undoubtedly, many of the most vulnerable refugees will remain immobile or seek immediate protection and humanitarian assistance in one of the refugee camps which they are likely to pass on their journey south. Thus, in essence, this line of argument proposes that only the most resilient refugees will ever reach a city like Johannesburg, in the southern-most state of Africa.[17]

The result of this viewpoint is that once refugees arrive in urban spaces in South Africa, UNHCR urban refugee policy, for all intents and purposes, ceases to apply. As a case in point, top officials in UNHCR South Africa did not see the 2009 and 2014 UNHCR urban policies applying to refugees in Johannesburg. It is 'not really an issue in South Africa because now people can live where they want – most people are actually living in urban centres',[18] the argument being that as refugees have freedom of movement, assistance from the global regime is not required.[19]

This construction of refugee movement into the urban space by the agency has led civil society in South Africa to conclude that UNHCR's approach to urban displacement is essentially that 'onward movement means being left on your own'.[20] A former Department of Home Affairs manager certainly felt this:

If you take initiative and travel further than you should in line with what is expected ... then you have too much agency to be a refugee – if you demonstrate [this] agency then you don't need our help.[21]

This quote aptly illustrates the risk inherent with this type of approach. As highlighted by civil society, when the topic of better access to services/protection for refugees is brought up with government officials, the typical response from the Department of Home Affairs is to reiterate the importance of *self-integration*.

Furthermore, this framing of refugees in urban areas as essentially having too much agency to be 'regime refugees' is inadvertently supporting recent shifts at the national level that are shrinking the asylum space and removing refugees from both the global regime and the national refugee framework. The risk is that as the influence of the refugee regime reduces, a void is created which is subsequently filled by the national immigration framework. Thus, a form of regime shifting similar to that examined previously in the context of Zambia, and re-introduced in the preceding chapter, is occurring in South Africa. As Betts (2009a) describes it, regime shifting is a form of *forum shopping* whereby a state attempts to address 'problems' which normally fall within the purview of one regime (in this case the refugee regime) by addressing them through another (in this case, the broader immigration regime). Whether by design or inference, the national government in South Africa is gradually detaching refugees from their refugee status, and from the refugee regime, by responding to all African migrants through using the national immigration framework. By essentially abstaining from engagement in the urban space and reinforcing the construction of urban refugees as entirely self-reliant, the UN agency is in danger of tacitly affirming this new approach to state-based reception.

Finally, this construction of urban refugees in South Africa as a solution to displacement fosters concerns that echo those that were brought up in relation to UNHCR's past pushes for self-reliance.[22] Similarly to previous approaches, UNHCR in Southern Africa is framing the 'refugee camp' as a site of reception and protection in a way that sets it up as antithetical to the 'urban space'. By extension, this also positions concepts of 'vulnerability' and 'self-reliance' in opposition to one another. This means that the mere presence of refugees in urban areas is enough to ascribe self-reliance, without the need for intervention from the regime. As such, rather than 'creating appropriate conditions for refugee self-sufficiency' (Meyer, 2006:14) in urban areas, UNHCR focuses its attention and resources on providing assistance in refugee camps. By contrast, in these confined spaces, individuals are framed as regime refugees, entirely dependent on aid and the regime. Ultimately, these opposing conceptualisations of the urban space/refugee camp by the UN agency have the potential to profoundly affect how the regime is understood at the sub-regional and regional level.

In conclusion, the relevance of UNHCR in the everyday practice of reception in South Africa post registration appears minimal. By moving to urban areas in South Africa, refugees are understood by UNHCR as essentially no longer needing assistance. This in turn is resulting in refugees being detached from the protection of the international governance regime, or even the national refugee legal framework. In this way, urban refugees are increasingly seen as part of the broader population of economic and illegal migrants. Thus, this approach is adding to the overall shrinking of the asylum space, with refugees running greater risks of arrest and harassment in urban centres. From a state perspective, this urban lens also removes obligations in relation to offering protection to refugees on its territory. Indeed, as set out in the previous section, the obligations at this stage of reception appear to fall mostly on the 'guest'.

The effect of national-run post-registration reception in urban spaces

This section considers the consequences of the institutional, material and ideational factors set out above, in terms of the role the national government and UNHCR play in post-registration reception in South Africa. In particular, how contemporary approaches to refugee reception in urban areas by key actors shape a refugee's ability to interact with local communities and economies in an attempt to pursue their own personal and economic aims. The section concludes by reflecting on how this overarching approach to refugees at the level of the urban space diverges from the broader approach seen at the national level to the perceived destabilising effect of large movements of refugees and migrants into cities post 2011.

Firstly, the assumption that, through agency and movement, minimal protection issues exist in cities in South Africa is not supported by the empirical research. This is particularly evident over the last decade, with policy changes at the national level shrinking the asylum space and increasing securitisation of all forms of African migrants in cities such as Johannesburg and Cape Town. Numerous interviews with leaders of local NGOs and migrant groups raised concerns over the general reception and protection being experienced by their clients/members in urban areas. A number of these issues appeared unique to refugees and forced migrants, for example, a lack of documentation or general confusion surrounding the validity of documentation (for refugees *and* law enforcement officers); issues surrounding opening bank accounts; gaining access to schools; and accessing healthcare.

Police and other law enforcement officers also regularly single out refugees and other forced migrants due to their status, intending to elicit bribes.[23] Experiencing extortion when trying to gain access to an RRO is all too frequent, with an implementing partner of UNHCR noting that their clients regularly have to 'pay a bribe to [a] security guard to get onto the premises'.[24] Finally, in the relation to localised forms of reception seen at the local or sub-local level, a human rights lawyer in Cape Town observed how these forms of urban citizenship do not remove the need for legal protection:

> I mean if you . . . if you're up at 4 a.m., 3 a.m. in the morning you must, you must walk . . . and see . . . in fact people have been camping out there because for them being documented, having an extension of their payment, is literally a lifeline.[25]

Thus, functioning state structures during the stages of registration and beyond remain indispensable to many refugees in urban spaces in South Africa, even if others prefer to find and rely entirely on alternative localised solutions.

Secondly, due to the attitude of non-interference in urban centres (shared by the national government and UNHCR), responsibility for the protection, support and supply of essential services falls on civil society. In reality, civil society is implementing key elements of the global refugee regime for substantial populations of forced migrants. By way of illustration, a local Catholic organisation in Johannesburg runs a busy shelter for refugee women and children, while also assisting their clients with livelihood projects. Moreover, the shelter regularly receives referrals of refugees in need of shelter and assistance from national-level state entities.

This example underscores two significant points concerning reception in the urban space. Firstly, not all refugees or refugee communities can independently meet their essential needs (including protection) in the urban space in South Africa. Indeed, with obligations imposed on them within the space by the state (including that of being a gracious and 'useful' guest), the granting of certain key norms, such as freedom of movement and the right to work, are not sufficient on their own to enable all refugees to achieve self-reliance. Secondly, civil society is replacing the functions and obligations of the state and the global refugee regime by implementing key elements of the global regime at the local level. In this way, implementation is in effect skipping the international and national levels and re-emerging at the sub-local level. This concept of implementation skipping levels is examined further in the second half of the chapter.

Finally, due to the inactivity by the state and UN agencies, combined with the increasingly hostile environment awaiting refugees and asylum-seekers upon arrival in urban spaces in South Africa, a UNHCR implementing partner has started 'resettling' refugees to refugee camps in neighbouring states. Specifically, small numbers of refugees are being relocated from Johannesburg to refugee camps in Botswana and Mozambique. The manager of the implementing partner organisation explained:

> Now recently I've had people coming to me saying, oh they can't look after their families and they need protection and they don't get it here. They would like to go to the refugee camp in Botswana and I'm working with [redacted] at UNHCR to see if we can move them there . . . listen – it is happening lots.[26]

This type of assistance is aimed at refugees who are struggling to adapt to the reality of a frenetic urban environment in South Africa. Indeed, in townships and informal settlements in Johannesburg and Cape Town where many refugees and other forced migrants move, they live with local communities who also find themselves cut off from any form of assistance or protection. Thus, for some refugees, the prospect (at least in the short-term) of living in a camp where services are provided is seen as the best available option.

Interviews confirmed that this form of sub-regional resettlement is being conducted in an informal ad hoc manner by one UNHCR implementing partner. Put in the context of the total number of forced migrants living in South Africa, this form of assistance is happening on a very small scale (contrary to the implication expressed in the quote above). Nevertheless, this phenomenon, which connects the urban space with the refugee camp in arguably new and somewhat surprising ways, merits further research. Also, and significantly for these purposes, it aptly illustrates the range of long-term issues that exist for refugees in urban spaces such as Johannesburg.

The first half of this chapter has examined the key factors behind why the government and UNHCR have maintained a non-interference approach to refugees in urban spaces in South Africa (beyond the initial registration phase). These causal mechanisms need to also be considered via a democratic lens. Scarce resources mean that the host state has little incentive to divert funds to a (relatively) small section of the population that lacks the right to vote. Thus, refugees have less of a voice at the national level than the voting public, and this public is currently harbouring increasingly strong anti-immigration sentiments. This results in refugees and forced migrants in cities in South Africa having very limited political space.[27]

The ongoing capacity issues in the urban space, the framing of an already 'generous' reception, and the conceptualisation of 'urban refugees' versus 'regime refugees' all also feed into the changes seen in refugee policy in South Africa since 2011. Indeed, the lack of a structured approach to mid- to long-term refugee reception, and the resulting temporary and cyclical nature of the movement in and out of urban spaces, have reinforced the current perception of instability in cities in South Africa. The delicate relationships that emerge between refugees, state bodies and local communities in this contested space are then challenged further when the number of newcomers increases. Thus, conflicting conceptions at the heart of refugee reception in urban spaces in South Africa interact with each other. The construction of the individual urban refugee (adopted to justify a policy of non-interference by the state and UNHCR) is ultimately being contested by an overarching national approach to cross-border migration which views all African migrants in the urban space through a bifocal security/stability lens.

Contemporary shifts in refugee policy at the local level: the City of Johannesburg

The second half of the chapter moves to investigate alternative contemporary shifts in refugee policy seen at the local level. Specifically, analysis is conducted on the role of the local government in post-registration reception in South Africa. As shown above, while the state and UNHCR have maintained the traditional non-interference policy in the sense of limited to no assistance for refugees in urban spaces, since 2011, the national government has also started to 'interfere' with reception by reducing the asylum space and restricting access. This assertion of sovereign power means that refugees are often removed from the space entirely or, much like with a refugee camp, are confined to specific spatial areas, such as informal settlements, where they live amongst other urban poor. Against this backdrop, this section asks whether by shifting focus to the level of the municipality, unique localised factors emerge that may create opportunities for alternative forms of state-based reception that diverge from dominant national policies.

A case study of the City of Johannesburg in Gauteng province is used to examine this proposition. Indeed, in the last fifteen to twenty years, there have been concrete attempts by the municipality to improve the mid- to long-term reception of all international migrants.[28] Thus, the section raises the possibility that 'the city' can be reimagined as a space of political rupture and localised citizenship for refugees in Southern Africa.

Decentralisation in South Africa

Decentralisation has spread rapidly across the majority world in the last few decades (Crook, 2003). This commitment to devolving decision-making and financial resources involves local governments managing mandates and budgets, running local government elections, raising taxes and then spending them locally (Smit and Pieterse, 2014). In South Africa, the National Constitution laid out the framework for local government and was followed by the 2000 municipal elections (Wittenberg, 2003). As a result, local government in South Africa retains an element of independence, with cities such as Johannesburg having power and authority in areas such as water and sanitation, and municipality planning. In terms of the reception of refugees and other migrants, most of the services available to them (for example, access to most forms of healthcare and education) falls on the national or provincial government to provide. Nevertheless, the Constitution does give some responsibility to the municipality for the social and economic development of the community (Landau, 2011).[29]

In terms of the actual implementation of policy based on these devolved powers, the results in South Africa are however quite poor (Koelble and Siddle, 2013). As seen more broadly in the region, this localised power is frequently undermined by financial constraints (Kasim and Agbola, 2017). Equally, at least until very recently, local government in South Africa was dominated by the ruling party (the ANC), which as an organisation remains highly centralised (Landau, 2011). Power has started to shift, however, at the city level, with the Democratic Alliance (DA) winning control of Cape Town in the Western Cape Province in 2006 and then Johannesburg in 2016.

Finally, while not the focus of this section, the provincial level also retains a degree of independence from the national government (as protected by the National Constitution) in South Africa. The nine provincial governments manage key social services such as education, health and social grants. Yet, when discussed, interviewees regularly portrayed the provincial level as merely an extension of the national level and thus it was not seen as playing an independent role in the reception of refugees in South Africa. Nevertheless, when the political party in charge of a provincial government is different from the ruling party at the national level, there appears to be some scope for alternative policies and approaches to refugee reception to emerge. For example, after winning control of Cape

Town in 2006, the DA then won the broader provincial elections in the Western Cape in 2009. In interviews, UNHCR officials observed how new working relationships with government bodies at the provincial level in the Western Cape had resulted in improved localised responses to xenophobic violence.

Ideational and institutional factors at the city level

Decentralisation creates the scope for achieving progressive humanitarian and development goals 'at sub-national levels, even during a period when leadership from central levels is limited' (Levy et al., 2015:6). Thus, while a national-level approach to a topic or issue (in this case refugee reception) may remain weak, the transfer of power to the local level opens up alternative possibilities. If this devolution and shift of power is matched with contrasting political ideals at the municipal level, then it may be possible to see real practical changes in how refugee reception is implemented in these localised sites.

Notably, from the late 2000s, the City of Johannesburg started to accept international movement (including refugees and forced migrations) as part of the fabric of the city. When referring to this shift in policy, a director of an NGO in Johannesburg suggested that there came a point when simply ignoring migrants or relying on self-integration tactics was no longer seen as a viable option at the city level:

> The city has a very important role to play and ignoring a section of the population means that you are not catering for them – and it could be a public health issue – there are lots of issues which [if] you then don't consider . . . could blow up in your face.[30]

This ideational shift in how migration into the city was conceptualised, coupled with the strong personalities of two ANC mayors – Amos Masondo (2000–2011) and Parks Tau (2011–16) – resulted in marked adjustments being made to how all migrants were received in Johannesburg.

Numerous initiatives were created in the late 2000s and early 2010s, which had a direct impact on the post-registration of refugees and their ability to find ways to engage with local communities and markets in neighbourhoods in Johannesburg. These initiatives included setting up a Migrant Help Desk in April 2007. Then, in 2010, the Johannesburg Migration Advisory Panel (JMAP) and the Johannesburg Migrants' Advisory Committee (JMAC) were both founded. At the time of writing, all three schemes remain active, albeit to varying degrees. JMAP is a forum of non-governmental organisations and city departments that meets monthly 'to look at challenges that confront migrants' (City of Johannesburg, 2017). The forum is used to determine where funding from the city's social funding initiative should be used. These discussions can then get elevated to JMAC, (a higher-level committee) which has the goal of 'facilitating the integration of plans of the various key departments that have an impact on the migrants in the various spheres of government' (City of Johannesburg, 2017:2). JMAC then also feeds up to the Mayor's Office.

The Help Desk was opened to provide numerous services to assist with the integration of cross-border migrants and to reduce the spread of xenophobia in the city.[31] One of the main roles it undertakes is the provision of information to migrants and refugees on where they can gain access to key services such as counselling, legal advice, housing and health. Significantly, the Help Desk has a policy of not asking the legal status of any cross-border migrant before assisting them. This differs sharply from approaches within the national government, where refugees and forced migrants consistently need to show documentation and evidence of their status. Without providing this they are often unable to access services available to citizens and run the risk of detention or deportation.

By utilising city-level funding, the three initiatives (Help Desk, JMAC and JMAP) have assisted in the creation and coordination of numerous events, dialogues, workshops and other initiatives aimed at improving the reception and integration of all forms of cross-border migrants. In addition, numerous attempts at improving social cohesion between local communities and migrant communities have been undertaken to help fight the increasing number of xenophobic outbreaks in neighbourhoods and townships around Johannesburg.

This willingness to engage and collaborate with migrants on the ground (that is, at the local and sub-local level) is also replicated at the international level. When speaking to UNHCR officials in South Africa it was evident that the UN agency has a healthier working relationship at this level of the state than with specific national-level government departments.

> At the local level – Johannesburg – we have had co-operations with municipalities in terms of fighting xenophobia . . . we do not have a problem there.[32]

Finally, several key stakeholders noted the importance of former Mayor Parks Tau in particular, as the driving force behind these initiatives. The former mayor managed to gain sufficient support for these ideational shifts by stressing that Johannesburg was 'a city built on migration' and these migrants 'were here and they needed to be integrated into the city'.[33]

> The idea ... is quite a good thing, the idea of acknowledging Johannesburg as a city built on migration ... tagline, 'how migrants can help the city and how the city can help migrants'.[34]

It is evident that by the late 2000s – at least in policy and approach – the City of Johannesburg had started to move away from the national-level approach to refugee reception in urban spaces. Indeed, this contrast between the form of reception at the local level and that offered at the national level highlights the lack of a 'clear coordinated coherent policy, to achieve some kind of social integration' for migrants or refugees at the national level.[35]

Continuing contestation

The previous section set out some key ideational and institutional differences in how the city level in South Africa (specifically Johannesburg) has understood and framed refugee and migrant reception, compared with national bodies and structures. In turn, these factors have been the main driving force for new reception policies to emerge in Johannesburg. Yet, the actual reception refugees receive at the city level via local state structures inevitably depends on the successful implementation of these policies. From key informant interviews and attendance at the helpdesk and numerous JMAP meetings, it is evident that there have been several points of blockage that have affected the execution of these city-run initiatives in the urban space. Significantly, the reasons for much of the contestation at the municipality level are a result of similar material, institutional and ideational factors found at the national level.

A mixture of local, national and provincial government departments provide services at the local level. Thus, refugees' access to services can differ vastly based on who the provider is and on the approach taken more broadly to the inclusion of refugees. This is particularly pertinent to several key public services that should, by law, be available to all refugees after initial registration.

> The problem is some of the services are not at the municipal level. Depending on what it is, for example education is provincial.[36]

As educational services are run and funded at the national and provincial level, a former manager of an RRO noted how various structural factors emanating from those levels create access issues (including exclusion mechanisms) for refugees and forced migrants.[37] Based on this division of labour, the city has had only limited success in unblocking certain barriers to inclusion (which have increased since 2011) that regularly prevent refugees from accessing key services such as education.[38] Another example is key health services, where the local government in Johannesburg is 'quite keen to provide services to asylum-seekers and refugees, [but] they have no control over the admission policy of a public hospital'.[39]

Finally, even when a large city like Johannesburg runs specific services, such as small-scale public health clinics, blockages regularly still occur at the point of delivery. This is often due to material and ideational factors such as capacity constraints in terms of funding and training, or anti-migrant sentiments at the point of service. This was the view of the manager of a UNHCR implementing partner organisation in Johannesburg:

> I think at the municipality level, they discuss these things and they come up with good resolutions but you know if you look for instance at health . . . it's up to them – to the staff – at a particular clinic, whether they are going to implement it or not.[40]

Due to these institutional, ideational and material constraints, a great deal of the work conducted by the city in terms of post-registration reception (such as the Migrant Help Desk) is focused on orientation, facilitating and sharing of information. Beyond this exchange of information, approval and coordination with national-level institutions (such as the Department of Home Affairs or Health) are usually required for refugees to see a real practical benefit. Collaboration between the different levels of the state is the part of the process where the system generally breaks down. As a case in point, national institutions frequently do not attend the JMAC. As a former employer of the Department of Home Affairs observed, there is an overall 'lack of coordination at the horizontal and vertical levels of government'.[41]

Shift in ideational approach at the city level

In 2016, power at the city level in Johannesburg shifted from the ANC, who had run the municipal council for twenty-two years since the end of apartheid, to the DA party. This change in power brought in a new city mayor, Herman Mashaba. At the time of his election, the city was suffering from several systemic issues concerning poverty, crime and unemployment. Part of his plan to tackle this overall sense of instability in the city was the adoption of a dramatically different approach to the movement of cross-border migrants into the urban space. Indeed, following his appointment there was a striking ideological shift in how all African migrants in the urban space were framed at the city level:

I have seen a big shift recently ... there was a recognition that people were here and they needed to be integrated into the city – but that has all changed with the new DA mayor.[42]

At the core of these policy shifts was a marked increase in the securitisation of all foreign nationals (excluding the highly skilled) and the insertion of xenophobic sentiment into public speeches and policy. Unquestionably, a key message from the Mayor's Office was the blaming of structural and systemic issues within the city (such as increases in crime, lack of jobs and the lack of housing) on refugees and other African migrants.

In terms of reception policies aimed at migrants and refugees, the Migrant Help Desk was effectively still running in the early 2020s, as well as JMAP and JMAC. Yet core changes in the overall policy at the city level were evident. These included: repeated raids on 'illegal' migrants; attempts to change legislation to expedite the removal of migrants from their accommodation, particularly from so-called 'hijacked buildings'; and stoking up xenophobic violence and attacks (Wilhelm-Solomon, 2017). This change in approach restricts access to the urban space for refugees.

An illustration of this shift in approach comes from an infamous speech covering cross-border migrants given by Herman Mashaba in 2017. In it, the mayor noted, 'they're holding our country to ransom and I'm going to be the last South African to allow it. I've got constraints as local government, because the national government has opened our borders to criminality' (as quoted in *Mail and Guardian*, 2017). This quote aptly demonstrates the engagement with the securitisation of cross-border migrants at the city level. It also shows how the municipality started reframing the movement of migrants into the city as the responsibility of the national government.[43] In doing so, this has the effect of removing responsibility from the Mayor's Office in relation to the reception of refugees in Johannesburg.

This change in approach, unsurprisingly, saw city-based reception on the ground regress further from global refugee regime norms. Indeed, the shifts seen in the national government's approach to the spatial restrictions of refugee reception were (and still are) being embraced and replicated at the city level (including through numerous community-level exclusion mechanisms). These policies ultimately feed into the impression that a refugee's stay in Johannesburg is inherently temporary, or worse, illegal. Furthermore, the approach of the Mayor's Office caused further ruptures between refugees and local communities, which inevitably impacts on a refugee's ability to successfully find forms of reception at the local and sub-local level and ultimately achieve their own personal and economic aims.

Reception at the city level: a mixed bag

This examination of local-level state-run refugee reception policies in urban spaces reveals some key issues that are worthy of further investigation. Firstly, the section tentatively suggests the possibility of regime-norm implementation skipping levels of the state where political structures are causing blockages or contestation and then reappearing and being implemented at lower levels (where different structures and pressures may exist). Forms of local-level state reception in Johannesburg have been able to reach refugees and other forced migrants who lack the correct legal paperwork – or who simply never attempted to engage with national-level processes. This preliminary finding also raises questions around how 'the state' is understood in relation to the global refugee regime and refugee reception and whether 'the state' and its interaction with the regime need rethinking/reconceptualising.

Secondly, the section shows how material, ideational and institutional factors that influence state-run reception are not exclusive to the national level. Indeed, through using the 'democracy-asylum' nexus, the recent regressive policy shifts noted at the city level were at least partially foreseeable. The appointment of the first-ever DA mayor came at a time of extremely low employment figures, high crime rates and increasing anxiety within the urban population about the perceived instability being caused by the numbers of African migrants in the city. Thus, the increased refugee movement, as permitted by national and local reception policies, created a disruptive presence in the urban space and adversely affected the opinion of the voting public. Concerned with the short-term gains of remaining in power, it is therefore unsurprising that the then mayor adopted approaches similar to the national level by blaming ongoing structural and systemic issues on 'non-rooted' persons such as migrants and refugees.[44]

This section contributes to the growing body of literature examining the role of the city as a possible space of improved reception and protection for refugees and other migrants. These new avenues of research are particularly pertinent now, given that states at the national level (both on the continent and globally) are continuing to retreat from international human rights obligations. This preliminary investigation into the City of Johannesburg shows the possibility of finding alternative and improved reception in response to differing pressures found at the level of the municipality. Nevertheless, the chapter also suggests some caution is needed in relation to recent attempts to frame the city space as a sanctuary for refugees. It is evident that the city is not immune from democratic pressures and other material, ideational and institutional factors that are present at the national level. Furthermore, alternative forms of reception at the city level appear to still be nested in larger geopolitical hierarchies at the national level. Thus, the need for vertical coordination between the different levels of the state on key provisions and services creates unique challenges. In sum, refugees in Johannesburg are far from experiencing an entirely different form of unconditional welcome at the city level nor, by extension, full implementation of the global refugee regime.

Post registration in South Africa: a precarious relationship between long-term guest and host

Once refugees become regularised in South Africa by obtaining legal documentation, they have access to a few key norms contained within the refugee regime, including freedom of movement. This generous welcome, at least on paper, allows refugees to freely move around the territory and locate other forms of reception at the local and sub-local level, post registration. Nevertheless, the chapter also reveals the emergence of delicate relationships in the urban space when the role and influence of the state and UNHCR at this later stage of reception are incorporated into the analysis.

Firstly, numerous inter-related key material and ideational factors combine to motivate the national government and UNHCR to maintain a non-interference approach to refugees in urban spaces (beyond the initial registration phase). These include ongoing capacity issues in the urban space and the framing of an already 'generous' reception. In addition, urban refugees are constructed as an entirely self-sufficient category of migrants by the national government and UNHCR. They therefore diverge fundamentally from the framing of 'regime refugees' seen in the refugee camp context in Southern Africa. This framing then further 'justifies' the decision by the national government and UNHCR to relinquish several key obligations relating to protection and integration as set out by the global refugee regime.

Secondly, because of the non-interference policy by the national government and UNHCR, urban refugees need to engage with local networks to find additional forms of reception at the local and sub-local level. Yet, this is also being restricted due to the xenophobic attitudes and violence that continues to grow within local communities. These communities are themselves frequently marginalised and often living in informal settlements and having to deal with increasingly 'anti-poor' rhetoric and actions by law enforcement agencies and politicians. As a result, alternative forms of reception at the sub-local level are not always available nor regarded as a sustainable strategy for all refugees.

This increasingly hostile localised 'welcome', coupled with the lack of engagement post registration at the national level, is causing multi-directional responses by refugees on the ground in South Africa. Refugees are regularly moving between different neighbourhoods and different urban settlements to find improved conditions (in terms of living space and employment). In addition, the combination of the spatial confinement of the global regime in the sub-region, the broad non-interference policy in cities such as Johannesburg, and the often-harsh realities of contemporary cities are together creating unconventional connections between the urban space and the refugee camp in Southern Africa. As revealed above, a small number of refugees are trading the city for the 'safety' of the refugee camp and the accompanying 'regime refugee' label.

Thirdly, urban reception, which this book frames as a process, can be understood in part as a tacit agreement or bargain made between the refugee and the host. Obligations stemming from this relationship between guest and host fall mainly on the guest. Refugees are granted temporary access to the urban space as visitors, with an implicit/unspoken understanding that they remain essentially silent. It is therefore extremely difficult for refugees to move past the level of visitor/guest in South Africa. Furthermore, increased levels of movement into the urban space will further contest and potentially rupture this host/guest relationship. Thus, a contradiction emerges in relation to refugee reception in the urban space in South Africa: on the one hand, freedom of movement is seen as creating agency (and the reason for non-interference policies) and yet on the other hand (as illustrated over the last two chapters), it is also seen as the cause of instability and insecurity. Thus, for the refugee, a highly conditional and volatile form of reception emerges in urban spaces; one that is prone to contestation and change and which ultimately reflects processes of negotiation and renegotiation between institutional actors.

Finally, the second half of the chapter illustrated how the local government in Johannesburg has had mixed results in implementing migrant programmes and better access to services at the local level. The role of strong personalities in the Mayor's Office was shown to be able to temporarily shift ideational thinking and institutional approaches towards migration and in doing so alter refugee reception in the city for the better. Yet, these localised policies and practices seem unable to 'end' reception on their own. Core services and policy decisions that affect refugees are retained at the national level. Also, with political change at the city level and the accompanying shift in rhetoric, this section has shown how the local level is not immune to democratic pressures. These levels of analysis (the national and local/sub-local) are deeply interconnected, with national pressures/politics filtering down and informing local debates and policies. These arguments will be examined further in the next and final chapter, which brings together analysis from across the book and draws out some practical implications for refugee advocates working on reception-related issues in Southern Africa.

Notes

1. See Punton and Shepard (2015).
2. In 2017, there were 215,860 asylum-seekers and 92,296 refugees or persons in refugee-like situations (UNHCR, 2018c). This is a substantial revision from previous numbers (above 1 million asylum-seekers), which is due to 'methodological changes' introduced in 2015 (World Bank, 2018a).
3. See City of Johannesburg (2013); Statistics South Africa (2012).
4. South Africa State Entities Interviewee 01.
5. South Africa State Entities Interviewee 01.
6. South Africa Civil Society and Refugee Groups Interviewee 17. This supports previous research by Landau (2018a); Landau and Amit (2014).
7. USD 91 million in 2012 to USD 76 million in 2017 (UNHCR, 2019c).
8. These include finding solutions to individual cases with special protection elements and ways to respond to xenophobia in urban spaces.
9. South Africa Civil Society and Refugee Groups Interviewee 03.
10. South Africa Civil Society and Refugee Groups Interviewee 03.
11. UNHCR is not permitted to assist refugees without documentation.
12. See public comments made by High Commissioner Filippo Grandi in 2019 (UNHCR, 2019d).
13. South Africa INGOs Interviewee 01.
14. Created by recent amendments to the 1998 Refugee Act.
15. South Africa Civil Society and Refugee Groups Interviewee 01.
16. See also Kuboyama (2008).
17. See also Landau (2018a); Kihato and Landau (2016).
18. South Africa INGOs Interviewee 01.
19. This interpretation of the 2009 urban policy dismisses sections of the policy that relate to the agency's role in assisting in self-reliance and gaining access to services (UNHCR, 2009).
20. South Africa Civil Society and Refugee Groups Interviewee 01.
21. South Africa State Entities Interviewee 02.
22. See UNHCR's Refugee Aid and Development (RAD) approach in the early 2000s (Meyer, 2006).
23. See also Chekero (2023).

24. South Africa Civil Society and Refugee Groups Interviewee 03.
25. South Africa Civil Society and Refugee Groups Interviewee 13.
26. South Africa Civil Society and Refugee Groups Interviewee 03.
27. See also Sanyal (2014).
28. In Cape Town, by contrast, there has been little movement in this area.
29. Section 152(1) and 153(a) of the South African Constitution.
30. South Africa Civil Society and Refugee Groups Interviewee 17.
31. See also World Bank (2018a).
32. South Africa International NGOs Interviewee 01.
33. South Africa Civil Society and Refugee Groups Interviewee 17.
34. South Africa Civil Society and Refugee Groups Interviewee 01.
35. South Africa Civil Society and Refugee Groups Interviewee 11.
36. South Africa State Entities Interviewee 02.
37. South Africa State Entities Interviewee 02. Access issues to schools and hospitals are not entirely down to national-level blockages. Access is also affected by individual school or hospital policy.
38. See also Landau et al. (2011).
39. South Africa State Entities Interviewee 02.
40. South Africa Civil Society and Refugee Groups Interviewee 03. Note that some health clinics are run by the city, while public hospitals are run by the state.
41. South Africa State Entities Interviewee 02.
42. South Africa Civil Society and Refugee Groups Interviewee 17.
43. See Landau et al. (2011).
44. Note that after the conclusion of the fieldwork, Mashaba resigned (November 2019).

Chapter 8

Conclusions and ways forward

This book has studied refugee reception through a state-focused analysis of responses to the arrival of refugees in Zambia and South Africa, close neighbours within the Southern Africa region. At its core, the book interrogates the question of why two SADC member states adopt such vastly different reception policies. Further, it addresses consequential concerns about the role these policies play in shaping how refugees pursue their personal and livelihood-related needs within the local context. In following these lines of enquiry, the refugee camp and the urban space were selected as focal points for the research, due to their prevalence as major reception sites in both case study countries and in Southern Africa more broadly.

Zambia and South Africa are both parties to key international conventions related to refugee protection and both permit UNHCR onto their territory. Thus, at first glance, one might expect a degree of uniformity or similarity in how they implement core elements of the global refugee regime (including norms and obligations). Yet, in law and official policy, wide variations exist in their responses to the arrival of refugees. By deploying a theory of norm implementation as a conceptual framework, the book develops a greater understanding of why differences between the countries' responses to refugees have emerged over time. Furthermore, by generating an understanding of reception that reflects the realities on the ground in Southern Africa, the preceding chapters build an analysis around what these reception policies mean in terms of specific reception sites and how they interact with, and shape, the multi-locational and multi-directional dynamics of contemporary refugee arrival and movement.

Four sets of general conclusions are presented in this final chapter. It begins by bringing together analysis from the case studies and the initial analytical work conducted to reframe our understanding of refugee reception in Southern Africa. This first section draws out a conceptualisation of reception based on the two key geographical sites investigated in Southern Africa. Next, the conclusions evaluate the analytical benefits and limitations of incorporating a theory of norm implementation into the analysis. The second half of the chapter pinpoints and examines the book's main findings in relation to the three pertinent academic debates set out in Chapter 2. Considering these findings in sequence serves to highlight and evaluate the contribution that the book makes to academic knowledge but also sets up the subsequent analysis of the implications of the book for national and international actors working with host states on the reception of refugees in Southern Africa.

Conceptualising reception in the refugee camp and urban spaces

Chapter 1 built on the 'context of reception' model (Portes and Böröcz, 1989) and research from the broader migration and human geography fields to advance a working understanding of refugee reception. This understanding was then used as a roadmap for exploring what refugee reception *is* from a theoretical standpoint. Previous academic work conducted in Africa that has looked at the forms of welcome given to refugees by states has habitually framed reception as a one-off event, such as the act of registration or the transferring of a refugee to a refugee camp. In contrast, this book employs a new approach that endeavours to reflect more accurately the changing nature of reception in Southern Africa today. It does this by acknowledging research into the role of human agency and mobility that forms connections between different sites of reception. It is no longer realistic (if it ever was) to understand persons who flee across a border as a homogeneous group whose movement abruptly ends once they arrive in a host state and/or refugee camp.

The book instead argues that reception is more than a one-off event or simply an act of finding shelter. Indeed, refugee movement in Southern Africa rarely amounts to just a one-directional singular journey. Key informants interviewed drew attention to the circular, sporadic and unpredictable nature of refugee movement taking place in the locations under scrutiny. For these reasons, the book sees reception as a *process* in which state, international and local actors shape a refugee's ability to access local communities and markets in an attempt to pursue their own personal and economic aims. This approach therefore recognises the plurality of actors involved in refugee reception. Although the focus here remains on state responses to refugees (both at the national and local level), it is evident that refugees in Southern Africa also find (or incorporate) alternative forms of reception at the local and sub-local level. The three subsections below use these findings to draw out a conceptualisation of refugee reception in Southern Africa, with a particular focus on the refugee camp and urban space and the complex relationships that emerge between (1) these reception sites and (2) refugees and host state structures.

Temporary versus permanent guest status

A core characteristic of reception in Southern Africa is the continual emphasis on refugees remaining fundamentally as guests on the territory. As a result, they rarely move past the level of 'visitor', with their stay in Zambia and South Africa retaining a precarious and conditional quality. This occurs in both the camp and urban settings. Differences emerge, however, in terms of understanding the temporary versus permanent character of refugees' stay in these spaces. As examined further later, in the urban space, host states view refugees' presence as temporary with access to that space understood as entirely provisional. In contrast, in the refugee camps in Zambia, while refugees still fundamentally remain as guests, there is nonetheless an understanding that their presence is likely to be long term.

Key to this observed difference is the way in which refugees are framed within the confines of the refugee camp. Large parts of the national government in Zambia continue to regard refugees as entirely separate from the political life of the state and as the responsibility of the international community. Thus, the main settlements in Zambia in many respects conform to contemporary work that has adopted Agamben's (1998) ideas on 'states of exception'. This framing of refugee camps is particularly pertinent today, with the settlements remaining the architecture through which political space, as well as geographical space, is regularly denied. This notion of reception in the refugee camp, while reflecting the bleak reality for many refugees in Southern Africa, is not of course the whole story. Daily access to local nearby communities allows some refugees in the settlements the mobility to engage in locally based livelihood activities and other refugees to utilise official travel pathways and take longer circular trips between the refugee camp and urban space. These officially sanctioned connections between the different reception sites and what they mean for conceptualising reception will be examined further below.

For the current discussion, the implications of these findings are twofold. Firstly, each reception site inevitably offers a contrasting form of reception. Yet, regardless of which space is encountered, refugees in

Zambia and South Africa remain as perpetual guests in the host state. Thus, while the form of reception may change over time (either through changes in policy or based on the agency of the individual refugee), the provisional form of residency offered on arrival endures long term. In line with previous research, the reception offered to refugees by states in Southern Africa, therefore, remains inherently qualified and conditional (Stronks, 2012). Indeed, this qualified form of reception may never truly end. Regardless of the specific modality of reception, refugees remain trapped as guests in someone else's house, reluctantly invited in by the owner but unable to move past this initial 'generous' welcome: a welcome that comes with permanent conditions and restrictions.

Secondly, the refugee camp allows the state to experience and project a sense of control over a 'non-rooted' population and their movement. While refugees stay inside the camp, there is little reason for the Zambian state to engage with or form relationships with the inhabitants, as the needs of the population are essentially handed over to the international community.[1] A genuine two-way host/guest relationship only occurs once a refugee leaves the camp. Indeed, in terms of understanding reception *inside* the refugee camp from a state-level analysis, the notion of these spaces as reception sites inside the territory but not necessary *of* the territory remains pertinent. Refugees are permitted to stay as permanent guests in Zambia, as long as they remain passive and immobile in these humanitarian spaces, with limited access to the political space of the state. As a result, the Zambian Government has little political or economic motivation for attempting to remove or repatriate refugees from the settlements. As investigated next, this is in sharp contrast to the urban space, where the implications of access being entirely provisional mean that a much more delicate and negotiated guest/host relationship emerges. Thus, in many ways the manner in which states view the permanent guest status of refugees in refugee camps actually speaks as much to how they view refugees in urban spaces as it does to the camp space.

Negotiating reception: the interplay between levels of reception in urban spaces

The multi-scalar analysis adopted by the book sheds light on how the reception of refugees in urban spaces in Southern Africa takes place at different levels and how those levels interact. The top tier (national level) informs and influences lower tiers (local and sub-local) and vice-versa. In South Africa, the granting of freedom of movement by the state allows refugees access to other forms of welcome at lower levels, whether this is through municipalities or other local government structures (as seen in Johannesburg, with mixed results) or through sub-local networks of local residents and/or refugee communities. Yet equally, the policy of non-interference in urban areas by the national government and UNHCR also makes these additional forms of reception *essential*. In turn, increased tensions and xenophobic attitudes within local communities not only create barriers to accessing services and labour markets for refugees and forced migrants, but due to the negative democratic feedback loops that are created, often filter up to the local and national levels and exert influence on policy and law.

These layered processes of reception, which interact and inform each other, are potentially unique to the urban space due to the conceptualisations of the 'urban refugee' and refugee movement by the state and UNHCR. Reception in both countries is conditioned via an 'invisible bargain' which refugees are forced to accept with the national government in urban spaces. On the host side, both South Africa and Zambia complete their part of the bargain by firstly permitting refugees onto their territories (via their much celebrated 'open door' policies) and by formalising their stay, albeit in a temporary way. Secondly, in South Africa this initial welcome is followed up by the state granting freedom of movement and access to the economy, which allows (at least in theory) immediate access to the urban space.

Access to the city is more complex in Zambia, with refugees having to apply for either a gate pass or an urban residency permit. However, once refugees have permission to move to the urban space in both states, the construction of urban refugees by both states and UNHCR means that most key international obligations that would usually fall on the 'host', are relinquished. In return for this access to the urban space, most of the responsibilities stemming from this host/guest relationship now fall on the guest. Urban refugees can live among the voting and 'rooted' public as visitors, but with the caveat that they must be self-reliant coupled with an implicit understanding that they must remain 'useful' but essentially silent. As a result, access to the political space remains limited.

These findings have implications for how we conceive refugee reception in urban spaces in Southern Africa, and potentially the wider continent. Reception needs to be understood in terms of this tacit and delicate trade-off (or bargain) between the refugee and the host state. Interactions and relations that develop between refugees, state and local actors enable access to local structures and communities. However, this access is premised on an entirely temporary basis, by state entities. Equally, these delicate relationships are frequently prone to change due to processes of negotiation and renegotiation between key actors in these reception spaces. Indeed, underlying causal mechanisms embedded within state (and international actors') behaviour continue to shape and alter these precarious relationships. For example, state- and community-level exclusion barriers often occur that enforce confinement to specific enclaves of the city or simply shrink access to the urban space entirely. Furthermore, while forms of belonging and 'local citizenship' are well documented at the local and sub-local level, these additional or alternative forms of reception appear to still be nested, to some extent, in larger geopolitical hierarchies at the national level. This is not to diminish the influential role such localised welcomes can have on the lives of refugees. Yet, due to their connectivity to higher up processes, they are unlikely to have the ability to completely reshape how refugees experience reception in urban spaces nor to offer a permanent solution to displacement.

Reception in urban spaces, therefore, remains fundamentally conditional, based on a fragile relationship between the host and temporary guest. Given that pathways to forms of permanent legal status remain remote, reception persists over the long term in these sites. Thus, the reception afforded to urban refugees in Southern Africa does not appear to substantially resolve the issue of displacement. As interrogated further below, these findings have consequences for how we understand the durable solution of local integration and the risks inherent in over-relying on concepts such as self-reliance and human agency when researching urban displacement.

The evolving symbiotic relationship between the refugee camp and the urban space

Research since the mid-2000s has shown how the refugee camp is a more dynamic and complex site of reception than was traditionally framed in the literature. Indeed, any analysis of contemporary refugee camps and related reception policies remains incomplete without also considering the areas surrounding the camps, and key urban spaces. This is in sharp contrast to previous long-standing depictions of the refugee camp and the urban space as being diametrically opposed and sealed off from one another. Recent reassessments of the refugee camp have predominantly focused on the reality on the ground by exploring how agency, mobility and technology connect this site to the rest of the host state. Thus, an objective of the book was to respond to the need for research investigating the intentions of the *host state* in relation to the recently documented forms of connectivity between the two reception sites.

The book submits that the purpose of refugee camps in Zambia is not to stop *all* movement, but that these designated sites of reception can in fact be understood as a method of regulating refugee movement into the interior and specifically into urban spaces. Thus, a multifaceted relationship emerges between the two reception sites – one that is *symbiotic*, with the activities in one site regularly affecting policy and practice in the other. In Zambia, the settlements are connected daily with local communities, the state and the wider world. COR is willing to allow this type of movement and interaction between refugees and citizens, albeit within certain limits. The result is that refugee movement in and around the urban space is regulated and controlled via the dominant camp reception policy. This has meant that the refugee camp creates the perception of stability required for *some* movement to be able to occur. Indeed, the camp space is in effect filtering the number of refugees in urban spaces and this helps to explain why the internal movement of refugees in Zambia is not currently being excessively securitised by the state.

As noted above, for states the movement of refugees and other 'non-rooted' persons is about moderation and management. Too much movement creates a destabilising effect, or at least the perception of instability and insecurity. For these reasons, states adopt various techniques to manage movement. Thus, states may see the refugee camp as a *mechanism for managing* movement. As a consequence, the findings suggest that we need to re-assess our understanding of why states in Southern Africa (and the wider continent) adopt camp-based reception policies. In contrast to previous literature that has supposed that states use refugee camps as the architecture to contain and remove all refugees from the interior, this book argues that camps need to be understood more as a way in which states can attempt to monitor and control the movement of refugees on their territory.

Every state attempts to manage the movement of 'non-rooted' persons on their territory. Indeed, freedom of movement is rarely envisaged without some recourse to limits or control. Yet with porous borders common across Southern Africa, coupled with an inability to adopt the external or internal border controls seen in the minority world,[2] states in the region have little choice but to resort to the camp space as a means of controlling unchecked movement into cities and towns. As a result, the refugee camp creates and maintains the order needed for some types of movement to be allowed in and around urban spaces. Crucially, the relationship between these different sites of reception remains delicately balanced: if numbers in the urban space increase rapidly or are perceived to reach an unsustainable level then a crackdown on urban reception can be expected, with refugees moved back to the camp space.

Reconsidering a norm implementation framework for refugee reception

The theory of norm implementation by Betts and Orchard (2014) was adopted and adapted to become the main conceptual framework. In line with the project's overarching constructivist epistemological position, the book's conceptual framework is rooted in theory and developed in reference to contemporary research. It ultimately represents an integrated way of examining reception.[3] Due to its emphasis on how international norms are implemented as prescribed actions at the national level, it is well suited to the book's state-focused approach to understanding state responses to refugees. Nevertheless, the theory itself is relatively new and has not previously been employed to investigate refugee reception. This section therefore critically reflects on the framework's value as an analytical tool, as an original contribution of the book and its utility for future work within forced migration studies.

The principal goal of integrating this theoretical work was to generate new insights into why states respond to the arrival of refugees in different ways through their reception policies. The conceptual framework was used to identify and examine key factors involved at various levels of the state (and beyond) that affect the implementation and running of state-based refugee reception policies. Thus, while attention remained predominantly at the national level (in line with the book's overarching approach), the incorporation of a multi-scalar lens created the flexibility to allow analysis to incorporate local-level concerns, as well as to scale up to the international level to understand broader regional and global pressures.

At the heart of the framework is the heuristic tripartite model, which sets out causal mechanisms (material, institutional and ideational) embedded within state behaviour that can reinforce, contest and/or constrain the implementation of international norms. This approach was beneficial in identifying and distinguishing between various material and political pressures that cause states to adopt diverse reception policies. In terms of causation (that is, how a particular mechanism directly affects the implementation of the regime or one of its norms), the reality on the ground meant that it was not possible to find neat causal links between individual factors and specific state-run refugee reception policies.

Instead, the conceptual framework helped to illuminate that reception policies at the national and local level are formed through ongoing and highly contingent processes of negotiation and renegotiation between key actors.[4] For example, as part of these negotiations in Zambia, different factors (such as material capacity concerns and the ideational power of former legal frameworks) reinforce each other and ultimately the overarching camp policy, outweighing contesting factors such as the ideational approach of COR (and UNHCR). In South Africa, the ideational power of the national legal framework is regularly contested by other factors (such as opposing material and ideational considerations, including security and stability concerns), to the degree that reception is slowly changing from being based on universal human rights to being based on nationalistic concerns. Thus, the framework has been used to: (1) identify and investigate individual factors; and (2) illustrate how some factors become interconnected and reinforce each other, while others cause contestation, creating tensions and potential variations or changes in reception.

As a result, a complex reality of interacting processes emerges. Indeed, the reception that refugees receive in Southern Africa cannot be understood as the mere function of a *factor* or a *precise set of factors*. Rather, the exact form of reception, whether that is at the national or local level, is the effect of circumstances whereby a particular combination of factors interact and/or contest with each other to create a given response.[5] These underlying factors result in state and international actors and structures and refugees forming precarious relationships, with these relationships continually shifting between something resembling stability and conditions of flux. Ultimately, this explains how national and local reception policies are often volatile in nature: rarely constant but rather prone to incremental or sudden shifts over time.

The adoption of the theory of norm implementation as the book's conceptual framework nevertheless has some potential limitations. Firstly, Betts and Orchard's theory places considerable weight on the 'global' and how international norms are implemented on the ground. In several respects, this emphasis was extremely useful in highlighting how and why key global refugee regime norms such as freedom of movement are frequently contested or blocked at the state and local level. Nevertheless, a reflexive approach to the conceptual framework throughout the life of the project was essential. During the preliminary framing exercise and the initial set of interviews in South Africa, it became apparent that there was a risk of overstating the regime's influence on refugee reception in Southern Africa. However, it is also important to note that the flexibility inherent within the framework created the opportunity for opposing arguments and alternative factors that emerged through the fieldwork to be observed and then fed back into the analysis. Thus, the focus of the research was broadened and relevant alternative factors at the national and local level (such as the role of national and municipality policy frameworks) were able to be included.

The adoption of a framework, to investigate reception policies in Southern Africa, which is based on a predominantly minority world understanding of international governance systems is nonetheless open to criticism. Indeed, Zambia and South Africa are developmental/hybrid states in transition, with their own normative agendas which regularly challenge the traditionally held views of international systems. As examined further below, national legal frameworks, policies and localised norms had a far greater influence on the reception received by refugees than did the key components of the global refugee regime.

Secondly, the conceptual framework and the heuristic tripartite model may not be granular enough for some researchers. The inability to show causal linkages between a specific factor and policy, or address issues of mapping and prediction, can be seen as a limitation. The inclusion of a process-tracing component to the framework in future research could be a way of reducing these concerns and, in turn, unearthing further understanding of specific policies.[6] Yet, whether a tool such as process-tracing would have developed clear lines of causation in the context of Southern Africa is open to debate. When considered as an option during the framing exercise of this project, this approach was ultimately dismissed due to its perceived rigidity and Western understanding of policy making. Indeed, the findings of the book follow Ragin's (1987) concerns around understanding social phenomena solely as a function of one or two key factors. Social phenomena (in this case, the reception offered to refugees in Southern Africa) are far too complex and intricate to be understood by simply tracing the origins of specific policies. Rather, as discussed above, state-based reception at the national and local level is the result of ongoing and highly contingent processes of negotiation and renegotiation.

In terms of its future application, a reliance on a Western understanding of the *role* and *importance* of international governance systems may serve to dissuade some researchers of the framework's applicability. This is particularly so, given that contemporary research on these topics in Africa is predominantly conducted from a ground-level perspective, which regularly offers radically different viewpoints compared to the sociocultural norms and institutions of mature Western states in the minority world. Also, the framework's approach to understanding contestation around the implementation of policy may not be sufficiently precise for some researchers. Nonetheless, for research that adopts a state-focused lens, the findings and critiques advanced here highlight the benefits and flexibility of an approach which encapsulates universal and essentialist behavioural characteristics of modern states. This is as true for mature states in the minority world, as it is for developmental/hybrid post-colonial states in the majority world. Indeed, the theory of norm implementation (and particularly its heuristic tripartite model) can be regarded as valuable for future projects that are interested in developing new understanding around state behaviour towards refugees and migrants.

Contributions to wider debates on refugee reception

Three academic debates were presented in the book, which illustrate ways in which research has investigated state and international level responses to refugees in Africa. These discussions centre on the role of the 'democracy-asylum' nexus in influencing state responses to refugees in Africa; the extent to which the global refugee regime shapes refugee reception policies; and the security and stability nexus. This section advances the book's key contributions to these debates and in doing so tentatively sets out the broader relevance of the findings, beyond the immediate case studies here considered.

Confirming the 'democracy-asylum' nexus

In 2009, Milner proposed the idea of a 'democracy-asylum' nexus to explain why states in Africa, during the 1980s and 1990s, moved from free-settlement reception approaches to containment approaches (such as the use of refugee camps).[7] In essence, he argued that the shift from authoritarian-style political settlements to more competitive ones led states on the continent to become more amenable to the growing anti-refugee and immigrant feelings within local voting populations – particularly in urban areas. In the fourteen years that have passed since Milner's research, the 'democracy-asylum' nexus has received little to no attention within the fields of forced migration and refugee studies. By embracing this work, this project was able to investigate the continuing relevance of the nexus and in doing so hopefully reinvigorate research in this area.

The case studies illustrate how the nexus remains an overarching concern for democratic political settlements in Southern Africa today. Indeed, a key finding is that the 'democracy-asylum' nexus plays a more dominant role in state responses to refugee movement than contemporary literature might suggest. In recognising this, the book supports Milner's conclusion that democracy is not always a good thing for refugees' human rights. In addition, the book has extended contemporary understanding on this topic by applying the nexus to examining the relationships between democratic structures (at the national and local level) and the reception of refugees in refugee camps and urban spaces.

In both case studies, albeit to differing degrees, the empirical evidence shows how the nexus with democratic politics is influencing national reception policy and practice within urban spaces. In South Africa, as state institutions at both the national and municipality level become more competitive and arguably democratic, the ruling parties, in attempts to remain in power, become focused on short-term gains and responding to the attitudes of the voting public. The South African case study highlights how key material and ideational factors, including capacity and security concerns related to the increasing urbanisation of refugee populations, feed into these democratic pressures at the national and local levels. In the context of poor economic performance, high levels of unemployment and perceived scarcity of resources, there is a growing wariness of 'outsiders moving in' that is shared by the voting public, the City of Johannesburg and the national government. As a result, officials at all levels of the state are currently engaged in public campaigns that blame a range of social, economic and political ills on cross-border African migration. Indeed, as Betts (2009b) suggests, through this construction of refugees as the enemy/outsider, they become used as an opportunity for ruling political settlements to garner support from urban constituencies.

Additional refugee movement into the urban space can therefore create negative democratic feedback loops. By implementing key norms contained within the global refugee regime, including democratic rights, the state effectively runs the risk of being 'punished' if movement creates instability (real or perceived) and adversely affects the opinion of the voting public. The 'democracy-asylum' nexus is thus intrinsically linked with the increasing global preoccupation around the stability of the nation state (even at the expense of universal human rights). This has resulted in a paradoxical situation whereby increases in democratic structures have been a catalyst for the decline in rights and access to the urban space for 'non-rooted' persons such as refugees in Southern Africa.

The idea of a 'democracy-asylum' nexus is also valuable in terms of developing an analysis of the evolving relationship between the refugee camp and urban space. Interviews in Zambia revealed how during the 1990s and early 2000s, key departments of the national government repeatedly became concerned about the number of refugees in large cities and the destabilising effect this might have on the urban space and the voting public. Thus, on numerous occasions, there was a reaction whereby large numbers of refugees were forced back into the settlements. This example reinforces the negative link observed between democratic structures and refugee reception, as well as the continued relevance of the nexus in the maintenance of camp policies, as observed by Milner (2009). Yet these historical patterns in Zambia also reveal the complexities surrounding responses to refugee movement. The pushbacks by the state were not about stopping *all* refugee movement (or containing all refugees), but rather about managing refugees and their movement. As observed above, there remains a delicate relationship between refugees and state structures in urban spaces in Southern Africa; too much movement into these spaces will always create a reaction.

The final way in which the book has expanded existing work on the 'democracy-asylum' nexus is by investigating the converse position to the phenomena observed by Milner. Specifically, does an opposite shift in the form of government – that is, from a competitive/democratic political settlement to a more authoritarian-style political settlement – open up the possibility of improved reception conditions for refugees? In essence, the book examined the hypothesis that when a political settlement moves towards an authoritarian style of governance, the government feels it can implement long-term programmes based on self-interest and ideological commitments without being overly concerned about challenges from opposition parties or the risk of losing re-election.

During Edgar Lungu's tenure as the President of Zambia between 2015 and 2021, Zambia witnessed 'democratic backsliding', whereby more and more power shifted to the Office of the President. These developments were troubling on numerous fronts, including the repression of opposition political parties, civil society and the press. Yet, due to the former president remaining ideologically committed to pan-Africanism, these shifts did offer an opportunity for better reception conditions for refugees. Indeed, this democratic backslide paradoxically created the political space for some positive moves towards refugee reception. In 2017, the state signed up to the Global Compact on Refugees, volunteering as one of the first countries to adopt the CRRF and committing to *consider* the long-term relaxation of the dominant settlement approach. In the same year, the state also opened the Mantapala settlement, with its focus on 'whole of society' and 'whole of government' approach. Time will tell whether these commitments will translate into long-term improvements in reception policies, particularly given some of the key concerns with the implementation of the Mantapala settlement, and the shift in power in 2021 to the new president, Hakainde Hichilema.

By advancing an analysis based on the 'democracy-asylum' nexus, these findings nevertheless suggest alternative approaches for UNHCR and other advocates of refugee rights in Southern Africa and further afield. Advocacy by international agencies in countries with political settlements like the one seen in Zambia between 2015 and 2021 is likely to be more successful if it is top-down, with less emphasis on pushing for international norms or the implementation of rights per se. Instead, emphasis should be on the president and on aligning improved reception conditions with existing ideologies and belief systems at this level. These findings do not, however, imply that authoritative political settlements are better for the overall reception of refugees. Rather, it is about finding an approach that works for the unique set of circumstances in a specific context. Thus, conversely, in a more democratic and competitive political settlement like South Africa, approaches to creating change would be better suited at the local level, for example, channelled through grassroots organisations and aimed at shifting the public perception of refugees and their role in the urban space.

The peripheral role of the global refugee regime in shaping refugee reception policies in Southern Africa

Turning to contemporary debates over the role of the 'global' in responses to the arrival of refugees in Africa, the book brings new understanding to the relationship between the global refugee regime (via its two main components: the 1951 Refugee Convention and UNHCR) and national and local reception policies in Southern Africa. Traditionally the global refugee regime has dominated research engaged with refugee arrival on the continent. However, this emphasis started to shift from the 2010s, with academic attention moving from the international to local and sub-local levels. From this ground-level perspective, the role of the global regime in relation to refugee protection and movement (especially in the urban space) is commonly dismissed entirely. Instead, contemporary research illustrates how refugees find alternative ways to survive and settle in cities via local networks and ad hoc local-level policy and practice.

The book brings new insights to both these distinct areas of research, by investigating the role of the regime in reception policies in Southern Africa from a state-focused perspective. Firstly, the global refugee regime has limited involvement in the day-to-day practice of reception in Zambia and South Africa. Thus, the book questions the continuing relevance of the 'global' in refugee reception in Southern Africa (particularly outside the refugee camp). Secondly, by appraising the role of the regime in reception, the case studies reveal the importance of national legal frameworks and policies in how reception is delivered to refugees on the ground.

When discussing legal and policy frameworks within the context of refugee protection in Africa, the emphasis in the literature has traditionally been at the international level, with commentators observing the role of the 1951 Refugee Convention. In contrast, analysis of the role and power of national and local frameworks, institutions and norms typically remain limited – or their influence on the ground is often dismissed as minor. For example, national law is regularly seen solely as a conduit for the international convention and rights. The book shows a different picture. Indeed, a key contribution is that in Southern Africa, international frameworks seem to have little influence or power over how state actors shape and implement reception policies. Analysis of the global refugee regime by legal scholars within the fields of refugee and forced migration studies often neglect that for many actors working in refugee protection, it remains a relatively remote concept. Instead, it is the national laws, policies and localised norms that are relevant in practice. Thus, in Zambia and South Africa national actors are implementing national and localised norms rather than international ones.

This finding means that while the book questions the relevance of international frameworks in the day-to-day practice of refugee reception in Southern Africa, it nonetheless stops short of dismissing the influence of all governance systems. Researchers such as Schmidt (2014) and Landau (2018a) suggest that attempts by refugees to settle in urban spaces in Africa are based predominantly on impromptu local policy/networks. As seen in the analysis investigating cities such as Johannesburg and Lusaka, these sub-local negotiations do indeed become an essential part of reception processes in Southern Africa. Nevertheless, the book questions whether some contemporary research conducted using a ground-level lens may underestimate the influence that national frameworks and policies have on key actors who engage daily with the reception of refugees. Indeed, as noted above, national-level forms of reception still inform and influence lower-tier ones.

As has become apparent through the case studies, it is not automatic that the global refugee regime retains relevance on the ground in Southern Africa. Indeed, if international frameworks have little influence on reception policies, where then does the regime appear and what is its added value? To develop this line of enquiry, the section turns to consider UNHCR, as the main international actor associated with the regime. The UN agency has equally been the centre of a great deal of academic attention from research addressing the welcome that refugees receive in Africa. In contrast, the role of the host state in refugee reception is frequently framed as a secondary or minor player.

The book found that UNHCR has less influence in Southern Africa than might be expected from existing literature. Indeed, the UN agency essentially adopts a non-interventionist policy in urban spaces within South Africa and Zambia.[8] This approach, in turn, all but confines the global refugee regime to the refugee camp. This finding highlights a key contradiction concerning the regime and refugee reception. The refugee camp was not originally conceived of as a core element of the global refugee regime. Indeed, most rights contained within the 1951 Refugee Convention relate to the integration of refugees into a host state (Aleinikoff and Zamore, 2019). Yet, although refugee camps are established through the policy decisions taken by host states and international donors and actors from the minority world, these sites have now become synonymous with the regime in Africa. Thus, at the heart of camp-based reception lies a paradox: the global refugee regime, which was designed to convey a wide range of rights to refugees, is confined to a site that it did not create. A site which, by its very presence, inhibits the full implementation of the regime in host countries. The implication of this finding for refugees in Southern Africa (and potentially on the wider continent) is that for them to gain access to the regime (and by extension international protection), they must give up their right to freedom of movement and in many respects dehumanise themselves.

In the context of Zambia, UNHCR is not, however, passive in the geographical confinement of the regime. Contrary to popular opinion in existing literature, the agency readily acquiesces to these restrictions. The host state has on numerous occasions been open to more urban programming or at least has not pushed back when UNHCR, its implementing partners and COR have implemented new initiatives in urban spaces. Yet for historical, material and ideational factors relating to protection and capacity concerns, the UN agency actively chooses to remain predominantly inside the refugee camp.

Turning to the urban space, the lack of a real presence by UNHCR in this reception site underpins and justifies the questioning of the continuing relevance of the global refugee regime in the everyday practice of refugee reception in Southern Africa. Equally, by not engaging with urban refugees in any meaningful way, UNHCR is reinforcing the conceptualisation of the 'regime refugee' as being a helpless, sedentary victim in need of international assistance that is delivered solely in refugee camps. When refugees exercise their agency and move to urban areas, they are, for all intents and purposes, leaving the confines of the regime. This is particularly evident in Zambia, where UNHCR explicitly sees refugees choosing between the regime and the urban space.

A similar situation occurs in South Africa, where there is an assumption within the UNHCR in-country office that if refugees required protection or humanitarian assistance, they would have stopped at a refugee camp in a neighbouring state in the region rather than continuing their journeys until arriving at the southern-most country in Africa. An objective of this construction is to confer sufficient agency onto the urban refugee to then relinquish some key obligations imposed by the global refugee regime involving protection and integration. In essence, by moving into cities there is an implication or expectation of self-reliance and resourcefulness. Yet, as highlighted previously, protection concerns remain in these spaces. This overarching approach by UNHCR in Southern Africa leaves most urban refugees to negotiate protection and find alternative forms of reception through the available local and sub-local policies and practices. While many refugees choose to avoid state and international actors and instead to self-settle in cities such as Johannesburg, refugee populations in the case studies have little choice in the matter post registration, as UNHCR actively elects not to engage in meaningful ways in the urban space.

Finally, the construction of the urban refugee as being entirely self-reliant is being replicated at the national level in South Africa. As observed by Schmidt (2014), international factors and domestic factors often interact with each other to influence policies aimed at refugees. In this case, the joint conceptualisation of the 'urban refugee' means that refugees' status is regularly confused with that of other migrants in urban spaces. Indeed, these findings imply that the approach to urban refugees by UNHCR in Southern Africa is reinforcing 'regime shifting' in urban spaces. This refers to the slow transfer of refugees from one governance regime to another, which is seeing urban refugees in both states being slowly moved from national refugee frameworks (and to a lesser extent the global refugee regime) to national migration frameworks. Consequently, this is reinforcing a dominant national-level conceptualisation of who a refugee is and where they reside – with 'regime refugees' in camp spaces and cross-border (often deemed illegal) migrants in urban spaces.

Based on these findings, the book questions the ongoing relevance of the global refugee regime in the reception of refugees in Southern Africa. In essence, the regime is being confined to the refugee camp. Yet, the refugee camp and urban spaces are becoming ever more connected in the region, with refugees regularly moving between these two reception sites. In turn, increasing numbers of refugees in the region (and on the continent), are rejecting the camp space altogether for cities and town. With the regime being contained within out-of-the-way geographical spaces, there is a danger of it becoming entirely irrelevant to the day-to-day practice of reception for large numbers of refugees in Southern Africa.

These findings also raise challenging questions for research looking at Africa that regularly adopts a Western understanding of refugee protection, with its focus (or at least point of departure) being the international level. In making this observation, it is acknowledged that this book itself is not immune from the same criticism. As an alternative, a reorientation towards the national and local levels, with a focus on the role of national and local law and policy, would go some way to avoiding the risk of over-inflating the influence of the 'global' on the protection of refugees. From this vantage point, the relationship between these national and local mechanisms, international norms and bodies and protection mechanisms found at the street level (through sub-local policies and networks) could all be examined with more specificity through a localised lens.

Evaluating the security and stability nexus

Research based on securitisation theory has been a valuable tool in understanding state behaviour towards refugee movement. In South Africa, the securitisation of refugees permeates all levels including state (national and local) and ground-level perspectives. Leaders at both the state and municipality level and local communities all regularly frame cross-border migrants as illegals or criminals. As noted above, these xenophobic narratives feed into state security discourses and are then reinforced by material and ideational concerns over scarce resources and services. The result has been a slow creeping shift in reception policy in South Africa that is seeing the state move away from a free-settlement approach. Indeed, this security lens has reached national-level policy documents and legislation, with the White Paper (DHA, 2017) proposing the removal of all asylum-seekers from the urban space.

The book nevertheless questions some of the broader assumptions that regularly stem from the literature on the securitisation of refugees. Firstly, discussions on securitisation and refugees often originate at the international level, with commentary concerning specific states lacking subtlety or specificity. Secondly, using the work of Vigneswaran and Quirk (2015) as a base, the book interrogated a growing assumption in the literature that states see *all* cross-border movement of low-skilled migrants and refugees as entirely negative. As identified in the case studies, the situation on the ground in Southern Africa is more complex, with several contradictions existing at the heart of responses to refugee movement. To respond to these points, the book's overarching state-focused perspective was utilised in conjunction with the introduction of the complementary concept of stability. The aim was to contribute to this body of literature by developing new strands of analysis on the relationship between refugee movement, state structures and reception policies in the context of Southern Africa.

Stability emerges as a dominant motivation behind how refugees are welcomed and treated in Southern Africa. Indeed, the perceived risk of instability and the overriding desire to maintain the status quo (that is, stability) is driving a great deal of national and local policy in relation to the reception of refugees. This finding has two important implications for contemporary debates on security and refugees. Firstly, understanding surrounding the state-based securitisation of refugee movement in the context of Southern Africa should be revisited. As noted above, contemporary research highlights how refugees and migrants are continuously framed as a security threat to a state or society (Buzan et al., 1998; Donnelly, 2017). Yet the reasons *why* states adopt this approach are less defined, with research often applying broader global or regional trends to state behaviour. For example, in the context of Africa, common reasons cited to explain why states adopt a security lens range from genuine direct and indirect security and capacity issues through to states using the presence of migrants as an 'opportunity' to shift blame for underlying structural issues elsewhere (Landau, 2006; Abebe et al., 2019; Chkam, 2016). All these issues materialised in the context of why state bodies at the local and national level in South Africa adopt securitisation tactics. Yet, concerns around stability were constantly raised *alongside* these other concerns. The empirical data showed that these concerns centred around overstretched services, overcrowding in urban spaces, negative impacts on labour markets, and democratic repercussions in terms of growing tensions within the voting public. Thus, stability emerges as an overarching reason why the state increasingly tries to control the movement of refugees – particularly in and around urban spaces.

Donnelly (2017) proposes that securitisation is a process that is continually negotiated. In this sense, the motivation behind adopting a security lens in respect of refugees is likely to change over time due to differing factors (including material, ideational and institutional) specific to the individual context. In Southern Africa, responses to the movement of refugees twenty years ago revolved around direct security concerns. Indeed, from the 1960s through to the 1980s, the sub-region witnessed a bloody history including the South African anti-apartheid struggle, Rhodesian/Zimbabwean counter-insurgency and liberation war and the Angolan civil war. Yet, with the sub-region now witnessing more peaceful times, the case studies show that when a security lens is used in South Africa, the overarching goal is now more broadly aimed at maintaining stability – or specifically countering the threat of instability that the increased movement of refugees might create.

The second implication arising from the motivating influence of stability over state reception policies is the volatile association that emerges between refugee movement and state structures in the urban space. This association is more nuanced than simply understanding state responses to all refugee movement through a security lens. The adoption of Kotef's (2015) work on the relationship between the movement of people ('rooted' and 'non-rooted') and state-based perceptions of stability was instrumental in arriving at these findings. All states attempt to constrain and manage population movement, especially if that movement originates from 'non-rooted' persons (Kotef, 2015). Thus, the movement of refugees (as 'non-rooted' persons) will always provoke a reaction, with efforts at controlling these specific movements framed as maintaining – or at least creating a perception of – stability and order, rather than restricting or denying freedom. In contrast, the internal migration of 'rooted' people, while equally likely to cause forms of instability if occurring in large numbers, is deemed as an essential freedom.

Prohibiting all movement is nevertheless equally improbable and unlikely to be the ultimate aim of a host state's reception policy. As noted above, to justify policies of non-interference, state officials and UNHCR in both countries understand the movement of refugees in urban spaces (at least on one level) as equating to full human agency. Furthermore, South Africa has essentially maintained a free-settlement approach since the end of the apartheid regime. In Zambia, some movement between the settlements and local communities and larger urban spaces has also always been accepted (either officially or through more tacit means). Indeed, the settlements have created the stability that has enabled this movement. Thus, the inclusion of a stability lens permits the analysis to go further, by engaging with the observed contradictions and paradoxes at the heart of states' responses to refugee movement. Stopping all refugee movement rarely appears to be the overarching aim of a reception policy. Rather, reception policies are focused on *managing* movement, to maintain a sense of stability.

These findings (in conjunction with the analysis above) show that a fragile balance emerges between the movement of refugees and responses by host states, with some movement accepted (or even encouraged) provided it adds 'value' and does not reach a level that is perceived as unstable. If levels increase too far and a sense of instability is created, then a rupture in the delicate host/guest relationship may occur. The result of this is restricted access for refugees, seen both in terms of the political space and actual geographical space. This reaffirms that urban reception in Southern Africa is a precarious form of reception.

Lastly, these findings have implications for academics (and policy advocates), with the push to convince states in the majority world to open up the urban space to refugees and forced migrants, continuing through livelihood and self-reliance initiatives. There is a need to be cognisant of this brittle association between refugee movement and perceptions of stability/instability. As seen in both case studies, increased movement into urban areas, without corresponding approaches to counter concerns over increased instability will likely cause negative responses at all levels of the state.

Implications for policy and practice relating to refugee reception

This final section builds on the previous section by developing some key implications of the book for national and international actors working on refugee reception. Firstly, these findings suggest the need for UNHCR and other humanitarian and development agencies to re-evaluate the relevance of international principles, such as the durable solution of local integration in a region like Southern Africa. Contemporary reception in this sub-region can no longer realistically be thought of as an initial step towards local integration. Key to this finding is the acknowledgement that the reception and longer-term stay of refugees in urban spaces are inherently precarious and temporary. Little assistance is provided by the state or UNHCR, with both entities maintaining policies of non-interference in these spaces. Indeed, the current pattern in both states is of delinking urban refugees from the global regime and treating them as economic or illegal migrants. This makes it hard to envisage the development of specific reception programmes for refugees, particularly at the national level. Furthermore, state- and community-level exclusion barriers regularly occur to enforce confinement to specific enclaves of the city or simply shrink access to the space entirely. Finally, states retain the ability to justify stricter approaches to managing refugee movement due to both the 'protector/protectee' dynamic and security reasons. The COVID-19 global pandemic only intensified these processes further (Maple et al., 2021). Indeed, the pandemic reinforced the notion that refugees are a destabilising presence on the territory and therefore constitute a group that can justifiably be managed, subjected to control or excluded entirely (Tesfai and de Gruchy, 2021; Moyo, Sebba and Zanker, 2021; Washinyira, 2022).

Secondly, the analysis also questions the value of local integration programmes in spaces where refugees and migrants regularly live in informal settlements or townships with locals who are also unable to access key services. Additionally, the patterns of refugee movements observed in cities like Johannesburg suggest that long-term integration programmes might not even be suitable for large portions of the refugee/forced migration population. Refugees frequently either opt to or are forced to (due to the unwelcoming reception) understand the city solely as a resource (Landau, 2018a). Due to the challenges faced in poor urban areas, refugees frequently continue to move between locations in search of better livelihood prospects. This renders the very notion of local integration or integration programming problematic (or at least out-dated) in the urban Southern African context.

As an alternative, the evidence suggests that the role of UNHCR (and other international agencies) following initial registration in the urban space might instead be better focused on convincing states to remove the barriers to accessing local services.[9] Certainly, this type of approach is not novel, with similar ideas promoted by UN agencies such as UNDP. Nevertheless, the book builds on these ideas by underscoring the need for *strategic and localised approaches*, whereby there is a requirement to first uncover and acknowledge the key material, ideational and institutional factors that play significant roles in creating barriers to access. Once identified, these factors should then be addressed and/or incorporated into responses.

In the context of the case studies, this approach could be implemented by engaging with historic constructions of refugees within key government departments in Zambia or by working first at the city level in South Africa, which then might feed up to the national level. Promoting an inclusive 'city' approach, rather than focusing on specific categories of persons, would allow international support to filter into existing state support systems that respond to the needs of all urban poor. In this way, forms of 'local citizenship' could work hand in hand with national and local government reception policy, to aid refugees in achieving personal and economic aims in these spaces – whether that is for the short or long term (Hovil and Maple, 2022). Approaches should also take into account the make-up of the political settlement in the host state. For example, working at the city level without first engaging the president and key individuals within the Department of Home Affairs would likely be less successful in Zambia.

There is a risk, nonetheless, that this approach could inadvertently serve to push refugees further away from the refugee label and more towards an economic or illegal migrant one. Protection concerns remain for many refugees in urban spaces in both case studies. Yet shifts in how UNHCR frames urban refugees may go a long way to recalibrate approaches to urban reception. The current construction (by academics and UNHCR) of the urban space and the refugees who reside in it as sites of opportunity and freedom, is feeding into the idea that refugees who make it to cities are no longer in need of protection. As Omata (2017) has observed, without an enabling environment and adequate resources, an over-reliance on agency can obscure or undermine ongoing protection concerns in these geographical spaces. Similar concerns exist around the importance placed on 'self-reliance' (a concept originating from policymakers), which again puts the onus on the refugee to find their own solutions, while concurrently appearing to remove obligations from states and UN bodies. As an alternative, UNHCR could focus on assisting urban refugees to achieve their 'personal and economic aims', while equally incorporating protection mechanisms into urban programming.

Finally, irrespective of exactly how international agencies and advocates attempt to improve implementation of the core norms from the global refugee regime in Southern Africa, at the heart of any advocacy there needs to be a recognition that the relationship between refugees as 'non-rooted' persons in these spaces and the state and local communities will likely remain fragile and prone to ruptures. States are always prone to exercise their sovereign rights by employing an element of control over the arrival and movement of refugees on their territory. This reality at the heart of refugee reception, therefore, needs to be front and centre of any advocacy to improve the implementation of refugee rights in host states.

Notes

1. This builds on the work of Karadawi (1999).
2. See for example, FitzGerald (2019).
3. See Imenda (2014).
4. See also Betts and Orchard (2014).
5. See also Lor (2011).
6. See also Collier (2011).
7. See also Crisp (2000).
8. With some notable exceptions, for example the work of UNHCR's implementing partners in Zambia.
9. See also Landau (2018a); Kihato and Landau (2016).

Bibliography

7NDP. 2018. *Seventh National Development Plan 2017–2021*. Republic of Zambia. Available: http://www.lse.ac.uk/GranthamInstitute/wp-content/uploads/2018/09/8721.pdf.

8NDP. 2022. *Eighth National Development Plan, 2022–2026*. Republic of Zambia, August.2022. Available: https://www.sh.gov.zm/wp-content/uploads/2022/09/EIGHTH-NATIONAL-DEVELOPMENT-PLAN-2022-2026-05-07-2022.pdf.

Abdelaaty, L. E. 2021. *Discrimination and Delegation: Explaining State Responses to Refugees*. Oxford: Oxford University Press.

Abdulai, A. G. and Hickey, S. 2016. The politics of development under competitive clientelism: Insights from Ghana's education sector. *African Affairs*, 115(458), 44–72.

Abebe, T. T. et al. 2019. The 1969 OAU Refugee Convention at 50: Report. *ISS Africa Report*, (19), 1–15.

Abrahams, C. 2016. Twenty years of social cohesion and nation-building in South Africa. *Journal of Southern African Studies*, 42(1), 95–107.

Acharya, A. 2004. How ideas spread: Whose norms matter? Norm localization and institutional change in Asian regionalism. *International Organization*, 58(2), 239–75.

Adelman, H. 1998. Why refugee warriors are threats. *The Journal of Conflict Studies*, 18(1), 49–69.

Adepoju, A. et al. 2007. Promoting integration through mobility: Free movement and the ECOWAS Protocol. *New Issues in Refugee Research*, 150. Available: https://www.refworld.org/reference/research/unhcr/2007/en/78362.

African Arguments. 2015. *The rise and paradoxes of pan-Africanism today*. Available: https://africanarguments.org/2015/06/30/the-rise-and-paradoxes-of-pan-africanism-today/15.

The African Wealth Report (AWR). 2020. *The African Wealth Report*. Available: https://www.intellidex.co.za/press-releases/the-african-wealth-report-2020/.

Agamben, G. 1998. *Homo Sacer: Sovereign Power and Bare Life*. Stanford: Stanford University Press.

Agamben, G. 2000. *Means Without End: Notes on Politics*. Minneapolis: University of Minnesota Press.

Agamben, G. 2005. *State of Exception*. Chicago: University of Chicago Press.

Agee, J. 2009. Developing qualitative research questions: a reflective process. *International Journal of Qualitative Studies in Education*, 22(4), 431–47.

Agier, M. 2008. *On the Margins of the World: The Refugee Experience Today*. Cambridge: Polity Press.

Agier, M. 2011. *Managing the Undesirables: Refugee Camps and Humanitarian Government*. Cambridge: Polity Press.

Alam, S. 2008. Majority world: Challenging the West's rhetoric of democracy. *Amerasia Journal*, 1, 34(1), 88–98.

Albert, M. 2010. Governance and prima facie refugee status determination: Clarifying the boundaries of temporary protection, group determination, and mass influx. *Refugee Survey Quarterly*, 29(1), 61–91.

Alderson, K. 2001. Making sense of state socialization. *Review of International Studies*, 27(3), 415–33.

Aleinikoff, A. 1995. State-centred refugee law: From resettlement to containment. In: Daniel, E. V. and Knudsen, J. C. eds. *Mistrusting Refugees*. Berkeley: University of California Press.

Aleinikoff, A. and Poellot, S. 2014. The responsibility to solve: The international community and protracted refugee situations. *Virginia Journal of International Law*, 54(2).

Aleinikoff, A. and Zamore, L. 2019. *The Arc of Protection: Reforming the International Refugee Regime*. Stanford: Stanford University Press.

Amit, R., 2011. *The Zimbabwean documentation process: Lessons learned*. ACMS. Available: https://citizenshiprightsafrica.org/the-zimbabwean-documentation-process-lessons-learned/.

Amit, R. 2012. *No way in: Barriers to access, service and administrative justice at South Africa's refugee reception offices*. ACMS. Available: https://ssrn.com/abstract=3274020.

Amit, R. 2015. *Queue here for corruption, measuring irregularities in South Africa's asylum system*. Lawyers for Human Rights and ACMS. Available: www.lhr.org.za/sites/lhr.org.za/files/lhracms_report-queue_here_for_corruption-july_2015.pdf.

Amuedo-Dorantes, C. et al. 2018. Refugee admissions and public safety: Are refugee settlement areas more prone to crime? *IZA Discussion Paper Series, No. 11612*. Available: https://www.iza.org/publications/dp/11612/refugee-admissions-and-public-safety-are-refugee-settlement-areas-more-prone-to-crime.

Anderson, B. 2010. Migration, immigration controls and the fashioning of precarious workers. *Work, Employment and Society*, 24(2), 300–17.

Arendt, H. 1951. *The Origins of Totalitarianism*. New York: Harcourt.

Arendt, H. 1958. *The Human Condition*. Chicago: University of Chicago Press.

Arar, R. and FitzGerald, D. S. 2023. *The Refugee System: A Sociological Approach*. Cambridge: Polity Press.

Asad, A. L. 2015. Contexts of reception, post-disaster migration, and socioeconomic mobility. *Population and Environment*, 36(3), 279–310.

Atkinson, R. and Flint, J. 2001. Accessing hidden and hard-to-reach populations: Snowball research strategies. *Social Research Update*, 33(1), 1–4.

Attride-Stirling, J. 2001. Thematic Networks: An analytic tool for qualitative research. *Qualitative Research*, 1, 385–405.

Bakewell, O. 2000. Repatriation and self-settled refugees in Zambia: Bringing solutions to the wrong problems. *Journal of Refugee Studies*, 13(4), 356–73.

Bakewell, O. 2002. *Review of CORD community services for Angolan refugees in Western Province, Zambia*. UNHCR. Available : https ://www.unhcr.org/uk/media/review-cord-community-services-angolan-refugees-western-province-zambia.

Bakewell, O. 2004. *Migration as a development strategy: A challenge to development NGOs*. Informed-NGO Funding and Policy Bulletin 10, 10–22.

Bakewell, O. 2007. Keeping them in their place: The ambivalent relationship between development and migration in Africa. *Working Paper Series 08*. International Migration Institute. Available: https://www.migrationinstitute.org/publications/wp-08-07.

Bakewell, O. 2014. Encampment and self-settlement. In: Fiddian-Qasmiyeh, E. et al. eds. *The Oxford Handbook of Refugee and Forced Migration Studies*. Oxford: Oxford University Press, 127–38.

Bakewell, O. 2018. Negotiating a space of belonging: A case study from the Zambia-Angolan borderlands. In: Bakewell, O. and Landau, L. B. eds. *Forging African Communities*. London: Palgrave Macmillan, 103–26.

Bakewell, O. and Jónsson, G. 2011. Migration, mobility, and the African city. *IMI Working Papers No. 50*. International Migration Institute. Available: https://ora.ox.ac.uk/objects/uuid:87e74a2b-81b3-4267-bd17-e5d0e94df889/download_file?file_format=pdf&safe_filename=WP50%2BMigration%2Bmobility%2Band%2Bthe%2Bafrican%2Bcity.pdf&type_of_work=Working+paper.

Bakken, I. and Rustad, S. 2018. Conflict trends in Africa, 1989–2017. *Conflict Trends, 6*. Oslo: Peace Research Institute. Available: https://reliefweb.int/report/world/conflict-trends-africa-1989-2017.

Ballard, R. et al. 2017. *Current dynamics of social cohesion within the city of Johannesburg*. Gauteng City Region Observatory (GCRO), Unpublished.

Banerjee, P. and Samaddar, R. 2018. Why critical forced migration studies has to be post-colonial by nature. In: Bloch, A. and Dona, G. eds. *Forced Migration: Current Issues and Debates*. Abingdon: Routledge, 44–59.

Barbelet, V. and Wake, C. 2017. *Livelihoods in displacement: From refugee perspectives to aid agency response*. Humanitarian Policy Group Report. Overseas Development Institute. Available : https ://www.refworld.org/reference/themreport/odi/2017/en/119539.

Barrientos, A. and Pellissery, S. 2012. Delivering effective social assistance: Does politics matter? *Effective States and Inclusive Development Research Centre Working Paper No. 9*. Available at: https://papers.ssrn.com/sol3/papers.cfm?abstract_id=2141880.

Barutciski, M. 2013. The limits to the UNHCR's supervisory role. In: Simeon, J. C. ed. *The UNHCR and the Supervision of International Refugee Law*. Cambridge: Cambridge University Press, 59–74.

Basok, T. 2009. Counter-hegemonic human rights discourses and migrant rights activism in the US and Canada. *International Journal of Comparative Sociology*, 50, 183–205.

Bauman, Z. 2002. In the lowly nowherevilles of liquid modernity: Comments on and around Agier. *Ethnography*, 3(3), 343–9.

BBC. 2019. *South Africa: How common are xenophobic attacks?* BBC News 2 October 2019. Available: https://www.bbc.com/news/world-africa-47800718.

Bebbington, A. et al. 2017. Political settlements and the governance of extractive industry: A comparative analysis of the longue durée in Africa and Latin America. *ESID Working Paper No. 81*. University of Manchester. Available: https://www.effective-states.org/wp-content/uploads/working_papers/final-pdfs/esid_wp_81_bebbington_et_al.pdf.

Becker, H. S. 2009. How to find out how to do qualitative research. *International Journal of Communication*, 3, 545–53.

Bennett, A. 2004. Case study methods: Design, use, and comparative advantages. In: Sprinzand, D. F. and Wolinsky-Nahmias, Y. eds. *Models, Numbers, and Cases: Methods for Studying International Relations*. Ann Arbor: University of Michigan Press, 19–55.

Bernard, R. H. 2011. *Research Methods in Anthropology*. Lanham: Altamira Press.

Betts, A. 2009a. Development assistance and refugees. Towards a north-south grand bargain? *Forced Migration Policy Briefing 2*. Oxford: Refugee Studies Centre (RSC).

Betts, A. 2009b. *Forced Migration and Global Politics*. Hoboken: Wiley-Blackwell.

Betts, A. 2013a. *Survival Migration: Failed Governance and the Crisis of Displacement.* Ithaca: Cornell University Press.

Betts, A. 2013b. Regime complexity and international organizations: UNHCR as a challenged institution. *Global Governance,* 19(1), 69–81.

Betts, A. 2014. From persecution to deprivation: How refugee norms adapt at implementation. In: Betts, A. and Orchard, P. eds. *Implementation and World Politics: How International Norms Change Practice.* Oxford: Oxford University Press, 29–49.

Betts, A. and Kaytaz, E. 2009. National and international responses to the Zimbabwean exodus: Implications for the refugee protection regime. *New Issues in Refugee Research,* Paper No 175. Available: https://www.unhcr.org/afr/research/working/4a76fc8a9/national-international-responses-zimbabwean-exodus-implications-refugee.html.

Betts, A. and Orchard, P. 2014. *Implementation and World Politics- How International Norms Change Practice.* Oxford: Oxford University Press.

Betts, A. et al. 2017. *Refugee Economies: Forced Displacement and Development.* Oxford: Oxford University Press.

Betts, A. et al. 2018. *Self-reliance in Kalobeyei? Socio-economic Outcomes for Refugees in North-West Kenya.* Oxford: RSC.

Betts, A. et al. 2019. *Refugee Economies in Uganda: What Difference Does the Self-reliance Model Make?* Oxford: RSC.

Bilotta, N. 2020. Anti-oppressive social work research: Prioritising refugee voices in Kakuma refugee camp. *Ethics and Social Welfare,*14(4), 397–414.

Black, R. 1998. Refugee camps not really reconsidered: A reply to Crisp and Jacobsen. *Forced Migration Review,* 3, Oxford: RSC.

Bloch, A. and Donà, G. 2018. Forced migration: Setting the scene. In: Bloch, A. and Donà, G. eds. *Forced Migration: Current Issues and Debates.* Abingdon: Routledge, 1–18.

Bloemraad, I. 2006. Becoming a citizen in the United States and Canada: Structured mobilization and immigrant political incorporation. *Social Forces,* 85(2), 667–95.

Boru, T. 2018. *The impact of industry concentration on performance, exploring a comprehensive bank performance model: The case of the Ethiopian banking sector.* PhD Thesis, University of South Africa.

Braun, V. and Clarke, V. 2006. Using thematic analysis in psychology. *Qualitative Research in Psychology,* 3(2), 77–101.

Brosché, J. and Nilsson, M. 2005. *Zambian Refugee Policy: Security, Repatriation and Local Integration.* Available: http://www.diva-portal.org/smash/get/diva2:1149513/FULLTEXT01.pdf.

Bryman, M. A. H. A. 2004. *Handbook of Data Analysis.* London: Sage.

Bucklaschuk, J. 2015. *A Literature Review of Local Partnerships and Welcoming Community Strategies*. Winnipeg: Immigration Partnership Winnipeg.

Burnell, P. 2005. *From Low-conflict Polity to Democratic Civil Peace? Explaining Zambian Exceptionalism*. Occasional Paper 58. University of Warwick. Available: http://wrap.warwick.ac.uk/896/1/WRAP _Burnell_7270220-180609-zambiaconflictas2.pdf.

Buzan, B. et al. 1998. *Security: A New Framework for Analysis*. London: Lynne Rienner Publishers.

Cadge, W. and Ecklund, E. H. 2007. Immigration and religion. *Annual Review of Sociology*, 33, 359–79.

Canefe, N. 2010. The fragmented nature of the international refugee regime and its consequences: A comparative analysis of the applications of the 1951 convention. In: Simeon, J. C. ed. *Critical Issues in International Refugee Law: Strategies Toward Interpretative Harmony*. Cambridge: Cambridge University Press, 174–210.

Cannon, B. J. and Fujibayashi, H. 2018. Security, structural factors and sovereignty: Analysing reactions to Kenya's decision to close the Dadaab refugee camp complex. *African Security Review*, 27(1), 20–41.

Cantor, D. J. and Chikwanha, F. 2019. Reconsidering African refugee law. *International Journal of Refugee Law*, 31(2–3), 182–260.

Carciotto, S., 2018. The regularization of Zimbabwean migrants: A case of permanent temporariness. *African Human Mobility Review*, 4(1), 1101–16.

Carciotto, S. and Ferraro, F. 2020. Building blocks and challenges for the implementation of the Global Compact on Refugees in Africa. *Journal on Migration and Human Security*, 8(1), 83–95.

Carciotto, S. and Mavura, M. 2022. *The Evolution of Migration Policy in Post-Apartheid South Africa: Emerging Themes and New Challenges*. Cape Town: Scalabrini Institute for Human Mobility in Africa Report.

Castles, S. 2015. International human mobility: Key issues and challenges. In: Castles, S. et al. eds. *Social Transformation and Migration: National and Local Experiences in South Korea, Turkey, Mexico and Australia*. New York: Springer, 3–14.

Chabal, P. and Daloz, J. P. 1999. *Africa Works: Disorder as Political Instrument*. London: International African Institute.

Chapotera, S. 2018. *Assessing opportunities and barriers of refugee local integration in Malawi*. MSc Dissertation, University of London.

Chatzipanagiotidou, E. and Murphy. F. 2022. Exhibiting displacement: Refugee art, methodological dubiety and the responsibility (not) to document loss. In: Grabska, K. and Clark-Kazak, C. eds. *Documenting Displacement: Questioning Methodological Boundaries in Forced*

Migration Research. Montreal: McGill-Queen's University Press, 81–103.

Cheeseman, N. 2017. Zambia slides towards authoritarianism as IMF props up government. *The Conversation*. Available: https://theconversation.com/zambia-slides-towards-authoritarianism-as-imf-props-up-government-79533.

Chekero, T. 2023. Borders and boundaries in daily urban mobility practices of refugees in Cape Town, South Africa. *Refugee Survey Quarterly*, 42(3), 361–81.

Chiasson, S. 2015. *Refugee freedom of movement restricted in Zambia*. Urban Refugees.Org. Available: http://urban-refugees.org/debate/refugee-freedom-movement-restricted-zambia/.

Chimni, B. S. 2009. The birth of a 'discipline': From refugee to forced migration studies. *Journal of Refugee studies*, 22(1), 11–29.

Chitupila, P. 2010. *Workshop discussion on refugee status determination (RSD) and rights in Southern and East Africa*. Uganda, 16–17 November 2010. Oxford: RSC. Available: https://www.rsc.ox.ac.uk/files/files-1/dp-rsd-zambia-2010.pdf.

Chkam, H. 2016. Aid and the perpetuation of refugee camps: The case of Dadaab in Kenya 1991–2011. *Refugee Survey Quarterly*, 35(2), 79–97.

City of Johannesburg. 2013. *2012/16 Integrated Development Plan: 2013/14 Review*. Johannesburg: City of Johannesburg. Available: https://www.joburg.org.za/documents_/Documents/Intergrated%20Development%20Plan/2013-16%20IDP%2017may2013%20final.pdf.

City of Johannesburg. 2017. Presentation slides from the Migration Sub-Unit, City of Johannesburg on Social Development, 18 November 2017.

Civicus. 2017. *Zambia: State of Emergency signifies worrying signs for civic space*. Zambia Council for Social Development. Available: https://www.civicus.org/index.php/media-resources/media-releases/2901-zambia-state-of-emergency-signifies-worrying-signs-for-civic-space.

Clark-Kazak, C. 2017. Ethical considerations: Research with people in situations of forced migration. *Refuge*, 33(2), 11–17.

Clark-Kazak, C. 2021. Ethics in forced migration research: Taking stock and potential ways forward. *Journal on Migration and Human Security*, 9(3), 125–38.

Clark-Kazak, C. 2023. *Research Across Borders: An Introduction to Interdisciplinary, Cross-cultural Methodology*. Toronto: University of Toronto Press.

Cohen, D. and Crabtree, B. 2006. *Using Qualitative Methods in Healthcare Research: A Comprehensive Guide for Designing, Writing, Reviewing* and *Reporting Qualitative Research*. Princeton: Robert Wood Johnson Foundation.

Collier, D. 1995. Translating quantitative methods for qualitative researchers: The case of selection bias. *American Political Science Review*, 89(2), 461–6.

Collier, D. 2011. Understanding process tracing. *PS: Political Science & Politics*, 44(4), 823–30.

Collier, D. and Mahoney, J. 1996. Insights and pitfalls: Selection bias in qualitative research. *World Politics*, 49(1), 56–91.

Collyer, M. 2014. Geographies of forced migration. In: Fiddian-Qasmiyeh, E. et al. eds. *The Oxford Handbook of Refugee and Forced Migration Studies*. Oxford: Oxford University Press, 112–26.

Collyer, M. and King, R. 2016. Narrating Europe's migration and refugee 'crisis'. *Human Geography: A New Radical Journal*, 9(2), 1–12.

Cortell, A. P. and Davis, J. W. 2005. When norms clash: International norms, domestic practices, and Japan's internalisation of the GATT/WTO. *Review of International Studies*, 31(1), 3–25.

Corti, L. et al. 2000. Confidentiality and informed consent: Issues for consideration in the preservation of and provision of access to qualitative data archives. *Forum Qualitative Sozialforschung/Forum: Qualitative Social Research*, 1(3).

Creswell, J. W. 2009. *Research design: Qualitative, Quantitative, and Mixed Methods Approaches*. Thousand Oaks: University of Nebraska–Lincoln.

Crisp, J. 2000. Africa's refugees: Patterns, problems and policy challenges. *New Issues in Refugee Research, Working Paper 28*. Available: https://www.unhcr.org/uk/research/working/3ae6a0c78/africas-refugees-patterns-problems-policy-challenges-jeff-crisp.html.

Crisp, J. 2003. No solution in sight: The problem of protracted refugee situations in Africa. *New Issues in Refugee Research, Working Paper 75*. UNHCR, Evaluation and Policy Analysis Unit.

Crisp, J. 2004. The local integration and local settlement of refugees: A conceptual and historical analysis. *New Issues in Refugee Research, Working Paper 102*. UNHCR, Evaluation and Policy Analysis Unit.

Crisp, J. 2006. Forced displacement in Africa: Dimensions, difficulties, and policy directions. *New Issues in Refugee Research, Working Paper 126*. Available: https://www.unhcr.org/afr/research/working/44b7b758f/forced-displacement-africa-dimensions-difficulties-policy-directions-jeff.html.

Crisp, J. 2008. Beyond the nexus: UNHCR's evolving perspective on Refugee protection and international migration. *New Issues in Refugee Research, Working Paper 155*. Available: https://www.unhcr

.org/uk/research/working/4818749a2/beyond-nexus-unhcrs-evolving-perspective-refugee-protection-international.html.
Crisp, J. 2010. Forced displacement in Africa: Dimensions, difficulties, and policy directions. *Refugee Survey Quarterly*, 29(3), 1–27.
Crisp, J. 2015. Too much information. *Forced Migration Current Awareness, guest post, 11 February*. Available: https://fm-cab.blogspot.com/search?q=jeff+crisp+too+much+information.
Crisp, J. 2017. Finding space for protection: An inside account of the evolution of UNHCR's urban refugee policy. *Refuge: Canada's Journal on Refugees*, 33(1), 87–96.
Crisp, J. and Jacobsen, K. 1998. Refugee camps reconsidered. *Forced Migration Review*, 3. Oxford: RSC.
Crisp, J. and Kiragu, E. 2010. *Refugee protection and international migration. A review of UNHCR's role in Malawi, Mozambique and South Africa*. UNHCR PDES. Available: https://www.unhcr.org/4c629c4d9.html.
Crook, R. C. 2003. Decentralisation and poverty reduction in Africa: The politics of local–central relations. *Public Administration and Development: The International Journal of Management Research and Practice*, 23(1), 77–88.
Crotty, M. 1998. *The Foundations of Social Research: Meaning and Perspective in the Research Process*. London: Sage.
Crouch, M. and McKenzie, H. 2006. The logic of small samples in interview-based qualitative research. *Social Science Information*, 45(4), 483–99.
Crush, J. and Chikanda, A. 2014. Forced Migration in Southern Africa. In: Fiddian-Qasmiyeh, E. et al. eds. *The Oxford Handbook of Refugee and Forced Migration Studies*. Oxford: Oxford University Press, 554–70.
Crush, J. et al. 2017. Benign neglect or active destruction? A critical analysis of refugee and informal sector policy and practice in South Africa. *African Human Mobility Review*, 3(2), 751–82.
d'Orsi, C. 2019. Refugee camps versus urban refugees: what's been said – and done. *The Conversation*. Available: https://theconversation.com/refugee-camps-versus-urban-refugees-whats-been-said-and-done-126069.
Da Costa, R. 2006. *Rights of refugees in the context of integration: Legal standards and recommendations*. UNHCR DIPS. Available: https://www.unhcr.org/44bb90882.pdf.
Daily Maverick, 2020a. Frozen futures: The uncertain and inhumane fate of Angolan refugees in SA. *Daily Maverick* 6 February 2008.

Available: https://www.dailymaverick.co.za/article/2020-02-06-frozen-futures-the-uncertain-and-inhumane-fate-of-angolan-refugees-in-sa/.

Daley, P. 2013. Refugees, IDPs and citizenship rights: The perils of humanitarianism in the African Great Lakes region. *Third World Quarterly*, 34(5), 893–912.

Darling, J. 2009. Becoming bare life: Asylum, hospitality, and the politics of encampment. *Environment and Planning D: Society and Space*, 27(4), 649–65.

Darling, J. 2017. Forced migration and the city: Irregularity, informality, and the politics of presence. *Progress in Human Geography*, 41(2), 178–1.

Darwin, C. 2005. *Report on the Situation of Refugees in Zambia*. AMERA. Available: https://www.matrixlaw.co.uk/wp-content/uploads/2016/03/20_10_2014_09_30_27_Report-Refugees-Zambia.pdf.

De Haas, H. 2009. Mobility and human development. *UNDP, Human Development Research Paper*, 2009/1. Available: http://hdr.undp.org/en/content/mobility-and-human-development.

de Wet, T. et al. 2011. Poor housing, good health: A comparison of formal and informal housing in Johannesburg, South Africa. *International Journal of Public Health*, 56(6), 625–33.

Deardorff, S. 2009. How long is too long? Questioning the legality of long-term encampment through a human rights lens. *Oxford RSC, Working paper series no. 54*. Available: https://www.rsc.ox.ac.uk/files/files-1/wp54-how-long-too-long-2009.pdf.

Deere, C. 2009. *The Implementation Game: The TRIPS Agreement and the Global Politics of Intellectual Property Reform in Developing Countries*. Oxford: Oxford University Press.

Delaney, D. and Leitner, H. 1997. The political construction of scale. *Political Geography*, 16(2), 93–7.

Derrida, J. 2000. Hospitality. *Angelaki*, 5(3), 3–18.

Derrida, J. 2005. The principle of hospitality. In: Derrida, J. ed. *Paper Machine*. Stanford: Stanford University Press, 66–9.

Derrida, J. and Dufourmantelle, A. 2000. *Of Hospitality*. Stanford: Stanford University Press.

DHA. 2016a. *Green Paper on international migration for South Africa*. Department of Home Affairs, June 2016. Available: http://www.dha.gov.za/files/GreenPaper_on_InternationalMigration-%2022062016.pdf.

DHA. 2016b. *2015 Asylum statistics; Analysis and trends – presentation to the Portfolio Committee of Homes Affairs*. Department of Home Affairs. Available: http://pmg-assets.s3-website-eu-west-1.amazonaws.com/160308Asylum.pdf.

DHA. 2017. *White Paper on International Migration for South Africa.* Department of Home Affairs, July 2017. Available: http://www.dha.gov.za/WhitePaperonInternationalMigration-20170602.pdf.

Diken, B. and Laustsen, C. B. 2005. *The Culture of Exception: Sociology Facing the Camp.* London: Routledge.

Donger, E. et al. 2017. *Refugee Youth in Lusaka: A Comprehensive Evaluation of Health and Wellbeing.* UNHCR et al. Available: https://www.hsph.harvard.edu/wp-content/uploads/sites/2464/2018/05/UNHCR-ZAMBIA-Report1.pdf.

Donnelly, F. 2017. In the name of (de)securitization: Speaking security to protect migrants, refugees and internally displaced persons? *International Review of the Red Cross*, 99(904), 241–61.

DTS. 2014. *Field evaluation of local integration of former refugees in Zambia.* U.S. Department of State. Available: https://2009-2017.state.gov/documents/organization/235057.pdf.

ESRC. 2017. *Refugee reception and integration.* Available: https://esrc.ukri.org/news-events-and-publications/evidence-briefings/refugee-reception-and-integration/.

Essed, P. and Wesenbeek, R. 2004. Contested refugee status: Human rights, ethics and social responsibilities. In: Essed, P. et al. eds. *Refugees and the Transformation of Societies: Agency, Policies, Ethics, and Politics (Vol. 13).* Oxford: Berghahn Books.

Fábos, A. and Kibreab, G. 2007. Urban refugees: Introduction. *Refuge: Canada's Periodical on Refugees*, 24(1), 1–19.

Fairclough, N. 2013. *Critical Discourse Analysis: The Critical Study of Language.* Abingdon: Routledge.

Fauvelle-Aymar, C. and Segatti, A. 2011. People, space and politics: An exploration of factors explaining the 2008 anti-foreigner violence in South Africa. In: Landau, L. B. ed. *Exorcising the Demons Within: Xenophobia, Violence, and Statecraft in Contemporary South Africa.* Johannesburg: Wits University Press.

Fedyuk, O. and Zentai, V. 2018. The interview in migration studies: A step towards a dialogue and knowledge co-production? In: Zapata-Barrero, R. and Yalaz, E. eds. *Qualitative Research in European Migration Studies.* New York: Springer Publishing, 171–88.

Fiddian-Qasmiyeh, E. 2015. *South-South Educational Migration, Humanitarianism and Development: Views from the Caribbean, North Africa and the Middle East.* Abingdon: Routledge.

Fiddian-Qasmiyeh, E. 2016. Refugee–refugee relations in contexts of overlapping displacement. *International Journal of Urban and Regional Research.* Available: https://www.ijurr.org/spotlight-on/the-urban

-refugee-crisis-reflections-on-cities-citizenship-and-the-displaced/refugee-refugee-relations-in-contexts-of-overlapping-displacement/.

Fiddian-Qasmiyeh, E. 2019. Looking forward: Disasters at 40. *Disasters*, 43, 36–60.

Fiddian-Qasmiyeh, E. 2020. Introduction: Recentering the South in studies of migration. *Migration and Society*, 3(1), 1–18.

Fiddian-Qasmiyeh, E. and Berg, M. L. 2018. Inaugural editorial. *Migration and Society*, 1(1), 5–7.

Field, J. R. C. 2010. Bridging the gap between refugee rights and reality: A proposal for developing international duties in the refugee context. *International Journal of Refugee Law*, 22(4), 512–57.

Fielden, A. 2008. Local integration: An under-reported solution to protracted refugee situations. *New Issues in Refugee Research*, 158. Available: https://www.unhcr.org/uk/research/working/486cc99f2/local-integration-under-reported-solution-protracted-refugee-situations.html.

Finnemore, M. and Sikkink, K. 1998. International norm dynamics and political change. *International Organization*, 52 (4), 887–917.

FitzGerald, D. S. 2019. *Refuge Beyond Reach: How Rich Democracies Repel Asylum Seekers*. New York: Oxford University Press.

Flahaux, M. L. and De Haas, H. 2016. African migration: Trends, patterns, drivers. *Comparative Migration Studies*, 4(1), 1–25.

Flick, U. 2006. *An Introduction to Qualitative Research*. Thousand Oaks: Sage.

Flick, U. ed. 2009. *The Sage Qualitative Research Kit: Collection*. Thousand Oaks: Sage.

Flyvbjerg, B. 2006. Five misunderstandings about case-study research. *Qualitative Inquiry*, 12(2), 219–45.

Forsythe, D. P. 2001. Humanitarian protection: The International Committee of the Red Cross and the United Nations High Commissioner for Refugees. *International Review of the Red Cross*, 83(843), 675–98.

Foucault, M. 1979. *Discipline and Punish: The Birth of the Prison*. New York: Vintage Books.

Freier, L. F., Micinski, N. R. and Tsourapas, G. 2021. Refugee commodification: The diffusion of refugee rent-seeking in the Global South. *Third World Quarterly*, 42(11), 2747–66.

Frischkorn, R. S. 2013. *We just aren't free: Urban refugees and integration in Lusaka, Zambia*. PhD Thesis, American University. Available: https://search.proquest.com/openview/53a80b73e20383339aec87787cf8fba3/1?pq-origsite=gscholar&cbl=18750&diss=y.

Frischkorn, R. S. 2015. Political economy of control: Urban refugees and the regulation of space in Lusaka, Zambia. *Economic Anthropology*, 2(1), 205–23.

Frontline Defenders. 2018. *Creeping towards authoritarianism? Impacts on human rights defenders and civil society in Zambia*. Available: https://www.frontlinedefenders.org/en/statement-report/creeping-towards-authoritarianism.

Gerring, J. 2008. Case selection for case-study analysis: Qualitative and quantitative techniques. In: Box-Steffensmeier, J. et al. eds. *The Oxford Handbook of Political Methodology*, Vol. 10. Oxford: Oxford University Press, 645–84.

Gill, N. et al. 2011. Introduction: Mobilities and forced migration. *Mobilities*, 6(3), 301–16.

Glasman, J. 2017. Seeing like a refugee agency: A short history of UNHCR classification in Central Africa (1961–2015). *Journal of Refugee Studies*, 30(2), 337–62.

Grabska, K. and Clark-Kazak, C. 2022. *Documenting Displacement: Questioning Methodological Boundaries in Forced Migration Research*. Montreal: McGill-Queen's University Press.

Grant, A. 2018. *Doing Excellent Social Research with Documents: Practical Examples and Guidance for Qualitative Researchers*. Abingdon: Routledge.

Gray, D. E. 2004. *Doing Research in the Real World*. London: Sage.

Gray, D. E. 2013. *Doing Research in the Real World*. London: Sage.

Grindheim, K. A. 2013. *Exploring the impacts of refugee camps on host communities: A Case Study of Kakuma Host Community in Kenya*. MA Thesis, University of Agder.

Grosfoguel, R. 2003. *Colonial Subjects: Puerto Ricans in a Global Perspective*. Berkeley: University of California Press.

Grosfoguel, R. 2004. Race and ethnicity or racialized ethnicities? Identities within global coloniality. *Ethnicities*, 4(3), 315–36.

Guarnizo, L. E. 2011. The fluid, multi-scalar, and contradictory construction of citizenship. In: Smith, M. P. and McQuarrie, M. eds. *Remaking Urban Citizenship: Organizations, Institutions, and the Right to the City*. New Brunswick: Transaction Publishers, 11–38.

Guarnizo, L. E. et al. 1999. Mistrust, fragmented solidarity, and transnational migration: Colombians in New York City and Los Angeles. *Ethnic and Racial Studies*, 22(2), 367–96.

Hagen, J. J., Michelis, I., Eggert, J. P. and Turner, L. 2023. Learning to say 'No': Privilege, entitlement and refusal in peace, (post) conflict and security research. *Critical Studies on Security*, 11(2), 1–19.

Hammerstad, A. 2010. UNHCR and the securitisation of forced migration. In: Betts, A. and Loescher, G. eds. *Refugees in International Relations*. Oxford: Oxford University Press.

Hammerstad, A. 2012. Securitisation from below: The relationship between immigration and foreign policy in South Africa's approach to the Zimbabwe crisis. *Conflict, Security & Development*, 12(1), 1–30.

Handmaker, L. A. et al. 2008. *Advancing Refugee Protection in South Africa (Human Rights in Context, Vol. 2)*. Oxford: Berghahn Books.

Hansen, A. 1979. Once the running stops: Assimilation of Angolan refugees into Zambian border villages. *Disasters*, 3(4), 369–74.

Hansen, A. 1982. Self-settled rural refugees in Africa: The case of Angolans in Zambian villages. In: Hansen, A. and Oliver-Smith, A. eds. *Involuntary Migration and Resettlement: The Problems and Responses of Dislocated People*. New York: Routledge.

Hansen, A. 1990. Refugee self-settlement versus settlement on government schemes: The long-term consequences for security, integration and economic development of Angolan refugees (1966–1989) in Zambia. *Discussion Paper-United Nations Research Institute for Social Development*, 17. Available: https://digitallibrary.un.org/record/421067?ln=en.

Harrell-Bond, B. 1998. Camps: Literature Review. *Forced Migration Review*, 2. Available: https://www.fmreview.org/sites/fmr/files/FMRdownloads/en/camps/harrellbond.pdf.

Hayden, B. 2006. What's in a name? The nature of the individual in refugee studies. *Journal of Refugee Studies*, 19(4), 471–87.

Hentschel, J. 1998. Distinguishing between types of data and methods of collecting them. *Policy Research Working Papers No. 1914 (World Bank)*. Available: http://documents1.worldbank.org/curated/en/575761468766463068/pdf/multi-page.pdf.

The Herald. 2023. *Motsoaledi's Decision to end ZEP Invalid and Unconstitutional, Rules High Court*. The Herald, Bernadette Wicks, 28 June.2023. Available: https://www.herald.co.zw/motsoaledis-decision-to-end-zep-invalid-and-unconstitutional-rules-high-court/.

Hickey, S. et al. 2015. (Introduction) Exploring the politics of inclusive development: Towards a new conceptual approach. In: Hickey, S. et al. eds. *The Politics of Inclusive Development: Interrogating the Evidence*. Oxford: Oxford University Press, 3–34.

Horst, C. 2004. Money and mobility: Transnational livelihood strategies of the Somali diaspora. *Global Migration Perspectives No. 9*. Available: https://www.refworld.org/docid/42ce49684.html.

Horwood, C. 2009. *In pursuit of the southern dream: Victims of necessity, assessment of the irregular movement of men from East Africa and the*

Horn to South Africa. Available: https://publications.iom.int/system/files/pdf/iomresearchassessment.pdf.

Hove, M. et al. 2013. The urban crisis in Sub-Saharan Africa: A threat to human security and sustainable development. *Stability*, 2(1), 1–14.

Hovil, L. 2007. Self-settled refugees in Uganda: An alternative approach to displacement? *Journal of Refugee Studies*, 20, 599–620.

Hovil, L. 2016. *Refugees, Conflict and the Search for Belonging*. London: Palgrave Macmillan.

Hovil, L. and Maple, N. 2022. Local integration: A durable solution in need of restoration? *Refugee Survey Quarterly*, 41(2), 238–66.

HPN/ODI. 2018. *Special feature: Humanitarian response in urban areas*. Available: https://odihpn.org/wp-content/uploads/2018/03/HE71_revised.pdf.

Hurd, I. 2008. Constructivism. In: Reus-Smit, C. and Snidal, D. eds. *The Oxford Handbook of International Relations*. Oxford: Oxford University Press, 298–316.

Hyndman, J. 2000. *Managing Displacement: Refugees and the Politics of Humanitarianism*. Minneapolis: University of Minnesota Press.

Hyndman, J. and Giles, W. 2011. Waiting for what? The feminization of asylum in protracted situations. *Gender, Place & Culture*, 18(3), 361–79.

Hyndman, J. and Mountz, A. 2008. Another brick in the wall? Neo-refoulement and the externalization of asylum by Australia and Europe. *Govern. Opposite*, 43(2), 249–69.

ICG. 1999. *Burundi's Peace Process: The Road from Arusha*, Central Africa Report, 12, November 1999. Available: https://www.crisisgroup.org/africa/central-africa/burundi/burundis-peace-process-road-arusha.

IFC. 2018. *Kakuma as a marketplace: A consumer and market study of a refugee camp and town in northwest Kenya*. Available: https://www.ifc.org/wps/wcm/connect/0f3e93fb-35dc-4a80-a955-6a7028d0f77f/20180427_Kakuma-as-a-Marketplace_v1.pdf?MOD=AJPERES&CVID=mc8eL2K.

Imenda, S. 2014. Is there a conceptual difference between theoretical and conceptual frameworks? *Journal of Social Sciences*, 38(2), 185–95.

Jackson, R. et al. 2019. *Introduction to International Relations: Theories and Approaches*. Oxford: Oxford University Press.

Jacobsen, K. 2002. Can refugees benefit the state? Refugee resources and African statebuilding. *The Journal of Modern African Studies*, 40(4), 577–96.

Jacobsen, K. 2005. *The Economic Life of Refugees*. Boulder, CO: Kumarian Press.

Jacobsen, K. 2017. Refugees in towns: Experiences of integration. *Forced Migration Review*, (56), 78–9.

Jamal, A. 2000. *Minimum standards and essential needs in protracted refugee situations. A review of the UNHCR programme in Kakuma, Kenya*. Available: https://reliefweb.int/sites/reliefweb.int/files/resources/151A73B63C254DE5C12571F800418928-UNHCR-Nov2000.pdf.

Jamal, A. 2003. Camps and freedoms: Long-term refugee situations in Africa. *Forced Migration Review*, 16(1), 4–6.

Jansen, B. J. 2016. The protracted refugee camp and the consolidation of a 'humanitarian urbanism'. *International Journal of Urban and Regional Research*. Available: https://www.ijurr.org/spotlight-on/the-urban-refugee-crisis-reflections-on-cities-citizenship-and-the-displaced/the-protracted-refugee-camp-and-the-consolidation-of-a-humanitarian-urbanism/.

Jaquenod, A. M. 2014. From the realist and liberal state to state fetishism in International Relations. The case of Argentine international insertion in the 1990s. *Proceedings of the FLACSO-ISA Joint International Conference*, July 2014. Available: http://web.isanet.org/Web/Conferences/FLACSO-ISA%20BuenosAires%202014/Archive/b86ae12e-b84c-4f9b-b888-356e43a9d488.pdf.

Jaworsky, B. et al. 2012. New perspectives on immigrant contexts of reception. *Nordic Journal of Migration Research*, 2(1), 78–88.

Jenkins, F. and de la Hunt, L. A. 2011. Detaining asylum-seekers: Perspectives on proposed reception centres for asylum-seekers in South Africa. In: Handmaker, J. et al. eds. *Advancing Refugee Protection in South Africa* (Vol. 2). New York: Berghahn Books, 167–85.

Jepson, N. and Henderson, J. 2016. *Critical transformations: Rethinking Zambian development*. Available: https://www.sheffield.ac.uk/media/36607/download?attachment.

Job, B. L. and Shesterinina, A. 2014. China as a global norm shaper. In: Betts, A. and Orchard, P. eds. *Implementation and World Politics: How International Norms Change Practice*. Oxford: Oxford University Press, 144–59.

Johnson, C. 2015. Failed asylum seekers in South Africa: Policy and practice. *African Human Mobility Review*, 1(2), 203–29.

Johnson, C. and Carciotto, S. 2018. The state of the asylum system in South Africa. In: O'Sullivan, M. and Stevens, D. eds. 2017. *States, the Law and Access to Refugee Protection: Fortresses and Fairness*. Oxford: Hart Publishing.

Josselson, R. and Lieblich, A. 2003. A framework for narrative research proposals in psychology. In: Josselson, A. et al. eds. *Up Close and*

Personal: The Teaching and Learning of Narrative Research. Washington, DC: American Psychological Association, 259–74.

Kagan, M. 2011.We live in a country of UNHCR: The UN surrogate state and refugee policy in the Middle East. *New Issues in Refugee Research*, 201. Available: https://www.unhcr.org/uk/research/working/4d5a8cde9/live-country-unhcr-un-surrogate-state-refugee-policy-middle-east-michael.html.

Kagan, M. 2013. *Why do we still have refugee camps?* Available: http://www.urban-refugees.org/debate/why-do-we-still-have-refugee-camps/.

Kagan, M. 2014. *New Year's question: Is Human Rights Law useful?* Available: https://rsdwatch.wordpress.com/2014/12/29/new-years-question-is-human-rights-law-useful/.

Kaiser, T. 2008. Sudanese refugees in Uganda and Kenya. In: Loescher, G. et al. eds. *Protracted Refugee Situations.* New York: United Nations University Press.

Kambela, L. 2016. *Angolan refugees in Zambia: Reflecting on local integration as a sustainable solution.* Available: https://www.eldis.org/document/A100112.

Karadawi, A. 1999. *Refugee Policy in Sudan 1967–1984.* Oxford: Berghahn Books.

Kasim, O. F. and Agbola, T. 2017. Decentralisation and local government reforms in Africa: Challenges, opportunities and the way forward. *Eastern Africa Social Science Research Review*, 33(1), 89–113.

Khan, F. and Lee, M. 2018. Policy shifts in the asylum process in South Africa resulting in hidden refugees and asylum seekers. *African Human Mobility Review*, 4(2), 1205–25.

Khan, F. and Rayner, N. 2020. *Country Fiche South Africa.* ASILE Project, University of Cape Town. Available: https://www.asileproject.eu/wp-content/uploads/2021/03/Country-Fiche_South-Africa_Final_Pub.pdf.

Khan, M. 2010. *Political Settlements and the Governance of Growth-enhancing Institutions.* Draft Working Paper. Available: https://eprints.soas.ac.uk/9968/1/Political_Settlements_internet.pdf.

Khan, M. 2011. The political settlement and its evolution in Bangladesh. Working Paper. Available: https://eprints.soas.ac.uk/12845/1/The_Political_Settlement_and_its_Evolution_in_Bangladesh.pdf.

Kibreab, G. 1989. Local settlements in Africa: A misconceived option? *Journal of Refugee Studies*, 2(4), 468–90.

Kibreab, G. 1996. Eritrean and Ethiopian urban refugees in Khartoum: What the eye refuses to see. *African Studies Review*, 39(3), 131–78.

Kibreab, G. 2007. Why governments prefer spatially segregated settlement sites for urban refugees. *Refuge: Canada's Journal on Refugees*, 24(1), 27–35.

Kihato, C. W. and Landau, L. B. 2016. Stealth humanitarianism: Negotiating politics, precarity, and performance management in protecting the urban displaced. *Journal of Refugee Studies*, 30(3), 407–25.

Kihato, C. W. and Landau, L. B. 2019. *The implications of Europe's 'containment development' for African cities*. Available: https://www.ispionline.it/en/pubblicazione/implications-europes-containment-development-african-cities-22988.

Klaaren, J. et al. 2008. Talking a new talk: A legislative history of the Refugees Act of 1998. In: Klaaren, J. et al. eds. *Advancing Refugee Protection in South Africa* (Vol. 2). New York: Berghahn Books, 47–60.

Klinck, J. A. 2009. Recognizing socio-economic refugees in South Africa: A principled and rights-based approach to Section 3 (b) of the Refugees Act. *International Journal of Refugee Law*, 21(4), 653–99.

Koelble, T. A. and Siddle, A. 2013. Why decentralization in South Africa has failed. *Governance*, 26(3), 343–6.

Kotef, H. 2015. *Movement and the Ordering of Freedom: On Liberal Governances of Mobility*. Durham, NC: Duke University Press.

Krause, U. 2017. Researching forced migration: Critical reflections on research ethics during fieldwork. *Oxford RSC, Working Paper Series, 123*. Available: https://www.rsc.ox.ac.uk/publications/researching-forced-migration-critical-reflections-on-research-ethics-during-fieldwork

Krause, U. and Gato, J. 2019. Escaping humanitarian aid in camps? Rethinking the links between refugees' encampment, urban self-settlement, coping and peace. *Die Friedens-Warte*, 92(1–2), 76–97.

Kreibaum, M. 2016. Their suffering, our burden? How Congolese refugees affect the Ugandan population. *World Development*, 78, 262–87.

Kuboyama, R. 2008. The transformation from restrictive to selective immigration policy in emerging national competition. Case of Japan in Asia-Pacific region state. *Centre on Migration, Citizenship and Development, Working Paper 61*. Available: https://www.ssoar.info/ssoar/handle/document/35345.

Kuch, A. 2016. Naturalization of Burundian refugees in Tanzania: The debates on local integration and the meaning of citizenship revisited. *Journal of Refugee Studies*, 30(3), 468–87.

Kumar, K. 1989. *Conducting key informant interviews in developing countries*. Available: https://citeseerx.ist.psu.edu/document?repid=rep1&type=pdf&doi=56f46fbe74c67985360c799cc767451a17a78327.

Kvale, S. 1996. *InterView: An Introduction to Qualitative Research Interviewing*. Thousand Oaks: Sage.

Landau, L. B. 2001. *Crisis and authority: A research agenda for exploring political transformation*. Available: https://reliefweb.int/report/united-republic-tanzania/crisis-and-authority-research-agenda-exploring-political.

Landau, L. B. 2006. Protection and dignity in Johannesburg: Shortcomings of South Africa's urban refugee policy. *Journal of Refugee Studies*, 19(3), 308–27.

Landau, L. B. 2007. Discrimination and development? Immigration, urbanisation and sustainable livelihoods in Johannesburg. *Development Southern Africa*, 24(1), 61–76.

Landau, L. B. 2011. Introducing the demons. In: Landau, L. B. ed. *Exorcising the Demons Within: Xenophobia, Violence and Statecraft in Contemporary South Africa*. Johannesburg: Wits University Press, 1–25.

Landau, L. B. 2014. Urban refugees and IDPs. In: Fiddian-Qasmiyeh, E. et al. eds. *The Oxford Handbook of Refugee and Forced Migration Studies*. Oxford: Oxford University Press, 139–50.

Landau, L. B. 2018a. Displacement and the pursuit of urban protection: Forced migration, fluidity and global cities. In: Bloch, A. and Dona, G. eds. *Forced Migration: Current Issues and Debates*. Abingdon: Routledge, 106–25.

Landau, L. B. 2018b. A chronotope of containment development: Europe's migrant crisis and Africa's reterritorialisation. *Antipode*, 51(1), 169–86.

Landau, L. B. and Amit, R. 2014. Wither policy? Southern African perspectives on understanding law, 'refugee' policy and protection. *Journal of Refugee Studies*, 27(4), 534–52.

Landau, L. B. and Freemantle, I. 2017. Shallow solidarities: Space and socialities of accommodation and exclusion in Nairobi and Johannesburg. In: Landau, L. B. and Bakewell, O. eds. *Forging African Communities*. London: Palgrave Macmillan, 277–302.

Landau, L. B. and Segatti, A.W. K. 2009. Human development impacts of migration: South Africa case study. *Human Development Research Paper (HDRP)* 5. Available: https://mpra.ub.uni-muenchen.de/19182/1/MPRA_paper_19182.pdf.

Landau, L. B. et al. 2011. Mobility and municipalities: Local authorities, local impacts, and the challenges of movement. In: Segatti, A. and Landau, L. eds. *Contemporary Migration to South Africa: A Regional Development Issue*. Washington, DC: The World Bank, 81–104.

Landau, L. et al. 2016. *Becoming Urban Humanitarians: Engaging Local Government to Protect Displaced People*. Available: https://www.urban.org/sites/default/files/publication/84356/Urban%20

Institute%20Research%20Report%20-%20Becoming%20Urban%20 Humanitarians_FINAL.pdf.
Laws, E. 2012. *Political Settlements, Elite Pacts and Governments of National Unity.* Available: https://www.dlprog.org/publications/research-papers/political-settlements-elite-pacts-and-governments-of-national-unity-a-conceptual-study.
Laws, E. and Leftwich, A. 2014. *Political settlements. Concept Brief 1.* Available: https://www.dlprog.org/publications/research-papers/political-settlements.
Lavers, T. and Hickey, S. 2015. Investigating the political economy of social protection expansion in Africa: At the intersection of transnational ideas and domestic politics. *Global Development Institute Working Paper Series.* The University of Manchester.
Leung, G. and Stone, M. 2009. Otherwise than hospitality: A disputation on the relation of ethics to law and politics. *Law and Critique*, 20(2), 193–206.
Levi, M. 1997. A model, a method, and a map: Rational choice in comparative and historical analysis. *Comparative Politics: Rationality, Culture, and Structure*, 28, 19–41.
Levitsky, S. and Way, L. A. 2010. Democracy's past and future: Why democracy needs a level playing field. *Journal of Democracy*, 21(1), 57–68.
Levy, B. et al. 2015. Governance and inequality: Benchmarking and interpreting South Africa's evolving political settlement. *Effective States and Inclusive Development Working Paper Series 51.* Available: http://www.effective-states.org/wp-content/uploads/working_papers/final-pdfs/esid_wp_51_levy_hirsch_woolard.pdf.
Lewis, C. 2012. *UNHCR and International Refugee Law: From Treaties to Innovation.* London: Routledge.
Lindley, A. 2011. Between a protracted and a crisis situation: Policy responses to Somali refugees in Kenya. *Refugee Survey Quarterly*, 30(4),14–39.
Loescher, G. 1992. *Refugee Movements and International Security.* International Institute for Strategic Studies. Available: https://www.tandfonline.com/doi/pdf/10.1080/05679329208449097.
Loescher, G. 2003. UNHCR at fifty: Refugee protection and world politics. In: Steiner, N. et al. eds. *Problems of Protection: The UNHCR, Refugees and Human Rights.* New York: Routledge, 3–18.
Loescher, G. et al. 2008. *The Politics and Practice of Refugee Protection into the 21st Century.* Available: https://www.rsc.ox.ac.uk/publications/the-united-nations-high-commissioner-for-refugees-unhcr-the-politics-and-practice-of-refugee-protection-into-the-21st-century.

Long, K. 2009. Early repatriation policy: Russian refugee return 1922–1924. *Journal of Refugee Studies*, 22(2), 133–54.
Long, K. 2014. Rethinking 'durable' solutions. In: Fiddian-Qasmiyeh, E. et al. eds. *The Oxford Handbook of Refugee and Forced Migration Studies*. Oxford: Oxford University Press, 475–87.
Long, K. 2019. More research and fewer experts: Global governance and international migration. In: Ruhs, M. et al. eds. *Bridging the Gaps: Linking Research to Public Debates and Policy Making on Migration and Integration*. Oxford: Oxford University Press, 222–40.
Long, K. and Crisp, J. 2011. In harm's way: The irregular movement of migrants to Southern Africa from the Horn and Great Lakes regions. *New Issues in Refugee Research*, 200. Available: https://www.unhcr.org/uk/research/working/4d395af89/harms-way-irregular-movement-migrants-southern-africa-horn-great-lakes.html.
Lor, P. J. 2011. *International and Comparative Librarianship: Concepts and Methods for Global Studies*. Munich: Walter de Gruyter, SAUR.
LSE, 2019. *Informed Consent*. LSE Guidelines, Research Ethics Policy and Procedures. Available: https://info.lse.ac.uk/staff/services/Policies-and-procedures/Assets/Documents/infCon.pdf.
Mackenzie, C. et al. 2007. Beyond "Do No Harm": The challenge of constructing ethical relationships in refugee research. *Journal of Refugee Studies*, 20(2), 299–319.
Maher, F. A. and Tetreault, M. K. 1994. *The Feminist Classroom: Dynamics Of Gender, Race, And Privilege*. New York: Basic Books.
Mail and Guardian, 2017. 'No one must be in SA without documentation' – Mashaba. 30 April. Available: https://mg.co.za/article/2018-04-30-no-one-must-be-in-sa-without-documentation-mashaba/.
Mail and Guardian, 2020. Refugees evicted from Cape Town church just want to leave South Africa. 3 March. Available: https://mg.co.za/article/2020-03-03-refugees-evicted-from-cape-town-church-just-want-to-leave-south-africa/.
Malkki, L. H. 1992. National geographic: The rooting of peoples and the territorialization of national identity among scholars and refugees. *Cultural Anthropology*, 7(1), 24–44.
Malkki, L. H. 1995. Refugees and exile: From 'refugee studies' to the national order of things. *Annual Review of Anthropology*, 24, 495–523.
Manby, B. 2016. *Citizenship Law in Africa*. Cape Town: African Minds.
Maple, N. 2016. Rights at risk: A thematic investigation into how states restrict the freedom of movement of refugees on the African Continent. *New Issues in Refugee Research, Research 281*. Available: https://www.unhcr.org/57ee60d57.pdf.

Maple, N. 2018. *What's behind Zambia's growing welcome to refugees.* Refugee Deeply. Available: https://www.newsdeeply.com/refugees/community/2018/06/12/whats-behind-zambias-growing-welcome-to-refugees.

Maple, N. 2023. *Zimbabwean forced migrants in South Africa: The continual search for solutions to long-term displacement.* RLI Blog. Available: https://rli.blogs.sas.ac.uk/2023/03/01/zimbabwean-forced-migrants-in-south-africa-the-continual-search-for-solutions-to-long-term-displacement/.

Maple, N., Reardon-Smith, S. and Black, R. 2021. Immobility and the containment of solutions: Reflections on the global compacts, mixed migration and the transformation of protection. *Interventions*, 23(2), 326–47.

Maple, N., Walker, R. and Vearey, J. 2021. *COVID-19 and Migration Governance in Africa.* Researching Migration and Coronavirus in Southern Africa Paper, 1, June 2021. Available: https://www.mahpsa.org/wp-content/uploads/2021/06/MiCoSA-Covid19-and-migration-governance-in-Africa-OccasionalPaper-2-June2021.pdf.

Maple, N., et al., 2023. The influence of the global refugee regime in Africa: Still 'Akin to a distant weather pattern'? *Refugee Survey Quarterly*, 42(3), 247–58.

Marcus, G. E. 1995. Ethnography in/of the world system: The emergence of multi-sited ethnography. *Annual Review of Anthropology*, 24(1), 95–117.

Martin, D. 2015. From spaces of exception to 'campscapes': Palestinian refugee camps and informal settlements in Beirut. *Political Geography*, 44, 9–18.

Martini, M. 2014. *Approaches to curbing corruption in tax administration in Africa.* Department for International Development. Available: https://assets.publishing.service.gov.uk/media/57a089a640f0b652dd000336/answer-2014-11.pdf.

Masuku, S. and Nkala, S. 2018. Patterns of the refugee cycle in Africa: A hazardous cycle with no end in sight? *Journal of African Union Studies*, 7(3), 87–105.

Mayblin, L. and Turner, J. 2020. *Migration Studies and Colonialism.* Cambridge: John Wiley & Sons.

Maystadt, J. F. and Verwimp, P. 2014. Winners and losers among a refugee-hosting population. *Economic Development and Cultural Change*, 62(4), 769–809.

Mbembe, A. 2018. *The idea of a borderless world.* Available: https://africasacountry.com/2018/11/the-idea-of-a-borderless-world.

McGahan, K. 2009. The securitization of migration in Malaysia. *APSA 2009 Toronto Meeting Paper*. Available: https://papers.ssrn.com/Sol3/papers.cfm?abstract_id=1449344

Merriam, S. B. 2009. *Qualitative Research: A Guide to Design and Implementation*. San Francisco: Jossey-Bass.

Meyer, S. 2006. The 'refugee aid and development' approach in Uganda: Empowerment and self-reliance of refugees in practice. *New Issues in Refugee Research*, 131. Available: https://www.unhcr.org/uk/research/working/4538eb172/refugee-aid-development-approach-uganda-empowerment-self-reliance-refugees.html.

Mfubu, P. 2018. *What does the 2017 Refugee Amendment Act mean for asylum seekers and refugees living in South Africa?* Available: https://www.saferspaces.org.za/blog/entry/what-does-the-2017-refugee-amendment-act-mean-for-asylum-seekers-and-refuge.

Miller, T. and Bell, L. 2002. Consenting to what? Issues of access, gate-keeping and 'informed' consent. *Ethics in Qualitative Research*, 53, 61–75.

Milner, J. 2000. Sharing the security burden: Towards the convergence of refugee protection and state security. *Oxford RSC, Working Paper Series*, 4. Available: https://www.rsc.ox.ac.uk/files/files-1/wp4-sharing-the-security-burden-2000.pdf.

Milner, J. 2009. *Refugees, the State and the Politics of Asylum in Africa*. London: Palgrave Macmillan.

Minca, C. 2015. Counter-camps and other spatialities. *Political Geography*, 49(90), 90–92.

Misago, J. P. 2016. Responding to xenophobic violence in post-apartheid South Africa: Barking up the wrong tree? *African Human Mobility Review*, 2(2), 443–67.

Misago, J. P., Monson, T., Polzer, T., and Landau, L. B. 2010. *Violence against Foreign Nationals in South Africa: Understanding Causes and Evaluating Responses*. Johannesburg: CoRMSA.

Montclos, M. and Kagwanja, P. M. 2000. Refugee camps or cities? The socio-economic dynamics of the Dadaab and Kakuma camps in Northern Kenya. *Journal of Refugee Studies*, 13(2), 205–22.

Mourad, L. and Norman, K. P. 2019. Transforming refugees into migrants: Institutional change and the politics of international protection. *European Journal of International Relations*, 26(3), 687–713.

Moyo, I. 2018. Zimbabwean dispensation, special and exemption permits in South Africa: On humanitarian logic, depoliticisation and invisibilisation of migrants. *Journal of Asian and African Studies*, 53(8), 1141–57.

Moyo, I. 2020. On borders and the liminality of undocumented Zimbabwean migrants in South Africa. *Journal of Immigrant and Refugee Studies*, 18(1), 60–74.

Moyo, K. and Botha, C. 2022. Refugee policy as infrastructure: The gulf between policy intent and implementation for refugees and asylum seekers in South Africa. In: Rugunanan, P. and Xulu-Gama, N. eds. *Migration in Southern Africa*. Berlin: Springer International Publishing, 77–89.

Moyo, K., Sebba, K. R. and Zanker, F. 2021. Who is watching? Refugee protection during a pandemic – responses from Uganda and South Africa, *Comparative Migration Studies*, 9(1), 1–19.

Moyo, K. and Zanker, F., 2020. *Political Contestations within South African Migration Governance*. Freiburg: Arnold-Bergstraesser-Institute. Available: https://www.arnold-bergstraesser.de/sites/default/files/political_contestations_within_south_african_migration_governance_moyo_and_zanker.pdf.

Mthembu-Salter, G. et al. 2014. *Counting the cost of securitising South Africa's immigration regime*. Available: https://assets.publishing.service.gov.uk/media/57a089d240f0b652dd000416/WP20_Mthembu-Salter.pdf.

Muggah, R. ed. 2009. *Security and Post-Conflict Reconstruction: Dealing with Fighters in the Aftermath of War*. New York: Routledge.

Muggah, R. and Kilcullen, D. 2016. *These are Africa's fastest-growing cities – and they'll make or break the continent*. Available: https://www.weforum.org/agenda/2016/05/africa-biggest-cities-fragility/.

Mulaudzi, M. 2015. *The missing link: State capacity, service delivery and the politics of the developmental state in South Africa*. Thesis, University of Johannesburg (South Africa).

Müller-Funk, L. 2021. Research with refugees in fragile political contexts: How ethical reflections impact methodological choices. *Journal of Refugee Studies*, 34(2), 2308–32.

Murtagh, L. 2007. Implementing a critically quasi-ethnographic approach. *Qualitative Report*, 12(2), 193–215.

Musuva, C. K. 2015. *International migration, xenophobia and the South African state*. PhD Dissertation, Stellenbosch University.

Mutesa, F. and Nchito, W. 2003. *Human Security and Poverty Reduction in Zambia*. Lusaka: University of Zambia Press.

Nancy, J. 2000. *Being Singular Plural*. Stanford: Stanford University Press.

Neimeyer, R. A. and Levitt, H. 2001. Constructivism/constructionism: methodology. In: Smelser, N. J. and Baltes, P. B. eds. *International*

Encyclopedia of the Social and Behavioral Sciences. Amsterdam: Elsevier, 724–8.

Neto, P. F. 2019. Displacement, refuge and urbanisation. From refugee camps to ecovillages. *Planning Theory and Practice*, 20(1), 123–6.

Newhouse, L. S. 2015. More than mere survival: Violence, humanitarian governance, and practical material politics in a Kenyan refugee camp. *Environment and Planning A*, 47(11), 2292–307.

Newman, E. 2003. Refugees, international security, and human vulnerability: Introduction and survey. In: Newman, E. and Van Selm, J. eds. *Refugees and Forced Displacement. International Security, Human Vulnerability, and the State*. Tokyo: UN University Press, 3–30.

Nowell, L. S., Norris, J. M., White, D. E. and Moules, N. J. 2017. Thematic analysis: Striving to meet the trustworthiness criteria. *International Journal of Qualitative Methods*, 16(1), 1–13.

Nshimbi, C. C. and Fioramonti, L. 2014. The will to integrate: South Africa's responses to regional migration from the SADC region. *African Development Review*, 26(S1), 52–63.

Nyers, P. 2006. The accidental citizen: Acts of sovereignty and (un)making citizenship. *Economy and Society*, 35(1), 22–41.

O'Driscoll, D. 2017. *Managing Risks in Securitisation of Refugees. K4D Report*. Available: https://assets.publishing.service.gov.uk/media/5a5f313ced915d7dfb57d029/224_Managing_risks_in_securitisation_of_refugees.pdf.

Obi, C. I. 2010. African migration as the search for a wonderful world: An emerging trans-global security threat? *African and Asian Studies*, 9(1/2), 128–48.

Ochieng, V. A. 2023. *An exploration of economic resilience among refugees and former refugees in Zambia*. MSc Dissertation, University of London.

OECD. 2017. *Who bears the cost of integrating refugees?* Available: https://www.oecd.org/els/mig/migration-policy-debates-13.pdf.

Oelgemöller, C. 2017. *The Evolution of Migration Management in the Global North*. London: Routledge.

Okoth-Obbo, G. 2001. Thirty years on: A legal review of the 1969 OAU Refugee Convention governing the specific aspects of refugee problems in Africa. *Refugee Survey Quarterly*, 20(1), 79–138.

Omata, N. 2017. *The Myth of Self-Reliance: Economic Lives Inside a Liberian Refugee Camp*. New York: Berghahn Books.

Omata, N. 2019. 'Over-researched' and 'under-researched' refugees. *Forced Migration Review*, 61. Available: https://www.fmreview.org/ethics/omata.

Omata, N. and Kaplan, J. D. 2013. Refugee livelihoods in Kampala, Nakivale and Kyangwali refugee settlements: Patterns of engagement with the private sector. *RSC, Working Paper Series, 80*. Available: https://www.rsc.ox.ac.uk/files/files-1/wp95-refugee-livelihoods-kampala-nakivale-kyangwali-2013.pdf.

Onuoha, G. 2008. *Resources and Development. The Role of the State in Sub-Saharan Africa*. Occasional Paper No 58. Johannesburg: Institute for Global Dialogue (IGD).

Osmers, J. 2015. *Cessation of Rwandan refugee status: Two years on*. Available: http://www.pambazuka.org/human-security/cessation-rwandan-refugee-status-two-years

Owens, P. 2009. Reclaiming 'bare life'? Against Agamben on refugees. *International Relations*, 23(4), 567–82.

Palmary, I. 2002. *Refugees, Safety and Xenophobia in South African Cities: The Role of Local Government*. Centre for the Study of Violence and Reconciliation. Available: https://www.files.ethz.ch/isn/104945/refugeessafteyand.pdf

Parilla, J. and Trujillo, J. L. 2015. *South Africa's global gateway: Profiling the Gauteng City-Region's international competitiveness and connections*. Available: https://www.brookings.edu/wp-content/uploads/2016/07/GCI_Johannesburg_Nov16REVfinal_LowRes-1.pdf.

Parliamentary Monitoring Group (PMG). 2021. *Refugee bodies on their work and challenges concerning refugees and asylum seekers; with Minister and Deputy Minister*, PMG, 02 March 2021. Available: https://pmg.org.za/committee-meeting/32404/.

Pasquetti, S. and Picker, G. 2017. Urban informality and confinement: Toward a relational framework. *International Sociology*, 32(4), 532–44.

Pavanello, S. et al. 2010. Hidden and exposed: Urban refugees in Nairobi, Kenya. *ODI Humanitarian Policy Group Working Paper*. Available: http://cdn-odi-production.s3-website-eu-west-1.amazonaws.com/media/documents/5858.pdf.

Phiri, C. 2016. *Is Zambia sliding away from the beacon of peace stand?* Available: https://thezambian.com/news/2016/07/12/is-zambia-sliding-away-from-the-beacon-of-peace-stand/.

Pitt-Rivers, J. 2012. The law of hospitality. *HAU: Journal of Ethnographic Theory*, 2(1), 501–17.

Pittaway, E. et al. 2010. 'Stop stealing our stories': The ethics of research with vulnerable groups. *Journal of Human Rights Practice*, 2(2), 229–51.

Polzer, T. 2007. Adapting to changing legal frameworks: Mozambican refugees in South Africa. *International Journal of Refugee Law*, 19, 22–50.

Polzer, T. 2009. Negotiating rights: The politics of local integration. *Refuge: Canada's Journal on Refugees*, 26(2), 92–106.

Polzer, T. and Segatti, A. 2011. From defending migrant rights to new political subjectivities: Gauteng migrants' organisations after May 2008. In: Landau, L. B. ed. *Exorcising the Demons Within: Xenophobia, Violence and Statecraft in Contemporary South Africa*. Johannesburg: Wits University Press, 200–225.

Porter, L. et al. 2019. Borders and refuge: Citizenship, mobility and planning in a volatile world. *Planning Theory and Practice*, 20(1), 99–128.

Portes, A. and Böröcz, J. 1989. Contemporary immigration: Theoretical perspectives on its determinants and modes of incorporation. *International Migration Review*, 23(3), 606–30.

Portes, A. and Landolt, P. 1996. *The Downside of Social Capital*. Washington, DC: The American Prospect. Available: https://vtechworks.lib.vt.edu/handle/10919/67453.

Portes, A. and Rumbaut, R. G. 2006. *Immigrant America: A Portrait*. Berkeley: University of California Press.

Pratt, B. and Loizos, P. 2003. *Choosing research methods: Data collection for development workers*. Oxfam Development Guidelines, 7. Available: https://policy-practice.oxfam.org/resources/choosing-research-methods-data-collection-for-development-workers-115358/

Pugh, J. 2011. *UNHCR and refugee rights protection in Ecuador: The effects of non-state institutional innovation on peacebuilding and human security*. APSA 2011 Annual Meeting Paper. Available: https://papers.ssrn.com/sol3/papers.cfm?abstract_id=1900446.

Punch, S. 2016. Exploring children's agency across majority and minority world contexts, reconceptualising agency and childhood. *New Perspectives in Childhood Studies*, (2)22, 183–96.

Punton, M. and Shepherd, A. 2015. *What is chronic poverty?* Findings from the Chronic Poverty Research Centre, ODI. Available: https://www.odi.org/publications/10485-what-chronic-poverty-findings-chronic-poverty-research-centre.

Quak, E. J. 2019. *Opposition political party approaches and international assistance against democratic backsliding*. Institute of Development Studies. Available: https://assets.publishing.service.gov.uk/media/5c8647f740f0b636938a0ec1/534_Opposition_Political_Parties_Approaches_in_Non-Democratic_Settings.pdf.

Ragin, C. C. 1987. *The Comparative Method: Moving Beyond Qualitative and Quantitative Strategies*. Berkeley: University of California Press.

Rahal, M. and White, B. T. 2022. UNHCR and the Algerian War of Independence: Postcolonial sovereignty and the globalization of the international refugee regime, 1954–63, *Journal of Global History*, 17(2), 331–52.

Ramadan, A. 2013. Spatialising the refugee camp. *Transnational Institute of British Geography*, 38(1), 65–77.

Ravenhill, J. 1990. The north-south balance of power. *International Affairs*, 66(4), 731–48.

Ravitch, S. M. and Riggan, M. 2016. *Reason and Rigor: How Conceptual Frameworks Guide Research*. London: Sage.

Reed, K. and Schenck, M. C. eds. 2023. *The Right to Research: Historical Narratives by Refugee and Global South Researchers*. Montreal: McGill-Queen's University Press.

Refugee Studies Centre, 2007. Ethical guidelines for good research practice. *Refugee Survey Quarterly*, 26(3), 162–72.

ReliefWeb. 2010. *300 Zimbabweans arriving in SA daily*. Available: https://reliefweb.int/report/zimbabwe/300-zimbabweans-arriving-sa-daily-msf.

Renzetti, C. and Lee, R. eds. 1993. *Researching Sensitive Topics*. Thousand Oaks: Sage.

Republic of Zambia. 2022. *Statement by Zambia, to the 73rd Session of the Executive Committee of the High Commissioner's Programme (Excom)*. Republic of Zambia, October 2022. Available: https://www.unhcr.org/in/sites/en-in/files/legacy-pdf/634437ad7.pdf.

Reus-Smit. C. 2005. Constructivism. In: Burchill, S. et al. eds. *Theories of International Relations*. 3rd ed. London: Macmillan International Higher Education, 188–212.

Richards, L. and Richards, T. 1994. From filing cabinet to computer. In: Bryman, A. and Burgess, R. G. eds. *Analyzing Qualitative Data*. London: Routledge, 146–72.

Robson, C. 2002. *Real World Research: A Resource for Social Scientists and Practitioner-Researchers*. Hoboken: Blackwell Publishing.

Rudestam, K. E. and Newton, R. R. 2007. *Surviving your Dissertation: A Comprehensive Guide to Content and Process*. Thousand Oaks: Sage.

Ruiz, I. and Vargas-Silva, C. 2015. The labor market impacts of forced migration. *American Economic Review*, 105(5), 581–6.

Rutinwa, B. 1999. The end of asylum? The changing nature of refugee policies in Africa. *New Issues in Refugee Research, Working Paper, 5*. Available: https://www.unhcr.org/uk/research/working/3ae6a0c34/end-asylum-changing-nature-refugee-policies-africa-bonaventure-rutinwa.html.

Rutinwa, B. 2002. Asylum and refugee policies in Southern Africa: A historical perspective. In: *Legal Resources Foundation, A Reference Guide to Refugee Law and Issues in Southern Africa*. Lusaka: Legal

Resources Foundation. Available: https://sarpn.org/EventPapers/april2002_imp/rutinwa/rutinwa.pdf

SAgov, 2020. *Local government*. Available at: https://www.gov.za/about-government/government-system/local-government.

Samaddar, R. 2018. Promises and paradoxes of a global gaze. *CRG Series on Policies and Practices*, 98, 1–23. Available: http://www.mcrg.ac.in/PP98.pdf.

Sanyal, R. 2014. Urbanizing refuge: Interrogating spaces of displacement. *International Journal of Urban and Regional Research*, 38(2), 558–72.

Sanyal, R. 2017. A no-camp policy: Interrogating informal settlements in Lebanon. *Geoforum*, 84, 117–25.

Sanyal, R. 2019. Planning for refugees in cities. *Planning Theory & Practice*, 20(1), 99–128.

Sarkar, A. 2017. *Displacement and the City*. World Peace Foundation, Reinventing Peace. Available: https://sites.tufts.edu/reinventingpeace/2017/03/10/displacement-and-the-city/.

Sassen, S. 1999. Whose city is it? In: Foo, A. F. et al. eds. *Sustainable Cities in the 21st century*. Singapore: NUS Press, 145–63.

Saunders, M. et al. 2007. *Research Methods for Business Students*. Harlow: Prentice Hall.

Saunders, N. 2014. Paradigm shift or business as usual? An historical reappraisal of the 'shift' to securitisation of refugee protection. *Refugee Survey Quarterly*, 33(3), 69–92.

Scalabrini, 2021. *Angola Special Permit Update*, Scalabrini Centre of Cape Town, 17 August 2021. Available: https://www.scalabrini.org.za/news/angola-special-permit-update/.

Scalettaris, G. 2009. Refugees and mobility. *Forced Migration Review*, 33, 58–9.

Schmidt, A. 2003. *Camps versus Settlements*. Forced Immigration. Available: https://sswm.info/sites/default/files/reference_attachments/SCHMIDT%202003%20Camps%20vs%20Settlements.pdf.

Schmidt, A. 2014. Status determination and recognition. In: Betts, A. and Orchard, P. eds. *Implementation and World Politics: How International Norms Change Practice*. Oxford: Oxford University Press, 248–68.

Schoenberger, E. 1991. The corporate interview as a research method in economic geography. *The Professional Geographer*, 43(2), 180–89.

Schwella, E. 2016. Federalism in South Africa: A complex context and continued challenges. In: Buhler et al. eds. *Federalism – a Success Story?* Munich: Hanns Seidel Foundation, 73–102.

Seawright, J. and Gerring, J. 2008. Case selection techniques in case study research: A menu of qualitative and quantitative options. *Political Research Quarterly*, 61(2), 294–308.

Seekings, J. and Nattrass, N. 2005. *Race, Class and Inequality in South Africa*. New Haven: Yale University Press.

Segatti, A. W. 2011. Reforming South African immigration policy in the post-apartheid period (1990–2006): What it means and what it takes. In: Segatti, A. W. and Landau, L. B. eds. *Migration in Post-Apartheid South Africa: Challenges and Questions to Policy-Makers*. Research Department, AFD, 32–6. Available: https://www.migration.org.za/wp-content/uploads/2017/08/Migration-in-Postapartheid-South-Africa-Challenges-and-Questions-to-Policy-Makers.pdf.

Segatti, A. W. 2013. Migration to South Africa: Regional challenges versus national instruments and interests. In: Segatti, A. W. and Landau, L. B. eds. *Contemporary Migration to South Africa: A Regional Development Issue*. Washington, DC: World Bank, 9–27.

Seidman-Zager, J. 2010. The securitization of asylum: Protecting UK residents. *Oxford RSC, Working Paper Series, 57*. Available: https://www.rsc.ox.ac.uk/files/files-1/wp57-securitization-of-asylum-2010.pdf.

Sewell, M. 1998. *The Use of Qualitative Interviews in Evaluation*. Tucson: University of Arizona. Available: https://cals.arizona.edu/sfcs/cyfernet/cyfar/Intervu5.htm.

Shapcott, R. 2010. *International Ethics: A Critical Introduction*. Cambridge: Polity Press.

Sharpe, M. 2018. *The Regional Law of Refugee Protection in Africa*. Oxford: Oxford University Press.

Siachiwena, H. 2021a. A Silent Revolution. *Journal of African Elections*, 20(2), 32–56.

Siachiwena, H. 2021b. *The good the bad and the alarming: Hichilemas first 100 days in Zambia*. African Arguments. 2 December 2021. Available: https://africanarguments.org/2021/12/the-good-the-bad-and-the-alarming-hichilemas-first-100-days-in-zambia/.

Sin, C. H. 2005. Seeking informed consent: Reflections on research practice. *Sociology*, 39(2), 277–94.

Slaughter, A. and Crisp, J. 2008. A surrogate state? The role of UNHCR in protracted refugee situations. In: Loescher, G. et al. eds. *Protracted Refugee Situations*. Tokyo: United Nations University Press, 123–40.

Smit, W. and Pieterse, D. E. 2014. Decentralisation and institutional reconfiguration in urban Africa. In: Pieterse, D. E. and Parnell, S. eds. *Africa's Urban Revolution*. London: Zed Books, 148–66.

Smith, M. 2004. Warehousing refugees: A denial of rights, a waste of humanity. *World Refugee Survey*, 38, 38–56.

Smith, T. R. 2003. The making of the South African (1998) Refugees Act. *Forced Migration Studies Programme Working Paper Series 5.* Johannesburg: University of the Witwatersrand.

Somerville, K. 2017. *Africa's Long Road Since Independence: The Many Histories of a Continent.* London: Penguin Books.

Sommers, M. 1999. Urbanization and its discontents: Urban refugees in Tanzania. *Forced Migration Review*, 4, 22–4.

Sommers, M. 2001. Young, male and Pentecostal: Urban refugees in Dar es Salaam, Tanzania. *Journal of Refugee Studies*, 14(4), 347–70.

Spiggle, S. 1994. Analysis and interpretation of qualitative data in consumer research. *Journal of Consumer Research*, 21(3), 491–503.

Spradley, J. 1979. Asking descriptive questions. *The Ethnographic Interview*, 1, 44–61.

Squire, V. 2011. From community cohesion to mobile solidarities: The City of Sanctuary network and the Strangers into Citizens campaign. *Political Studies*, 59, 290–307.

Stake, R. E. 2003. Case studies. In: Denzin, N. K. and Lincoln, Y. S. eds. *Strategies of Qualitative Inquiry.* Thousand Oaks: Sage, 119–50.

Statistics South Africa. 2012. *Census 2011: Census in brief.* Pretoria. Available: http://www.statssa.gov.za/census/census_2011/census _products/Census_2011_Census_in_brief.pdf.

Stedman, S. J. and Tanner, F. 2004. *Refugee Manipulation: War, Politics, and the Abuse of Human Suffering.* Washington, DC: Brookings Institution Press.

Stein, B. and Clark, L. 1990. Refugee integration and older refugee settlements in Africa. *A paper presented at the 1990 meeting of the American Anthropological Association, New Orleans*, Michigan State University. Available: https://msu.edu/course/pls/461/stein/FINAL.html.

Stevens, J. 2006. Prisons of the stateless. The derelictions of UNCHR. *New Left Review*, 42, 53–67.

Straus, S. 2012. Wars do end! Changing patterns of political violence in sub-Saharan Africa. *African Affairs*, 111(443), 179–201.

Stronks, M. C. 2012. The question of Salah Sheekh: Derrida's hospitality and migration law. *International Journal of Law in Context*, 8(1), 73–95.

Sturridge, C. 2011. Mobility and durable solutions: A case study of Afghan and Somali refugees. *New Issues in Refugee Research, Research Paper No 204*. Geneva: UNHCR. Available: https://www .unhcr.org/uk/research/working/4d7657899/mobility-durable -solutions-case-study-afghan-somali-refugees-caitlin-sturridge.html.

Subulwa, A. G. 2013. Settlement, protracted displacement, and repatriation at Mayukwayukwa in western Zambia. *African Geographical Review*, 32(1), 29–43.

Subulwa, A. G. 2019. Urban refugees. In: Orum, A. et al. eds. *The Wiley Blackwell Encyclopedia of Urban and Regional Studies*. Wiley Online Library. Available: https://onlinelibrary.wiley.com/doi/10.1002/9781118568446.eurs0542.

Tati, G. 2008. The immigration issues in the post-apartheid South Africa: Discourses, policies and social repercussions. *Space Populations Societies*, 3, 423–40.

Tesfai, A and de Gruchy, T. 2021. Migration and Covid-19: New and continuing concerns with South Africa's response to the pandemic, MiCoSA Issue Brief 4. African Centre for Migration and Society. Available: https://www.mahpsa.org/wp-content/uploads/2021/10/MiCoSA-Issue-brief4-new-continuing-concerns-with-SAs-response-to-the-pandemic.pdf.

Thebe, V. 2017. 'Two steps forward, one step back': Zimbabwean migration and South Africa's regularising programme. *Journal of International Migration and Integration*, 18(2), 613–22.

Thorne, S. 2000. Data analysis in qualitative research. *Evidence Based Nursing*, 3, 68–70.

Thorsen, K.T. 2016. *Field Report from Visit to Meheba Refugee Settlement in North Western Province of Zambia*. Oslo: Refugee Alliance.

Travers, M. 2001. *Qualitative Research through Case Studies*. London: Sage.

Tsourapas, G. 2019. How migration deals lead to refugee commodification. *Refugees Deeply*. Available: https://deeply.thenewhumanitarian.org/refugees/community/2019/02/13/how-migration-deals-lead-to-refugee-commodification.

Turner, S. 2016. What is a refugee camp? Explorations of the limits and effects of the camp. *Journal of Refugee Studies*, 29(2), 139–48.

UNCDF. 2018. *Can digitization of social cash transfers improve the lives of refugees in Zambia?* Available: https://www.uncdf.org/article/3347/article-can-digitization-of-social-cash-transfers-improve-the-lives-of-refugees-in-zambia.

UNGA. 2016. *71/1. New York Declaration for Refugees and Migrants*. Resolution adopted by the General Assembly on 19 September 2016. General Assembly, 3 October 2016 A/RES/71/1. Available: https://www.unhcr.org/57e39d987.

UNGA. 2018. *13 September 2018 Report of the United Nations High Commissioner for Refugees Part II Global Compact on Refugees*. General Assembly, 13 September 2018. A/73/12 (Part II). Available: https://www.unhcr.org/uk/media/report-united-nations-high-commissioner-refugees-part-ii-global-compact-refugees.

UN-Habitat, 2012. *Fiscal Decentralisation in Zambia*. The Global Urban Economic Dialogue Series. Available: https://unhabitat.org/sites/default/files/download-manager-files/Fiscal%20 Decentralisation%20in%20Zambia.pdf.

UNHCR. 1994. *Activities Financed by Voluntary Funds: Report for 1993–1994 and Proposed Budget Programmes and Budget for 1995*. Section 23 – Zambia. UN General Assembly. Available: http://www.unhcr.org/4de638d99.html.

UNHCR. 1997. *The State of the World's Refugees: A Humanitarian Agenda*. New York: Oxford University Press.

UNHCR. 2004. *Addressing Irregular Secondary Movements of Refugees and Asylum-seekers*. UNHCR Convention Plus Issues Paper. Available: https://www.refworld.org/pdfid/471de35b2.pdf.

UNHCR. 2005. *Handbook For Self Reliance*. Available: https://www.unhcr.org/44bf7b012.pdf.

UNHCR. 2006a. *Angolan Repatriation from Zambia Resumes for Final Year*. Available: https://www.unhcr.org/uk/news/latest/2006/8/44e1e4faa/angolan-repatriation-zambia-resumes-final-year.html.

UNHCR, 2006b. *State of the World's Refugees 2006*. Available: https://www.unhcr.org/publications/sowr/4a4dc1a89/state-worlds-refugees-2006-human-displacement-new-millennium.html.

UNHCR. 2009. *UNHCR Policy on Refugee Protection and Solutions in Urban Areas*. Available: https://www.unhcr.org/uk/protection/hcdialogue%20/4ab356ab6/unhcr-policy-refugee-protection-solutions-urban-areas.html.

UNHCR. 2012. *Zambia Begins Granting Angolan Refugees Permanent Residency*. Available: https://www.unhcr.org/uk/news/latest/2012/12/50e162899/zambia-begins-granting-angolan-refugees-permanent-residency.html.

UNHCR. 2014a. *UNHCR Policy on Alternatives to Camps*. Available: http://www.refworld.org/docid/5423ded84.html.

UNHCR. 2014b. *Strategic Framework for the Local Integration of Former Refugees in Zambia*. UNHCR. Available: https://docplayer.net/12344584-Strategic-framework-for-the-local-integration-of-former-refugees-in-zambia.html.

UNHCR. 2015a. *Statistical Yearbook 2014, 14th edition*. Available: http://www.unhcr.org/uk/statistics/country/566584fc9/unhcr-statistical-yearbook-2014-14th-edition.html.

UNHCR. 2015b. UNHCR Global Appeal 2015 Update. Available: https://www.unhcr.org/uk/media/unhcr-global-appeal-2015-update-populations-concern-unhcr.

UNHCR. 2015c. Onward Movement of Asylum Seekers and Refugees, in *Discussion Paper prepared for the Expert Roundtable on Onward Movement Graduate Institute of International and Development Studies*. Geneva, 1–2 October 2015. Available: https://www.refworld.org/pdfid/563080eb4.pdf.

UNHCR. 2016a. *Global Trends: Forced Displacement in 2015*. UNHCR. Available: https://www.unhcr.org/uk/media/unhcr-global-trends-2015

UNHCR. 2016b. *On Eve of South Sudan 5th Anniversary, Forced Displacement Continues to Rise*. Available: http://www.unhcr.org/uk/news/briefing/2016/7/577f6b0c16/eve-south-sudan-5th-anniversary-forced-displacement-continues-rise.html.

UNHCR. 2017a. Submission by the UNHCR For the Office of the High Commissioner for Human Rights' Compilation Report. *Universal Periodic Review: 3rd Cycle, 28th Session*. Zambia. Available: https://www.refworld.org/docid/5a12ae242.html.

UNHCR. 2017b. *UNHCR Global Report, Global Summaries, Africa*. Available: https://www.unhcr.org/uk/publications/fundraising/5b30b9d07/unhcr-global-report-2017-africa-regional-summary.html.

UNHCR. 2018a. *Highlighted Underfunded Situations*. Available: https://reporting.unhcr.org/sites/default/files/UNHCR%20Brochure%20on%20Underfunded%20Situations%20-%20September%202018.pdf.

UNHCR. 2018b. *UNHCR Turkey Factsheet*. Available: https://reliefweb.int/report/turkey/unhcr-turkey-factsheet-august-2018.

UNHCR. 2018c. *UNHCR Global Report, Global Summaries, Africa*. Available: https://www.unhcr.org/uk/the-global-report.html.

UNHCR. 2019a. *Zambia / Global Focus*. Available: https://www.unhcr.org/sites/default/files/legacy-pdf/4c0903ca9.pdf.

UNHCR. 2019b. *Burundi Situation*. Available: https://data.unhcr.org/en/documents/details/69972.

UNHCR. 2019c. Southern Africa. *UNHCR Global Report 2019*, 82–5. Available: https://reporting.unhcr.org/sites/default/files/gr2019/pdf/GR2019_English_Full_lowres.pdf.

UNHCR. 2019d. *Africa Bureau Director's Speech, March Standing Committee, 2019*. Available: https://www.unhcr.org/5c80fa944.pdf.

UNHCR. 2020. *Global Trends: Forced Displacement in 2019*. Geneva: UNHCR. Available: https://www.unhcr.org/flagship-reports/globaltrends/globaltrends2019/#:~:text=At%20the%20end%20of%202019%2C%20Syrians%20continued%20to%20be%20by,six%20million%20internally%20displaced%20people).

UNHCR, 2021a. *Work to Revamp the Asylum System Begins in South Africa*, UNHCR Press Release, 8 March 2021. Available:

https://reliefweb.int/sites/reliefweb.int/files/resources/Press%20 Release_UNHCR_Work%20begins%20to%20revamp%20the%20 asylum%20system%20in%20South%20Africa_08Mar21.pdf.
UNHCR. 2021b. *Country Strategy Evaluation: Zambia*. UNHCR Final Report, December 2021. Available: https://reliefweb.int/report/zambia /unhcr-country-strategy-evaluation-zambia-final-report-december -2021.
UNHCR. 2022. *Operational Update, Zambia*. UNHCR, September 2022. Available: https://reporting.unhcr.org/zambia-operational-update.
UNHCR. 2023a. *Regional Factual Sheet: Southern Africa*. UNHCR. May 2023. Available: https://reporting.unhcr.org/southern-africa -factsheet-5195.
UNHCR. 2023b. South Africa. UNHCR. May 2023. Available: https://www .unhcr.org/countries/south-africa.
USDS, 2023. *2022 Country Reports on Human Rights Practices: Zambia*. U.S. Department of State. Available: https://www.state.gov/reports /2022-country-reports-on-human-rights-practices/zambia.
Vale, P. 2002. The movement, modernity and new international relations writing in South Africa. *International Affairs*, 78(3), 585–93.
Vale, P. and Taylor, I. 1999. South Africa's post-apartheid foreign policy five years on – from pariah state to 'just another country'? *The Round Table*, 88(352), 629–34.
Van Amersfoort, H. and Van Niekerk, M. 2006. Immigration as a colonial inheritance: Post-colonial immigrants in the Netherlands, 1945–2002. *Journal of Ethnic and Migration Studies*, 32(3), 323–46.
van der Waldt, G. 2020. Constructing conceptual frameworks in social science research. *The Journal for Transdisciplinary Research in Southern Africa*, 16(1), 1–9.
van Garderen, J. 2004. Refugee protection in Africa. *Human Rights Law in Africa Online*, 1(1), 839–42.
van Garderen, J. and Ebenstein, J. 2011. Regional Developments: Africa. In: Zimmerman, A. ed. *The 1951 Convention Relating to the Status of Refugees and its 1967 Protocol. A Commentary*. Oxford: Oxford University Press, 185–203.
Van Hear, N. 1998. Report. Refugee protection and immigration control: Addressing the asylum dilemma. *Refugee Survey Quarterly*, 17(3), 1–27.
Van Noorloos, F. and Kloosterboer, M. 2018. Africa's new cities: The contested future of urbanisation. *Urban Studies*, 55(6), 1223–41.
Varsanyi, M. W. 2006. Interrogating 'urban citizenship' vis-à-vis undocumented migration. *Citizenship Studies*, 10(2), 229–49.
Vearey, J. 2017. Urban health in Johannesburg: Migration, exclusion and inequality. *Urban Forum*, 28(1), 1–4.

Vearey, J. et al. 2017. Analysing local-level responses to migration and urban health in Hillbrow: The Johannesburg Migrant Health Forum. *BMC Public Health*, 17(3), 89–93.

Verdirame, G. and Harrell-Bond, B. 2005. *Rights in Exile. Janus-faced Humanitarianism. Studies in Forced Migration*, 17. Oxford: Berghahn Books.

Verdirame, G. and Pobjoy, J. 2013. *A Rejoinder*. Urban Refugee.Org. Available: http://urban-refugees.org/debate/rejoinder/.

Veroff, J. 2010a. Crimes, conflicts and courts: The administration of justice in a Zambian refugee settlement. *New Issues in Refugee Research*, 192. Available: https://www.unhcr.org/research/working/4cd7bfa99/crimes-conflicts-courts-administration-justice-zambian-refugee-settlement.html.

Veroff, J. 2010b. *Justice administration in Meheba refugee settlement: Refugee perceptions, preferences, and strategic decisions*. PhD Thesis, Oxford University.

Vigneswaran, D. 2008. A foot in the door: Access to asylum in South Africa. *Refuge: Canada's Journal on Refugees*, 25(2), 41–52.

Vigneswaran, D. and Quirk, J. 2015. *Mobility Makes States: Migration and Power in Africa*. Philadelphia: University of Pennsylvania Press.

Waldinger, R. 2001. *Strangers at the Gate: New Immigrants in Urban America*. Oakland: University of California Press.

Walker, K. E. 2014. The role of geographic context in the local politics of US immigration. *Journal of Ethnics and Migration Studies*, 40, 1040–59.

Ward, P. 2014. Refugee cities: Reflections on the development and impact of UNHCR urban refugee policy in the Middle East. *Refugee Survey Quarterly*, 33(1), 77–93.

Washinyira, T. 2022. Refugees left in limbo without protection as they battle to renew asylum documents through home affairs online system. *Daily Maverick*, 4 February 2022. Available: https://www.dailymaverick.co.za/article/2022-02-04-refugees-left-in-limbo-without-protection-as-they-battle-to-renew-asylum-documents-through-home-affairs-online-system/.

WEF. 2017. *Migration and Its Impact on Cities*. World Economic Forum report. Available: https://www.weforum.org/reports/migration-and-its-impact-on-cities.

Weiner, M., 1992. Security, stability, and international migration. *International Security*, 17(3), 91–126.

Whitaker, B. E. 1999. *Disjuncutured Boundaries*. PhD Thesis, University of North Carolina.

Whitaker, B. E. 2002. Refugees in Western Tanzania: The distribution of burdens and benefits among local hosts. *Journal of Refugee Studies*, 15(4), 339–58.
Wilhelm-Solomon, M. 2017. The ruinous vitalism of the urban form: Ontological orientations in inner-city Johannesburg. *Critical African Studies*, 9(2), 174–91.
Williamson. R. 2015. Towards a multi-scalar methodology: The challenges of studying social transformation and international migration. In: Castles, S. et al. eds. *Social Transformation and Migration: National and Local Experiences in South Korea, Turkey, Mexico and Australia*. London: Palgrave Macmillan, 17–32.
Wittenberg, M. 2003. *Decentralisation in South Africa*. Johannesburg: University of Witwatersrand.
WorldAtlas. 2019. *Geography Statistics of Zambia*. Available: https://www.worldatlas.com/webimage/countrys/africa/zambia/zmlandst.htm.
World Bank. 2018a. *Mixed Migration, Forced Displacement and Job Outcomes in South Africa*. Available: http://documents.worldbank.org/curated/en/247261530129173904/main-report.
World Bank. 2018b. *Overcoming Poverty and Inequality in South Africa: An Assessment of Drivers, Constraints and Opportunities*. Available: http://documents.worldbank.org/curated/en/530481521735906534/Overcoming-Poverty-and-Inequality-in-South-Africa-An-Assessment-of-Drivers-Constraints-and-Opportunities.
World Bank. 2019. *New Country Partnership Framework to Support Zambia Achieve Inclusive Growth*. Available: https://www.worldbank.org/en/news/press-release/2019/02/14/new-country-partnership-framework-to-support-zambia-achieve-inclusive-growth.
World Vision et al., 2019. *Summary Report of Online Meeting on Advancing Local Integration in Zambia*. World Vision, ICVA and UNHCR, 17 June 2021. Available: https://globalcompactrefugees.org/sites/default/files/2021-10/Summary-Report_Zambia-LI_Meeting_17%20June%202021.pdf.
Yin, R. K. 1994. *Case Study Research: Design and Methods*. London: Sage.
Zanker, F. 2019. Managing or restricting movement? Diverging approaches of African and European migration governance. *Comparative Migration Studies*, 7, 1–18.
Zanker, F. L. and Moyo, K. 2020. The Corona virus and migration governance in South Africa: Business as usual? *Africa Spectrum*, 55(1), 100–112.
Zetter, R. 2015. *Protection in Crisis: Forced Migration and Protection in a Global Era*. Migration Policy Institute. Available: https://www

.migrationpolicy.org/research/protection-crisis-forced-migration-and-protection-global-era.

Zetter, R. and Deikun, G. 2010. Meeting humanitarian challenges in urban areas. *Forced Migration Review*, 34, 5–8.

Zetter, R. and Ruaudel, H. 2016. Refugees' right to work and access to labor markets – An assessment. *The KNOMAD Working Paper Series*. Available: https://www.knomad.org/publication/refugees-right-work-and-access-labor-markets-assessment-part-1.

Zieck, M. 2018. Refugees and the right to freedom of movement: From flight to return. *Michigan Journal of International Law*, 39, 19–119.

Ziegler, R. 2020. Access to effective refugee protection in South Africa: Legislative commitment, policy realities, judicial rectifications? *Constitutional Court Review*, 10(1), 65–106.

Zolberg, A. R. et al. 1989. *Escape from Violence: Conflict and the Refugee Crisis in the Developing World*. Oxford: Oxford University Press.

Index

A

African National Congress, 13, 151, 162, 164, 193–4, 197
African Union, 42n10
Agamben, Giorgio, 31–2, 51, 95, 207
Angola, 8, 10, 46, 92, 95, 223
Angolan refugees, 95, 126, 114n5, 147n34, 177n41
anonymity, 84–5, 185
Arendt, Hannah, 28, 31, 123

B

Bantustan, 177n39
border areas, 10, 13, 23, 56
Botswana, 8, 191

C

Cape Town, 157, 171–2, 180, 183, 193, 203n28
Caritas Zambia, 121
Cash Based Interventions, 121, 146n12
Central Africa, 7, 57, 155
cholera, 83
citizens, 63, 90, 101, 107
citizenship, 36, 93, 132, 162, 182
civil society, 8, 11–12, 68, 73, 76, 77, 85, 105, 110–11, 190–91
colonialism, 10, 12, 20n17, 28, 47, 104, 163, 214
Commission for Refugees (Zambia), 91, 94–5, 114n16, 129, 131, 136–8
comparative case studies, 7–15
compliance, 37, 94
Comprehensive Refugee Response Framework, 11, 54, 83, 139–40, 217
confidentiality, 84–5
constructivism, 6, 68, 69, 212
containment, 47, 66n9, 123, 215
Convention relating to the Status of Refugees (1951), 9, 36, 38–9
 implementation in Africa, 52–3, 55, 218
 implementation in Zambia, 9, 91, 97
 implementation in South Africa, 12, 151, 164
Copenhagen School, 59. *See also* securitisation
COVID-19 global pandemic, 225

D

data collection, 72–7
decentralisation, 48–9, 193–4
decolonisation, 46–8
'democracy-asylum' nexus, 16, 46–9, 60, 64, 139, 143, 163, 199, 215–18
Democratic Alliance (DA), 20n20, 193
Democratic Republic of the Congo
 history, 10
 unrest, 83, 92, 102, 114n42, 126, 138, 140
democratization, 47–8, 64, 163, 175
Department of Home Affairs (South Africa)
 access to, 12, 75
 'Backlog Project', 161
 capacity issues, 166
 corruption, 167
 and encampment, 162–3, 173
 engagement with UNHCR, 159–61
 generous reception, 153–4, 159, 185, 188
 national security concerns, 169–71
 shrinking asylum system, 13, 169–75
Department of Immigration (Zambia), 94–5, 134–5
dualism, 90, 113n2

E

East Africa, 7, 43, 103, 108, 187
employment rights of refugees, 2, 8, 13, 19, 36, 41, 90, 107, 125, 130, 140, 163, 173, 180, 199, 201
elections, 11, 12, 13, 47–9, 59, 108, 110, 139, 193, 194, 197, 217
encampment, 1, 3, 9, 16, 50–51, 56, 64
epistemological position, 6, 68, 212
Eritrean migrants and refugees, 7
ethical considerations, 67–8, 84–6
Ethiopia, 8, 155
Ethiopian migrants and refugees, 7
ethnography, 6, 68, 69
European Union, 42n1
extractivism, 82

F

faith-based organisations, 115n60, 173, 190–91

framing exercise, 69–70
freedom of movement, 2–3, 8, 9, 11, 13, 51, 97–8, 107, 130, 137–8, 146n29, 162
free-settlement, 1, 3, 12, 46–8

G

Gauteng province, 181, 192
generalisability, 14–15, 24, 80
Global Compact on Refugees, 11, 54, 139–40, 161, 217
Global Refugee Forum, 161
Global refugee regime
 implementation of norms, 3, 22–3, 29, 35, 37–8
 shaping reception policies, 28, 49–55, 112, 152–3, 158–9, 175, 218–22
 'regime refugee', 123–4, 144, 188, 201, 207, 220
 'urban refugee', 187–9, 192, 209, 220–21, 225
Great Lakes Region, 7, 156

H

Hichilema, Hakainde, 12, 217
'Homelands' 162, 177n39. *See also* Bantustan
Horn of Africa, 7, 53, 156, 187
hospitality, 27, 30, 33–4, 47, 94, 185
human agency, 18, 32, 187, 206–8, 210, 220, 224
human rights, 2, 47–8, 61, 64, 75, 152, 162, 164–5, 213, 215–16

I

integration, 19, 26–7, 139, 143, 153, 180, 195, 200, 220–21, 226. *See also* local integration
informal interviews, 68–70, 77, 86n3, 109
informed consent, 84–5
interviewing, 68, 72, 74–6, 78, 81–2, 84, 86

J

Johannesburg
 economy, 181
 Migrant Help Desk, 194–5, 197, 198
 Migrants' Advisory Committee, 194–5
 migration, 12, 108, 157–8, 180–82
 Migration Advisory Panel, 194–5, 196
 refugee reception offices, 13, 150, 171–2
 role of Mayor, 194–6, 197–8, 199
 site of refugee reception, 13, 20n20, 180–83, 192–200, 209
 xenophobia, 85, 195, 198

K

Kaunda, Kenneth, 46
Kenya, 8, 54, 107, 115n55
Kenyan refugee camps, 9, 32, 58
key informant interviews, 68, 69, 71–2, 73–6
Kotef, Hagar, 62–4, 223–4

L

legal documentation, 29, 34, 164, 179, 189–90, 195, 199–200, 210
local government, 3, 11, 13, 140–1, 192–200, 209, 226
local integration, 181, 210, 225–6
 de facto local integration, 33
localised citizenship, 4, 62, 153–4, 190, 192, 210, 226
Lungu, Edgar, 11–13, 83, 110–11, 139–40, 217
Lusaka, 73, 74, 76, 83, 91, 108, 110, 121–2, 129

M

majority world, 20n4
Malawi, 8, 28
Mantapala refugee settlement, 11, 118, 138–43, 145, 217
Mashaba, Herman, 197–8, 203n44
Mawere, Abdon, 137–8
Mayukwayukwa refugee settlement, 11, 20n14, 92, 103, 122, 127, 140, 147n41
Meheba refugee settlement, 11, 12, 20n14, 92, 93, 103, 127–8, 140
Ministry of Community Development and Social Services (Zambia), 95, 120–21, 125
minority world, 20n4
mobility, 23–4, 25–6, 33, 60, 64, 206–7, 210
Mozambique, 10, 46, 57, 191
Mozambican refugees, 10, 105, 151, 155
multi-scalar lens, 5, 17, 24–5, 34, 39–41, 208–9, 212
Musina, 157, 176n24

N

New York Declaration for Refugees and Migrants, 11, 54, 83, 139–40
non-refoulement, 51, 151, 163

O

Office of the Vice President (Zambia), 91, 95, 143, 217
Organisation of African Unity Convention Governing Specific Aspects of Refugee Problems in Africa, 46, 52, 90, 91, 97, 151, 164

P

Pan-Africanism, 11, 18, 46, 49, 139, 162–3, 165, 174–5, 217
path dependency, 105
political settlements, 47, 65n3
  authoritarian political settlements, 11, 47–9, 60, 139, 215, 218–19
  competitive political settlements, 48, 59–60, 183, 215–18
positionality, 67, 79, 81–2
prima facie refugee status, 91–2
principle of 'do no harm', 68, 82
process tracing, 214
provincial government, 11, 42n10, 91, 193–4, 196

Q

quasi-ethnographic methods, 69, 77

R

reception
  as a process, 3, 15, 21, 24, 25–6, 35, 167, 201, 206, 209–10
  'context of reception' approach, 23–6, 206
  'open-door' policy in Africa, 2, 10, 28, 35, 46–7, 149, 151, 209
  qualified welcome, 27–8, 92–3, 132–4, 174, 191–2, 207–8
reflexivity, 70–1
refoulement, 93, 163
refugee camps
  in the 1980s, 3
  academic focus, 4, 30, 90
  armed elements, 56
  bare life, 31–3, 90, 123, 207
  international support, 98–9, 102–4
  links to the urban space, 4, 34–6, 113, 118, 129, 191, 210–11
  reception space, 28, 31–2, 211, 219–20
  and 'refugee warriors', 56–7
  security concerns, 56–8
  and settlements, 9
  UNHCR role, 4, 50–2, 218–22
refugee commodification, 66n9, 186
refugee definition, 28, 91, 97, 151, 164
refugee-led initiatives, 5
refugee movement, 16–19, 61–2, 216–18
refugee participation in research, 85–6
refugee status determination processes, 65n6, 91–2, 113n5, 150–51, 152–3, 159, 173
'refugee warriors', 56–8, 105
regime shifting, 136, 138, 164, 188, 221
regime stretching, 164
reliability, 72, 79–81

repatriation, 48, 126, 151
research design, 67, 69–77
research questions, 69–73, 76, 79, 80
resettlement, 163, 178n70, 184, 191
Rwanda, 10, 105
Rwandan refugees, 92, 95, 107, 126, 147n34

S

sampling, 73–4
  purposive sampling, 73–4
  snowball sampling, 73–4
'secondary' movement, 7, 53
security and securitisation
  direct security concerns, 56–8, 104–6, 157, 171, 223
  in forced migration literature, 55–60, 222
  indirect security concerns, 55, 56–9, 104–6, 136
  in Kenya, 58
  migration as a security threat, 5
  refugees as a security threat, 59–64, 223
  securitisation theory, 16, 59–60, 222–5
  securitisers, 60
  in South Africa, 165, 167–71, 222–5
  in Zambia, 104–11, 222–5
self reliance, 43n11, 93, 117, 121, 140, 187–8, 190, 210, 221, 226
social cohesion, 33, 195
Somali refugees, 7, 57, 155
South Africa
  1998 Refugee Act, 18, 151–2, 155, 161, 165, 171, 174, 175, 177n26, 202n14
  Apartheid regime, 18, 151, 159, 162–3, 169, 175, 177n29, 182, 223
  border areas, 13, 152, 157, 162, 173
  delays in asylum claims, 161, 166–7, 171–2, 176n22
  immigration Act, 168, 173, 178n58
  migrant groups, 168, 184–6
  National Constitution, 152, 161–12, 174, 176n5, 193
  police and law enforcement, 154, 190
  processing centres at the border, 13, 150, 162, 173, 178n79
  refugee camps, 155, 162–5, 191,
  refugee reception offices, 152–3, 158, 160, 167, 171–2, 177n71
  registration of refugees, 150–8, 160, 166–7, 172–3, 174–5
  social assistance programmes, 182–3
  xenophobic violence, 14, 83, 85, 163, 165, 178n70, 195, 198

Southern Africa
  borders, 7
  as a case study, 6–14
  reception of refugees, 6–8, 41, 53, 155, 176n1
Southern African Development Community (SADC), 1, 7, 42n10, 105, 185
stability, 60–5, 171–2, 208, 210–11, 216, 222–5
state sovereignty, 89, 93
sustainable farming, 103, 121–3, 125

T

Tanzania, 57, 155n53, 155n55
Tau, Parks, 194–6
taxation, 100–101, 182, 193
thematic analysis, 78–9
travel documents, 2, 131, 172
triangulation, 67, 72, 81
theory of norm implementation
  adapting to refugee reception policies, 5, 15–16, 36–9, 212–15
  as a conceptual framework, 71, 212–15
  the heuristic tripartite model, 37–9, 41–2, 212–13

U

Uganda, 8, 54, 176n24
Ugandan refugee camps, 9
United Nations High Commissioner for Refugees (UNHCR)
  academic focus, 4, 50–5, 218–19
  conditional welcome, 28, 31–2, 219–22
  implementing partners, 108, 124, 135–6, 176n9, 184, 191, 220, 227n8
  role in Africa, 50–5
  South Africa, 12, 151, 158–61, 183–5, 187–9, 200, 202n11, 209, 219–22
  urban policy, 53–6, 187, 202n19
  Zambia, 9, 96, 113n5; 113n6, 115n49, 120–4, 125–8, 135–6, 219–22
urban space
  academic focus, 4–5, 30–1, 32–3, 219
  indirect security concerns, 57–9, 169
  links to refugee camps, 4, 34–6, 113, 210–11
  reception space, 33–4, 208–10, 220–21
  sanctuary cities, 34, 199
urbanisation, 4, 33, 43, 53, 107, 216

V

validity, 41, 72, 79–81
vulnerability, 121, 125, 146n12, 176n9, 184, 187

W

Western Cape, 193–4

X

xenophobia, 14, 48, 59, 83, 106, 163, 174, 209

Z

Zambia
  the 1970 Refugee (Control) Act, 90, 94–8, 104–5, 134–5
  access to urban area, 98, 99–101, 108–9
  border areas, 94, 99, 101–2, 104, 106, 109, 138
  border crossings, 91, 106, 108
  as a case study, 9–12
  elections, 12, 108, 110, 139, 217
  gate passes, 96, 122, 128–34, 143, 147n36, 209
  independence, 10
  legal framework relating to refugees, 90–2, 94–7
  National Development Plans, 120, 146n3
  police and law enforcement, 91, 95, 97
  Refugees Act No.1 of 2017, 91, 94–8, 114n14, 134, 147n40; n49
  registration of refugees, 90–4
  strategic framework for the local integration of former refugees, 114n15, 147n34
  urban residence permits, 92, 96, 128–34
  xenophobia, 108, 122
  Zambia Initiative, 147n41
Zimbabwe, 10, 105, 156–7, 176n22, 176n24, 223
Zimbabwean migrants
  treatment in South Africa, 12, 156–8, 163–4
  Zimbabwean Dispensation Permit, 156, 164
  Zimbabwean Exemption Permit, 164, 177n44
  Zimbabwean Special Dispensation Permit, 164

www.ingramcontent.com/pod-product-compliance
Lightning Source LLC
LaVergne TN
LVHW050008140426
836100LV00010B/54